Breaking The Wall Of Silence

How New History Challenges Israel's Narrative

Hichem Karoui

Global East-West. London

Copyright © 2025 by Hichem Karoui.

The Mediterranean Notebooks. A Global East-West Series. London.

All rights reserved.

No portion of this book may be reproduced in any form without written permission from the publisher or author, except as permitted by copyright law.

Contents

Dedication	V
Foreword	1
Introduction The Role of History in Shaping National Identity	7
1. The Rise of the New Historians A Scholarly Revolution Begins	29
2. Benny Morris and the Reconsideration of 1948	55
3. Ilan Pappé Unveiling the Ethnic Cleansing Argument	77
4. Avi Shlaim Critique on Israeli Diplomacy and Military Strategy	99
5. Simha Flapan Rethinking National Myths	119
6. Revisiting the 'David vs. Goliath' Paradigm	147
7. The Palestinian Exodus Causes and Controversies	171
8. Fierce Backlash Intellectual Battles and Public Debate	195

9. Historical Truth as a Pathway to Peace 219
   Historical Truth as a Pathway to Peace: Challenges and Possibilities

10. Israeli Society 247
    Struggling With an Uncomfortable Past

11. The Fall of The Extremist Narratives at the Hands of the New Historians 273

12. Israel: A Lie Debunked 297
    A Society About To Implode

Conclusion 321
Political Implications in Today's Israel in the Wake of Gaza Genocide

Contents

Dedication	V
Foreword	1
Introduction The Role of History in Shaping National Identity	7
1. The Rise of the New Historians A Scholarly Revolution Begins	29
2. Benny Morris and the Reconsideration of 1948	55
3. Ilan Pappé Unveiling the Ethnic Cleansing Argument	77
4. Avi Shlaim Critique on Israeli Diplomacy and Military Strategy	99
5. Simha Flapan Rethinking National Myths	119
6. Revisiting the 'David vs. Goliath' Paradigm	147
7. The Palestinian Exodus Causes and Controversies	171
8. Fierce Backlash Intellectual Battles and Public Debate	195

9. Historical Truth as a Pathway to Peace 219
   Historical Truth as a Pathway to Peace: Challenges and Possibilities

10. Israeli Society 247
    Struggling With an Uncomfortable Past

11. The Fall of The Extremist Narratives at the Hands of the New Historians 273

12. Israel: A Lie Debunked 297
    A Society About To Implode

Conclusion 321
Political Implications in Today's Israel in the Wake of Gaza Genocide

To the **New Historians** who opened our eyes to the fact that in the Israeli society there are many people who stand for justice, freedom and peace; who put their hands in those of the Palestinians and the Arabs and walk together to build the great wall against fascism.
They have my respect and that of all those who fight for the triumph of justice and truth.

Foreword

The chapters of this book have been written at different times and places, which explains the different approach. Most were initially meant to be published separately as essays in a "long read" magazine. But at the last moment, I changed my mind and decided to keep them in the shade until I decided what to do with them. Finally, I opted for a book, as the Gaza genocide is still going on. Another book about the former "victim" becoming a torturer? Unfortunately, there are not so numerous.

Western governments are still living in the lie. I don't say the denial because it is pretty the same thing. After all, lying to one self is like lying to others, or worse. But there is another reason. It is not the New Israeli Historians who describe Israel as "a lie", as you will discover in this book. A lie that many people believe it will go on forever. Nevertheless, the history of "the Jewish state" – as described by Netanyahu and his clique – has taken a decisive turn since the beginning of the murderous, unjust and immoral war against the population of Gaza.

Israel has never been as isolated as it is today in the Western world, precisely. If many of the Western governments did not wake up, their populations did. Fortunately. There are still people unwilling to condone or forgive the criminals who bomb hospitals, schools, and kill children, women and elder people. Democratic governments know that continuing to ignore what Israel is doing would lead them to an impasse. Not just a moral impasse, but a political one as well. One of those deadlocks that may cause social upheaval and, ultimately, loss of control and power. That's why some of them announced recently that they will recognise the State of Palestine.

Despite, the chaos they created, Israel's extremists continue to dream of ruling the entire Middle East, with the support of those, at thousands of miles, who dream of making America great again, while their country is approaching collapse, squeezed by all kinds of plagues!

Making America great again (MAGA)? Is it a joke? Excuse-me, maybe I did not understand well. When exactly in History was America great? You know, all the great civilisations reach their climax by their humanist magnitude, contributing to the progress of all the other nations. What did the USA do in this context for the Africans, the Asians, and even for those who live on the southern continent, apart from invading, plundering, and leaving behind millions of people dead? You may mention technology, Internet, AI, etc. It is true these are achievements certainly, but not for humanism, not offered generously for free, but well, because it makes profit for the Big corporations and the Big capital behind them. Did the "Great America" offer anything for free? Just give us a time in history showing the US humanist achievements. Was that during the bombing of Vietnam, Laos and Cambodia, for example? Or during the bombing of Afghanistan or during the invasion of Iraq? Oh! I almost forgot the great American achievement that showed up in Africa, tearing millions of men and women away from their ancestral land to enslave them for the benefit of the humanist cotton and corn plantations. That's also the sign of a great civilisation. Or perhaps when the settlers wiped out millions of indigenous lives from the earth's surface in America? We don't know exactly how many were killed because there were no media at the time. At least today, we know approximatively how many died and continue to die in Gaza, if not by the bombs and bullets, then by deliberate starving, to "make Israel great again"... For it seems obvious that the Israeli extremists are on the same path, walking in the steps of "the Great America".

Why not? They already have the ethical model designed and ready to apply. It is a gift from the MAGA fanatics to those who pretend to be descendants of the Holocaust's survivors.

Don't live anyone of them alive: Netanyahu has even mentioned a text from the Bible about killing the babies and the animals. No wonder that he is wanted by the *International Criminal Court* (ICC).

I have been blamed by a "colleague" from the academia because, according to him, I committed suicide in publishing a book titled: "The Right To Resist" which is a collection of essays written under the urgency of the war against the people of Gaza, including an essay titled "Zionism and Fascism". That last section of the book precisely is thoroughly documented with over a hundred of sources and references, many of them are Israeli (today famous), while I did not cite a single Arabic book or article. However, I understand that some people in academia and elsewhere become overzealous in the defence of the wrong if defending the right clashes with the steak. Obviously, the steak is more important than justice, freedom and truth. Its value is sure, while one is never sure with those "abstracts", although all democratic nations claim they represent their constitutive foundations, which I believe historically true. Hopefully, nowadays, democratic leaders do not understand history as just the past, but also as the present and the future. If so, the same values apply everywhere, and it is our duty to make the globe more an inclusive place, without excluding anybody, particularly the Palestinians struggling to make their voice heard. For, like all humans, they deserve to enjoy the same values that democratic nations enjoy.

Anyway, I don't want to deprive anybody from the right to keep his steak coming. I don't blame. I understand.

Today, I come back with a group of academics who did not mind losing their steak for the sake of doing their job of researcher. We should recognise that it is not easy in a locked society like Israel to have the courage to say something that is not just different from the official narrative, but also clashing with it.

The truth is a risk that only prophets, saints and heroes can indulge in. So far, we did not expect modest social scientists to take it, against the government and the anchored beliefs and myths of the people.

But they just did it. They are called in Israel and elsewhere: The New Historians.

I tried to present them the best I can. I am not sure whether I made a comprehensive analysis of their works. Yet, it is a modest contribution in introducing them to the readers, maybe this helps open the eyes of more people on the tragedy still going on for 77 years.

I am confident those who love freedom and justice exist everywhere in this world. Not only that, but I am also quite certain that Freedom and Justice for the Palestinian people

will triumph.
   Free Palestine!

Hichem Karoui, August 2025 (Southern France).

Introduction
The Role of History in Shaping National Identity

As the collective memory of a people, history wields decisive influence over the formation and reinforcement of national identity. Through curated stories that connect origins, achievements, and trials, communities weave a shared past into their cultural, social, and political lifeworld. The resulting narrative becomes the stage on which national character is rehearsed, determining the inward self-image of citizens and the outward posture they adopt toward other nations. Those who craft these accounts—historians, educators, and political leaders—offer the cultural scaffolding on which a unified identity is raised. At their best, these narratives evoke a common moral and political horizon. Yet, the meaning of history is never monolithic. Divergent interpretations of decisive events may compete for the allegiance of the public, splintering the national story and exposing latent fractures within society. Selective remembering or forgetting of certain facts compounds the problem, enshrining inequities and refreshing old prejudices. Understood in this light, history's influence is not merely to enlighten, but to engineer the terms on which collective memory is contested and consensus is secured or denied.

Its influence is felt not only within the arguments and evidentiary choices that historians articulate, but equally within the channels through which these arguments are transmitted and subject to collective interpretation. Pedagogical choices in school curricula, the rhetorical framing employed in monuments and memorials, and the cinematic and televisual representations that circulate in global popular culture together elevate and suppress particular dimensions of a collective past, thereby moulding the self-image a polity espouses. Moreover, the relationship between historiography and national self-understanding transcends territorial boundaries, affecting diplomatic posture and transnational reputations. A polity's reconstructed past may elicit either approbation or condemnation, consolidating or fragmenting geopolitical coalitions. Consequently, an attentive analysis of the historiographical variables that undergird national identity is indispensable for any nuanced grasp of the structural conflicts and affinities that characterise both domestic pluralities and the global arena.

Narratives as Lenses: How Stories Frame Our Understanding of the Past

Throughout the sweep of history, stories have been indispensable in forming our perception of bygone times. They function, symbolically, as transparent glass through which entire epochs come into view. Just as the tint of a lens subtly modifies the colour of the landscape, so do stories modulate our interpretation of incidents, determining not only what is seen but the affective and cognitive reactions that follow.

Stories structure the transmission of historical knowledge, articulating it in a form that transcends discrete dates and figures. They crystallise the lived experience of former generations, permitting us to approach remote epochs as if they still breathed. Whether they endure in the chant of a village elder, the pages of a chronicle, or the frames of a film, stories weave a fabric of continuity, forging an intimate attachment between the listener and the vanished.

Crucially, these lenses are anything but fixed; they are revised and reconfigured as contexts shift. Ideals, prejudices, and aspirations that lie far from the original moment coexist in the retelling, and the story is remade to suit the present. Such fluidity means that the same series of events may nourish differing national memories, competing identities, or partisan ideologies. Yet, for all their pliability, stories remain indispensable; they furnish the coordinates that give events their depth, their significance, and, ultimately, their grasp upon our imagination.

The strength of narratives resides in their capacity to present intricate ideas and emotions in an accessible format. When history is rendered as a story, it permits individuals to inhabit the psyches of people separated by distance and time, cultivating an emotional resonance that mere facts often cannot achieve. Narratives likewise facilitate critical self-reflection, urging readers to ponder the ramifications of past actions and their persistent reverberations in present-day life.

In addition, narratives play a vital role in shaping both national and cultural identities. By perpetuating common memories and fostering intergenerational solidarity, they constitute the emotional and intellectual infrastructure of a coherent national character. When communities succeed in articulating potent and persuasive stories, they reinforce a collective identity anchored in shared traditions, beliefs, and values.

Yet multiple and often contradictory narratives can simultaneously contest the same historical episodes, each striving for acceptance and authority. This contest of stories highlights the plurality of lenses through which the past can be perceived, and reminds us that no single account can claim absolute truth. By interrogating these competing versions, individuals can refine their comprehension of historical complexity and achieve a fuller understanding of the forces that continue to inform contemporary society.

In conclusion, narratives function as critical tools for clarifying the past, guiding our interaction with it, and influencing our contemporary perspective. Their reach is extensive, touching distinct domains of individual lives and shared remembrance. Recognising the force of narratives is therefore vital for grasping the layered character of historical comprehension and the effects it exerts upon societies around the globe.

Historians, as custodians of understanding, face the ongoing challenge of reconciling subjective interpretation with the aspiration for objective analysis of the past. The intricacies of the discipline require them to function as deliberate evaluators of evidence, balancing their personal insights against an archive of empirical documentation to produce layered accounts. Central to their craft is the duty to recognise and disclose the biases that, however unacknowledged, colour every reconstruction. A historian's perspective is always shaped by the lattice of personal beliefs and sociocultural circumstance; therefore, the effort to attain impartial representation must be resolute. Yet, the demand for objectivity does not advocate for emotional distance; it invites the scholar to be critically conscious of their positionality and to assess how it may colour the interpretation of particular events. Such reflexive awareness empowers historians to move beyond their predispositions, to deliberate with competing perspectives, and to deepen the collective enquiry into the past. The objective discipline is further reinforced by rigorous archival practice: meticulous selection, evaluation, and triangulation of evidence are required to ensure that narrative construction rests upon the verifiable rather than the speculative. At the same time, an acknowledgement of subjectivity affirms the complexity and richness of lived experience that form the substratum of every historical process.

Accepting subjectivity does not undermine the integrity of history; it rather acknowledges the layered emotional and experiential dimensions that historical events invariably carry. Such an acceptance opens the discursive space for multiple voices and viewpoints, thereby revealing the past's inherent multidimensionality. When historians attend to the diverse ways individuals have experienced, remembered, and recorded historical events, they foster empathy that transcends purely impersonal verification. The ongoing historian's responsibility of integrating subjective interpretation with objective evidence is consequently a fluid, responsive practice. It mandates unwavering self-reflection, intellectual modesty, and an enduring commitment to revealing truth's stratified nature. By finely calibrating these dimensions, historians negotiate the subtle interplay of personal insight and empirical verification, thereby advancing an understanding of history that is both more complete and more humane.

Evolving Historical Interpretations: From Fixed Scripts to Fluid Narratives

The trajectory of modern historiography illustrates how understandings of the past have progressively replaced rigid, prescriptive narratives with flexible, revisable stories. Earlier scholarship treated history as a kaleidoscope of events linked by discernible causality, yet current inquiries foreground the contingency, uncertainty, and interplay of differing forces that misfit linear explanation. This intellectual turning point reflects a generalised commitment to pluralism, fostered by the wish to question sedimented interpretations often grounded in the assumptions of a single, dominant culture. Central to the transformation is the acceptance that multiple truths can coexist, thereby discrediting authoritative accounts that masquerade as the sole record. When historians foreground divergent experiences and conflicting interpretations, the past is rendered more textured, revealing the variegated fabric of human action and meaning. Fluid narratives, in turn, summon the previously unheard, permitting previously subordinated voices to modify the conventional scripts that dominated mainstream discourse. The rejection of fixed frameworks is moreover mirrored in the current appetite for interdisciplinary enquiry: historians now routinely engage anthropology, sociology, literary studies, and other fields, allowing them to interrogate and enrich the contours of familiar subjects and to situate the historian's own decisions about evidence amid broader social and intellectual forces.

A multidisciplinary lens on the past expands the horizon of enquiry while furnishing scholars with fresh analytic instruments capable of addressing complex, intersecting processes. Simultaneously, the dynamic character of present-day historiography compels continued re-evaluation of established paradigms. Such re-evaluation confronts scholars with unsettling realities, requiring them to scrutinise long-accepted assumptions about pivotal events and key actors. Through repeated, critical reassessment, historical accounts can evolve in responsiveness to both new empirical findings and shifting civic priorities. The emerging tendency toward fluid, contingent narratives does not compromise accuracy; rather, it enlarges the historical record by soliciting a broader array of voices and experiences. Yet, as this methodological transition unfolds, scholars must guard against the excesses of both dogmatic relativism and unprincipled revisionism. The central challenge lies in harmonising an embrace of multiplicity with the strict observance of evidentiary discipline. Only by rooting contingent narratives in thorough research and continuous critical appraisal can the discipline safeguard its scholarly rigour. The movement beyond monolithic representations toward open, alterable accounts marks a theoretical re-orientation in the practice of the discipline. It calls the community to accept historiographical diversity, to confront the past's inherent contradictions, and to accept the permanence of reinterpretation—all of which together yield a richer, more complete, and more egalitarian grasp of the historical record.

Memory and Myth: Bridging Personal Remembrance with Collective History

Memory and myth orchestrate an ongoing dialogue between intimate recollection and the broader historical record, revealing how personal experience can be absorbed into the communal narrative. Memory, in its intimate register, archives the particularities of lived experience—sensations, emotions, and the subtleties of a moment which, though ephemeral, remain vivid for the individual. Yet, once such recollections confront decisive historical occurrences—wars, revolutions, migrations—they are often recast, acquiring the language and contours of myth. They are no longer simply remembered; they are remembered in a certain way, retouched by the filters of collective meaning, and thus integrated into the collective imagination. That fusion offers the individual a place in the grander chronicle, while simultaneously reconfiguring the communal account by incorporating a mote of personal truth. The result is a living, mutable archive where personal and public memories sustain one another, informing individual identity while reconstituting the ongoing story of the nation or culture.

This mutual constitution of memory and myth can be traced across heterogeneous cultures, where decisive junctures are perpetually migratory—layered with metaphor, infused with communal sentiment, and tethered to civic self-understanding. Each retelling and re-invigoration of the past—through ritual, education, or oratory—contributes to what Pierre Nora called the "lieux de mémoire," forming reservoirs of meaning that outlast the events themselves. Such collective recollections, though often gilded with heroic or redemptive motifs, offer civic consolation, fortifying the nation against the anxieties of its lived divisions. Yet, that very consolation may be frail, for it can occlude the asymmetries that the past has bequeathed: the stories of the subaltern, the lost, and the forsaken are frequently excised or rendered inaudible.

The reach of memory and myth, however, extends far beyond the archives of the past; it becomes a decisive actor within the arenas of power. Political rhetoric frequently invokes the spectre of founding sacrifices, magnifying the past to lend urgency to present claims. Statues, monuments, and commemorative dates translate intimate bereavements into collective ritual, while public memory—institutions, curricula, and media—reproduces the selection and arrangement of the past that citizens will inherit. In such transactions, what is remembered and how it is remembered is not a disinterested exercise; it arms or disarms citizens, legitimises or contests sovereign forms, and forges or fractures the bonds by which societies sustain themselves.

The rituals, commemorative structures, and national commemorative days that conspicuously mark the passage of historic events weave those events tightly into the societal fabric. However, this same mechanism may inadvertently license the persistence of inaccuracies, the silencing of critical perspectives, and the entrenchment of polarising commemorative scripts. Consequently, the convergence of memory, myth, and disciplined enquiry solicits sustained and sceptical examination, urging us to mediate the friction between broadly accepted narratives and the discrete, often contradicting, testimonies of lived experience.

The Impact of Political Context on Historical Narratives

Current historiography is increasingly attentive to this convergence of memory and myth, paying careful attention to their imprint on popular and scholarly historical consciousness. By integrating survivor accounts, oral-recorded memory, and explicitly oppositional narratives, historians disentangle the sedimented layers of recollection, testing and often displacing inherited simplifications. This scholarly programme not only adds depth to our knowledge of prior experience; it cultivates an elastic and ethically attentive historical practice that affirms the significance of previously marginal voices. Through such enquiry, we recognise that individual and social memory are not antithetical realms but mutually saturating dimensions, thus opening the horizon for a history rooted in critical regard for the variegated character of its subjects.

Political circumstances invariably leave their imprint upon historical scholarship, framing every act of interpretation. Political environments direct historians in the choice of sources, the prominence accorded to certain events, and the framing of causation, thereby privileging some voices and marginalising others. Consequently, accounts of the past resonate beyond academic discipline, acquiring a currency in present-day discourse.

A principal channel for political influence is the production of state-authorised historiography. Regimes—whether democratic, authoritarian, or colonial—frequently devise narratives that legitimate their authority, evoke nationalist sentiment, or rationalise conquest. Such accounts become embedded in educational systems, commemorative practices, and public monuments, producing a collective memory that often calcifies into national identity. In the process, the past is polished, omissions and recalibrated in conformity with contemporary objectives, producing what Jean-François Chiappe has termed a vision that reinforces the state and suppresses the contradictory.

Historical narratives are always sensitive to the interplay between political ideologies and institutional power. When ideologically divided societies confront their past, the result is often a contest of competing interpretations, each faction attempting to author a version of history that substantiates its own claims and discredits the adversary. Such a zero-sum struggle distorts the evidentiary record, complicating the task of arriving at a dispassionate account and entrenching societal fractures that impede both collective memory and durable reconciliation. Mistrust is thus institutionalised, as rival communities come to inhabit mutually exclusive pasts that inhibit common futures.

The political environment further conditions both the direction and the breadth of historical enquiry. Accounts that interrogate the premises of prevailing power arrangements are often met with institutional resistance—be it through formal censorship, funding cuts, or the strategic silence of sanctioned memory. In these circumstances, the canon contracts, and alternative testimonies are exiled to the margins. In contrast, a polity characterised by substantive political openness permits a dialogue of sources, enabling historians to recover suppressed voices and to render a multidimensional past that acknowledges conflict without surrendering to it. Only such an environment allows the discipline to fulfil its epistemic and ethical responsibilities to the societies it seeks to illuminate.

Analysing how political contexts influence historical narratives reveals that scholarly enquiry and the collective memory of the past are dynamic and susceptible to external pressures. Acknowledging and rigorously assessing the distortions potentially inflicted by prevailing political environments is essential to fostering an understanding of history that is both fuller and more faithful. Such an undertaking must engage with multiple perspectives and safeguard the past against its co-optation by partisan agendas.

Challenge to Dominant Regimes: The Advent of Novel Discourses

For generations, historical scholarship has rested upon hegemonic paradigms that both determine academic hierarchies and contribute to the sedimentation of national collective memories. Hitherto confident narratives, anointed as authoritative or canonical, are now confronted by the ascendancy of emergent discourses that invite sustained and rigorous critique. This chapter investigates the conditions that have allowed such discursive innovation to flourish, situating it within longer intellectual and social currents. The emergence of these counter-discourses constitutes not an ancillary shift, but a watershed moment in the discipline, as researchers intentionally excavate neglected strata of evidence and resuscitate voices long relegated to silence or marginalisation. This excavatory enterprise, animated by both scholarly rigour and ethical imperative, refuses the neutrality often ascribed to the historian and instead assumes a confrontational posture toward sedimented certainties. The resultant upheaval destabilises canonical narratives and prompts a recalibration of the ethical obligations historians owe to both the evidence and the societies that memorialise it. By traversing and, where necessary, transgressing the delimitations of received historical discourse, these initiatives expand the discursive horizon, permit the circulation of previously incommensurable perspectives, and foster genuinely intercultural exchange. In the act of assembling these newly composite accounts, they cultivate a tempered yet tenacious empathy that insists upon recognising the contradictory and fractured nature of human agency and historical temporality.

The steady erosion of accepted dogmas has converted history from a fixed repository of past certainties into a vibrant forum for radical reinterpretation, fertilising a plural field of narratives that mirror the mosaic of human experience. Armed with these emergent discourses, historians and scholars have commenced a deeper expedition, illuminating long-silenced episodes and teasing apart the subtleties of celebrated events. This broadened panoramic account empowers the collective present with a richer, more iridescent grasp of its antecedents, thereby nurturing a profound respect for the intricacies of historical truth. Questioning settled orthodoxy initiates not only a renewal of archival and interpretive zeal, but also auditions for public consciousness that extend far past the walls of the seminar room. Such inquiries invigorate civic conversation, sharpening attention to the layers and hesitations that any act of historical presentation must bear, and compelling audiences to question pervasive, monochromatic interpretations. In this way, the same inquiries that unsettle certainties invariably motivate broader movements, fuelled by an elemental quest for equity and authenticity. By amassing the previously inaudible and negotiating the discordant, these efforts cultivate solidarity and compassionate grasp, aspiring to a collective, dialogically-formed comprehension of the past and of its stubborn reverberations in the living present.

Ultimately, the emergence of new discourses accomplishes far more than a mere correction of the historical record; it stands as a witness to the continued resilience and flexibility of historical narratives, thereby confirming that collective memory is not a fixed archive but a vibrant, evolving dialogue that is always alert to the possibilities of reinterpretation and rediscovery.

Why History Matters: Narratives as Tools for Social Change

The processes by which societies negotiate their destinies are invariably influenced by how they remember and narrate their pasts. Historical narratives are potent instruments that can exert a lasting and transformative pressure on collective consciousness. Each re-examination and new articulation of a past event provides societies with an opportunity to interrogate unquestioned customs, to contest entrenched hierarchies, and to appreciate the complicated interdependencies that characterize human behaviour. Thus, history operates simultaneously as a reflective surface and as a directional instrument, permitting communities to see what they once were and to deliberate upon what they might yet become.

At the core of history's power is its capacity to nurture empathy and reciprocal recognition among heterogeneous groups. When the stories of the politically and socially marginalised are made visible, the distance between past suffering and present responsibility is bridged. Audiences are invited to inhabit lives that they have not lived, to confront injury that they have not inflicted, and to acknowledge that the reverberations of past injustices are neither cancelled by time nor rendered irrelevant by geography. In documenting such experiences, history creates a communal memory that can galvanise collective action; the injustices of yesterday become the imperatives of today. Civil societies, therefore, draw upon the scholarly and popular memory of injustice to refine their commitments to equity, cohesion, and democratic integrity.

Moreover, historical analysis functions as a critical vantage point for evaluating current predicaments. A systematic interrogation of prior institutions, legislative frameworks, and social movements allows policymakers and citizens alike to extract pertinent lessons applicable to present deliberations and interventions. By tracing the mechanisms that produced earlier injustices and periodic crises, we amass a body of knowledge that enhances our capacity to confront similar phenomena now unfolding within our own societies. In this manner, the study of the past is recast as a generative process that transforms memory into a foundation for evidence-based dialogue, legislative revision, and anticipatory action designed to counter entrenched inequalities.

In addition, history imposes a disciplined imperative for accountability and restorative justice. When societies confront the discomfiting verities of their earlier conduct, they are pressed to recognise the persistent scars and inequities that have often been concealed beneath rhetorical reassurances. A collective reckoning with these injustices constitutes a necessary precondition for healing and for the construction of a shared political culture oriented toward equity. Consequently, the historical record becomes not merely a repository of dates and events, but a strategic archive of admonitions and imperatives, marking the perils of indifference and the redemptive capacities that emerge through coordinated, collective action.

In sum, the study of history carries immense significance because it can unite communities, cultivate empathy, guide current decisions, and promote both reconciliation and justice. As guardians of our collective memory, we bear a moral responsibility to extract and apply the insights woven into historical accounts, transforming them into instruments that deepen comprehension and propel meaningful reforms in society.

Revisiting yesterday in the name of knowledge demands of scholarship the highest ethical vigilance. Each era, scrutinised through the prism of the present, reveals choices, structures, and catastrophes whose legacies lay out the parameters of contemporary life and future possibility. To examine the past ethically is first to concede that the writing of history is never a neutral craft; the frame, the periodisation, the language, the selective citation, and the silences that scholars permit themselves and others participate in the shaping of collective memory and identity. Duty therefore urges us not only to render the past intelligibly, but to weigh whose intelligibility is being rendered and why. Such responsibility motions the investigator beyond dispassionate analysis to attunement to the wounds, obfuscations, and insulation that earlier generations bequeathed to us. Along the way, the historian, consciously or not, takes up the challenge of transforming inherited discord into acknowledged conflict, thereby opening pathways out of the stalemate that a long, unexamined past can sponsor. Integrity, empathy, and a scrupulous fidelity to evidence converge to sustain the scholar in this enterprise. Turbulences and taboos emerge; the tension of balancing multiplicity of views and the burden of historic wrongs weighs heavily. Yet, the necessity of rebuilding, sentence by loaded sentence, a more ethical public memory remains non-negotiable.

Such memory must remain a work in progress, fuelled by the ethical precept not to settle for dominant accounts but to expand what the archive, the monument, the curriculum, or the digital corpus is prepared to recognise. Ethical history therefore invites, on every page and in every lecture, the simultaneous recognition of structural power and personal grief. It summons the analyst to excavate not only policies and campaigns but the daily intimacies of suffering, resilience, and resistance that official chronicles routinely elide. By foregrounding those whose laughter and mourning, whose errors and reckonings, whose very absence have produced the normalised outlines of the past, scholarship refuses the complacency of "already known" truth and remains open to the possibility of a gentler but more insistent historiography.

By bringing once-hidden stories to light, historical research can work to amend past silences and to begin redressing historic wrongs. Through such illumination, scholars can initiate a reconciliation process that is indispensable to the lasting welfare of entire communities. Engaging with this obligation also requires confronting the enduring legacies of colonialism, imperial dominion, and the myriad forms of systemic oppression that still shape the present.

This responsibility demands that historians remain attentive to how their findings affect living groups, and that they refuse to construct narratives that sustain injury or distort reality. It calls for prioritising the voices, experiences, and agency of those who have been previously silenced, and for scrutinising how past interpretations have been conscripted to serve regimes of domination. By situating their work within this moral framework, scholars can chart courses through troubled legacies that prioritise understanding, inclusivity, and justice. When ethical reflection informs every stage of the enquiry, the past may be recast in forms that nourish a future defined by equity and compassion. Such a reconstitution invites both individual and collective introspection, empowering societies to advance with an informed recognition of our mutual and entangled histories.

Facing the Past: The Ethical Imperative in Re-examining History

Entering a new chapter of enquiry, we must accept that our comprehension of the past is never fixed. The trajectory of history-writing in the coming decades promises to reveal ignored viewpoints and latent narratives that have so far evaded notice. This trajectory itself affirms history's persistent capacity to influence the present and to inform our future choices. Scholars are therefore positioned to probe the finer textures of lived experience, to elevate previously silenced voices, and to retune our communal recollection.

Such persistent pursuit of historical verity requires both those within the discipline and its interlocutors to subject familiar assumptions to sustained scrutiny. The limits of conventional historiography will be tested, permitting the arrival of new analyses and questions. At the same time, developing digital tools are widening access to primary material and facilitating the distribution of findings, a convergence that transcends previously impermeable geographic and cultural frontiers.

In the midst of ongoing intellectual ferment, historians confront escalating ethical dilemmas, particularly when investigating sensitive and contested episodes. Balancing scholarly integrity with acute awareness of the meaningful lives still shaped by the past remains the foremost duty. With the discipline expanding in scope, the demand for interdisciplinary collaboration intensifies; historians increasingly draw fruitfully on sociology, psychology, anthropology, and other fields to deepen and complicate their interpretations of historical phenomena.

The responsible historian cannot isolate scholarly enquiry from societal conversation. History, by informing concepts of national identity and the practices of governance, invariably confronts present realities. Trained historians must thus participate in public dialogue, providing tempered accounts and analytic rigour capable of informing public judgment and, in turn, strengthening social cohesion.

When we consider the future, the reach of historical scholarship clearly extends beyond the academy. By rendering the past in all its complexity, historians cultivate empathetic engagement, promote processes of reconciliation, and question entrenched biases. Appreciating the ongoing trajectory of the discipline requires awareness of the transformative force embedded in historical narratives, for these accounts have the temperamental capacity to evoke reflection and to spur constructive change within society.

In closing, the trajectory of historical research reveals a future characterised by enduring discovery, critical reflection, and vibrant public engagement. As we venture into the yet-unmapped domains of the past, we must steadfastly resolve to disentangle the complex strata of the human record while safeguarding the rigorous standards that anchor our discipline.

1
The Rise of the New Historians
A Scholarly Revolution Begins

The Context of Traditional Israeli Historiography

Classical Israeli historiography, emerging in the aftermath of the state's founding and shaped by its nationalist imperatives, foregrounded celebratory accounts and origin myths while marginalising the critical scrutiny of contentious occurrences (Shapira 1995; Gelber 2004). The prevailing historiographical scheme reified the Zionist enterprise as a saga of enduring struggle, communal sacrifice, and final triumph framed in quasi-redemptive terms, yet it consistently curated the evidence so as to minimise, if not entirely efface, the experiences and grievances of subsumed communities, above all the Palestinians (Flapan 1987; Segev 1986). This selective archiving and interpreting consequently insulated a narrative of Jewish righteousness and victimhood, occluding alternative perspectives and stifling dissent within scholarly arenas and the public sphere (Silberstein 1999).

During the greater part of the twentieth century, Israeli historiography and the enterprise of national cohesion were functionally co-determined. The prevailing scholarship articulated a past that, while ostensibly descriptive, served the instrumental ends of collective identity and state legitimation (Kimmerling 2001; Shlaim 1995). By valorising one interpretation and silencing others, the scholarly edifice fostered a populace that subscribed to a unified, purpose-driven narrative. This implicatory concord, however, exacted the price of wilful amnesia or doctrinal evasion of the past's more fraught dimensions, inhibiting the interrogation of traumatic events and the re-examination of axiomatic certainties (Shapira 1995; Gelber 2004).

Conventional Israeli historiography thereby underscored a starkly divided rendering of past events, framing them as pure triumphs or unqualified transgressions. This monochromatic framing frequently obscured, or relegated as regrettable footnotes, the subtler, ambivalent, or morally confounding layers of the record (Segev 1986; Shlaim 2000). It significantly undervalued the necessity of contesting rival elucidations and of continuously subjecting canonized accounts to reassessment, thereby limiting the historical discourse and dulling sensitivity to the legacy of the past (Shapira 1995).

Correspondingly, the formal education apparatus and dominant media outlets established a dominant channel through which the orthodox historicist paradigm was repeated and entrenched, thereby moulding the civic imagination around decisive epochs. By circulating a streamlined and depurated account, these agencies sustained a communal remembrance that comported with the authorized script, while systematically sidelining the testimonies and perspectives that resisted its boundaries (Kimmerling 2001; Silberstein 1999).

Dominated by overt nationalism and ideology, the traditional paradigm constructed a hermetically sealed interpretive space, which constrained critical engagement and produced a scholarship that fortuitously served the state's political and social imperatives. Against this backdrop, the New Historians emerged as the first systematic and sustained rupture with the earlier paradigm, compelling a deep and often unsettling reconsideration of the nation's historical self-understanding (Flapan 1987; Shlaim 1988; Morris 1988).

Intellectual Seeds of Change: The Climate of the 1980s

The 1980s represented a decisive moment in the historiography of the Israeli-Palestinian conflict. As the global order began to fragment, the intellectual climate within Israel was invigorated by a compound of external and intra-communal perturbations. An expanding civil society, increasing access to archival material, and the gradual normalization of postmodern reflexivity produced an atmosphere of reconsideration (Silberstein 1999; Shlaim 1995). Within this milieu, the New Historians, never a homogeneous collective, nonetheless politicised the act of historical writing, turning the archive itself into a contested site of contemporary memory (Morris 1988; Flapan 1987).

Following the Lebanon War and the First Intifada, a distinctive atmosphere of self-scrutiny settled over the Israeli public (Schiff and Ya'ari 1984; Beinin and Lockman 1989). The repercussions of these confrontations prompted scholars and lay observers alike to reconsider what had long been regarded as settled chronicle. Concurrently, the resurgence of post-colonial and revisionist methodologies within worldwide historiography supplied an intellectual milieu in which fresh, sometimes troubling, accounts of the Zionist narrative began to flourish (Said 1978; Shafir 1989).

The momentum of this enquiry was greatly amplified by the incremental opening of state-held files. Newly rediscovered documents illuminated previously shadowed dimensions of the national saga, permitting a more finely calibrated dissection of incidents surrounding the birth of the Israeli state (Shlaim 1988; Morris 1988). The release of archival materials in the UK under what was then a 30-year rule (now the 20-year rule) and via the Israel State Archives broadened the evidentiary base for these debates (The National Archives (UK) n.d.; Israel State Archives n.d.).

Furthermore, the domestic political context in Israel underwent a discernible transformation during these years. The early 1980s saw the emergence of a more engaged and critically self-aware civil society, characterised in part by a markedly bolder academic community (Silberstein 1999; Kimmerling 2001). The intersection of these developments produced a public sphere in which dissent became more tolerable and scholarly enquiry more resolute, thereby creating a conducive environment for the New Historians to interrogate previously uncontested narratives (Shapira 1995; Segev 1986).

Within this environment, historians of exceptional distinction—Benny Morris, Ilan Pappé, Avi Shlaim, and Simha Flapan—embarked upon investigations that broke decisively with dominant interpretations (Morris 1988; Flapan 1987; Shlaim 1988; Pappé 1988). Their foundational studies reframed chronology and causation and raised ethical and epistemological questions that reverberated beyond academia (Shlaim 1995). The intellectual turbulence they inspired and the new critical lexicon they introduced resulted in a discernible recomposition of the discipline, extending the geographic and temporal boundaries of Middle Eastern historiography.

Unearthing New Evidence: Access to Declassified Documents

The second wave of Israeli historiographical reconceptualisation arose distinctly during the 1980s, when expanded access to declassified governmental, military, and diplomatic records permitted researchers to interrogate events previously cloaked in institutional opacity (Morris 1988; Shlaim 1988). The gradual release of these files, from the Israel State Archives and foreign archives such as the UK's National Archives, coincided with the maturation of the discipline (The National Archives (UK) n.d.; Israel State Archives n.d.). Newly unveiled cables, military situation reports, and inter-agency memoranda disclosed previously muted actors and unreported decisions that underpinned momentous crises (Morris 1986a; Morris 1986b).

Scrutinising the documents, historians were compelled to recalibrate the chronological and causal underpinnings of phenomena such as the 1948 war, the creation of the Israeli security doctrine, and the 1982 Lebanon invasion. Each previously redacted entry similarly destabilised foundational categories—whether the left's celebrated national liberation or the right's teleological reconstruction—thus demonstrating the contingencies obscured by former ideologues.

The historiographical discipline, now underpinned by verifiable archival sources, moved from grand syntheses toward granular micro-studies and comparative security assessments (Morris 2008). Civil-society efforts have since documented barriers and opportunities around archival access, further shaping the terrain of research (Akevot Institute n.d.).

Ironically, the very state that the scholarship examined in critical modes thus became a primary archivist of its own historiographical undoing, creating the conditions for a synthesis less reducible to a singular national narrative and more attuned to the tactic of contradiction, agency, and forgetting. The residual task remains to integrate these fragments within broader regional and global constellations, continually averting the temptation to sediment the new narrative into a conservable orthodoxy.

Access to previously classified materials resonated beyond universities, stirring public discussion and interrogating commonly held beliefs. Once archival safeguards faded, historians set out on an overdue voyage, illuminating stories that had mellowed in the dark (Segev 1986; Flapan 1987). The flush of new documentation triggered a shift in the discipline, obliging investigators to formulate new questions and methods (Shlaim 1995).

The sudden appearance of withheld information in these

folders amounted to a summons for a thorough reassessment of both public assertions and refutations. The layered verities uncovered within the old, sealed files obligate the scholarly domain to pause, reflect, and recommit, standing on the brink of an interpretive upheaval that promises to redraw the familiarity of the past.

Challenging Orthodox Narratives: The Role of International Scholarship

The emergence of the New Historians constituted a watershed in reconfiguring historical writing on Israel. International scholarship unsettled orthodox accounts by introducing neglected archives, marginal voices, and new theoretical orientations—postcolonial critique, memory studies, and nationalism studies (Said 1978; Shafir 1989; Peters and Newman 2013). Comparative and transnational methods diversified the questions asked and complicated the narrative, highlighting the coexistence of contradicting memories and the fragility of authoritative claims (Shlaim 1995; Peters and Newman 2013).

The research produced beyond Israel offered a calibrated vantage point from which the formative years of the state could be re-assessed, revealing lines of causation and agency that had previously been muted. Distinctive methodological and theoretical orientations brought to the study of land, population, and conflict invited historians to interrogate the premises on which the older synthesis had rested. Whether through the lens of post-colonial critique, memory studies, or the critique of nationalism, the incorporation of international scholarship encouraged the gradual disaggregation of monolithic accounts and highlighted the coexistence of contradicting memories, thereby exposing the fragility of previously authoritative claims.

Contemporary historiography now benefits from exchanges among scholars trained in diverse traditions—via published debates, workshops, and digital forums—that transcend narrow national frames (Peters and Newman 2013). The result is cumulative knowledge that recognises the historical landscape as internally contested (Shlaim 1995). This collaborative venture continues to re-frame our conception of the past while establishing a methodological reflex that, in turn, interrogates the present.

Through sustained scholarly dialogue and the slow, cumulative work of exchange, the frame of historical enquiry widened so as to include a greater range of voices and interpretations, thereby renewing the search for historical truth. This jointly conducted work did more than enrich the discipline itself; it reached a public eager to re-examine well-defended narratives confronted by new, carefully verified findings.

The effect of this international contribution was to prompt a decisive re-evaluation of inherited accounts, instituting a measured restructuring of the questions historians asked. As outside perspectives were increasingly taken up, they re-organised the field of Israeli historiography and invited a more plural and layered representation of the past. The continuing engagement of non-local scholarship thus became both the occasion and the instrument of a critical re-weighting of narratives, illustrating the capacity of joint intellectual labour to alter our shared conception of historical reality.

Early Pioneers: Key Figures and Their Works

The rise of the New Historians in Israel constituted a watershed moment in the historiography of the Israeli-Palestinian encounter, interrogating dominant narratives and presenting referentially alternative interpretations of foundational episodes. This revisionist wave originated with a group of scholars prepared to probe hitherto marginalised archives, to return to primary documents, and to subject the moral certainties of the younger state to rigorous empirical re-examination.

Benny Morris's The Birth of the Palestinian Refugee Problem, 1947–1949 (1988; revised 2004) catalogued the processes of displacement during the 1948 war with systematic attention to Israeli, Arab, and international sources (Morris 1988; 2004). Through a meticulously assembled combination of Israeli military records, Arab testimony, and press accounts on specific operations, Morris interrogated the interplay of agency and coercion, revealing a multidimensional tableau illuminating mechanisms of flight, expulsion, and pre-war demographic tension (Morris 1986a; 1986b; 2008). The result was, for some, a painful dislodgment of soothing fables; for others, a more granular and, in the end, more credible narrative.

Ilan Pappé, extending Morris's methodological underpinnings, advanced a more assertive stratigraphic claim: the intentionality of a planned and systematic transfer of the Arab population, which he crystallised in The Ethnic

Cleansing of Palestine. His interpretation, underpinned by declassified military correspondence and the memoirs of the state's senior officers, reclassified the events of 1948 from the register of collateral tragedy to that of premeditated administrative action (Pappé 2006; 1988). Pappé's conclusions animate ongoing polemics, and, by displacing the controversy from the margins of the academic guild to the heart of public discussion, underscored the New Historians' wider cultural impact.

Avi Shlaim, widely respected for his incisive critique of Israeli diplomatic and military strategy, introduced a perspective that challenged the customary idolisation of Israeli conduct and thus encouraged a fundamental reevaluation of the record (Shlaim 1988; 2000).

Simha Flapan concentrated on disclosing the concealed facets of Zionist policy and their ramifications for the local population, discrediting the hegemonic national myths upheld by conventional historiography (Flapan 1987).

Such scholars of the first generation reoriented the intellectual terrain and cleared a path for a decisive reconfiguration of historical studies, laying a durable groundwork for subsequent scholars. Through fearless engagement with contentious topics and assiduous examination of the sources, they succeeded in inaugurating an era of enquiry that continues to inform contemporary understandings of the Israeli-Palestinian conflict and its wider significance. Their publications remain compelling affirmations of the efficacy of dissenting scholarship and the transformative capacity of disciplined historical research.

From Margin to Mainstream: Gaining Academic Currency

The movement of historically marginalised scholars to respected centres of historiographical discussion marks an extraordinary enrichment of the discipline. This reconceptualisation was not incidental; it emerged from sustained attempts to interrogate dominant paradigms and to articulate alternative chronological understandings. With each substantive publication and scholarly colloquium, the once-niche arguments acquired sufficient critical mass to obligate peer researchers to engage them and, over time, to revise settled historiographical positions.

Key to the concomitant widening of their reach was the strategic publication of monographs, edited collections, and articles in leading journals, coupled with their sustained presence at multidisciplinary conferences. When distinguished university presses and journals subjected their work to rigorous peer review and granted it prominence, it gained the imprimatur necessary to enter graduate syllabi and undergraduate readings (Shlaim 1995; Peters and Newman 2013). **Awarding fellowships and research grants to these scholars further entrenched their findings at the curricular, intellectual, and administrative levels, thus translating intellectual marginality into scholarly orthodoxy and guiding the formation of successor generations of researchers** (Morris 2004; Shlaim 2000).

The newer generation of historians actively employed

digital and broadcast media —op-eds, documentaries, and popular histories— **to share their research beyond university lecture halls and library walls** (Segev 2000). **This direct outreach, combined with analytically rich yet narratively compelling presentations, attracted readers and viewers eager for more complex and less monolithic portrayals of the past. As a result, their interpretations circulated through newspapers, podcasts, and documentary series, fostering wider intellectual curiosity while inviting a reinvestment in the contingencies and conflicts that earlier textbooks tended to elide. Public debates and commemorative controversies then became venues for the professional circulation of their research, amplifying its civic relevance while complicating previously unchallenged civic myths.**

Despite their successes, these historians encountered concerted pushback from defenders of established narratives, who marshalled institutional authority and disciplinary inertia to dismiss their methods and motives. The newcomers responded not with defensive rhetoric but with transparent citation, methodological self-reflexivity, and a readiness to revise (Karsh 1997; Shapira 1995; Teveth 1989). **Their perseverance, coupled with a series of carefully staged public interventions—from roundtable symposiums to opinion pieces juxtaposing archival evidence against politically charged recollection—earned the confidence of a much larger constituency. Over time, their contributions altered the benchmarks of professional dialogue while embedding a more contested conception of memory in the nation's everyday conversations about the past.**

Setting the Stage for a Paradigm Shift in Historical Studies

The 1980s witnessed a shift from conventional narrative frameworks to more critically engaged, analytically pluralist historiography. Scholars broadened their lens to include structures of power, everyday practice, and transnational forces (Shafir 1989; Said 1978). Methodological innovations—oral history, material culture, microhistory—lent depth to reconstructions and unsettled orthodoxies (Peters and Newman 2013; Beinin and Lockman 1989). Cross-border collaborations and conferences enabled comparative challenges to dominant narratives, fostering a sustained, reciprocal critique (Peters and Newman 2013; Shlaim 1995).

Drawing on a kaleidoscopic array of disciplinary methods and documentary forms, practitioners peeled away stratified representations to reveal the voices and experiences that mainstream accounts had rendered inaudible. The readiness to confront politically and emotionally charged omissions, and to unsettle entrenched disciplinary orthodoxies, proved a decisive factor in conditioning the emergence of a new historiographical paradigm.

Navigating this intellectually charged topography, leading researchers intentionally widened the analytical aperture to include the heteronomous structures of power and everyday practice that frame any given event. The attendant reconceptualisation of the past as a densely interwoven field served to exhibit the mutual constitution of the laboratory of local actors and the imperatives of transnational constellations. Methodologically, innovations such as the systematic collection of oral testimonies, the critical integration of material culture, and sensitive readings of stratified archaeology lent depth and granularity to the reconstructions, transcending reductive periodisation and additive historiography. The cumulative effect was a historiographical moment that hinted at, and in some places inched toward, a definitively new disciplinary sensibility.

The international scholarly community has thus functioned as a vital incubator for intellectual exchange, enabling a comparative challenge to dominant historical narratives. Through cross-border collaborative research projects, conferences, and electronic forums, historians were encouraged to articulate their questions alongside those originating in different disciplinary and national settings. The resulting articulation of divergent yet overlapping interpretations compelled each scholar to confront and reflect on their own situated assumptions, resulting in a sustained, reciprocal critique. Such acute forms of intellectual cross-fertilization encouraged a re-definition of historiographical boundaries and fostered the imagination of new calibrations of evidence and argument.

Simultaneously, the methodical re-examination of archival materials, in concert with a sustained critique of colonial legacies, led to a broadening of the questions historians were willing to entertain. Increasing sensitivity to the entangled power relations that structure both documents and their interpretation permitted a movement beyond a narrow reliance on legitimising evidence. This development configured a historiographical field increasingly capable of displacing grand narratives that sedimented dominant ideologies and amplifying those accounts that were, until recently, relegated to the margins. The cumulative effect of these twin processes—a methodological enquiry into documents and an ethical interrogation of power—invited a re-setting of scholarly priorities away from the reproduction of consensus and toward the interrogation of silence.

The transitional phase that preceded the paradigm shift in historical scholarship was marked by an exceptional willingness to reconstruct narratives, an insistence on examining inherited doctrinal assumptions, and an unwavering quest for evidentiary truth. This foundational reconfiguration of methodological and interpretative commitments established the conditions for a subsequent phase of enquiry, whose evolving forms now persistently reorient and deepen our grasp of preceding epochs.

The Impact of Global Events on Scholarly Perspectives

The 20th century was punctuated by a sequence of global upheavals that irreversibly reframed the intellectual landscape of historiography. The sequelae of two world wars, the disintegration of empires, decolonisation, and the attendant sculpting of new national borders generated a matrix within which historians were repeatedly compelled to recalibrate their vantage points. Collectively, these phenomena exposed the fragility and partiality of earlier interpretive frameworks.

Such Global upheavals—two world wars, decolonisation, the Cold War, human rights movements, and accelerating globalisation—reframed historical enquiry and challenged Eurocentric narratives (Said 1978; Shafir 1989). **The need to situate these phenomena alongside global currents fostered a scholarly environment that affirmed the necessity of comparative and transnational methodologies. The result was a historiographical expansion that valorised contingency and interdependence over isolated sovereignty.**

Among these global transformations, the decay of formal colonial rule and the subsequent forging of post-colonial entities exercised the most far-reaching influence. The collapse of imperial authority invited historians to excavate the sediment of colonial rule, the subtler registers of indigenous agency, and the uneven legacies left to the emergent polities. In the process, historiography was gradually de-centred; traditional Eurocentric narratives were not merely supplemented, but recast, as the voices of previously marginalised actors gained analytical and symbolic prominence. Historians increasingly adopted comparative and transnational approaches that foregrounded contingency and interdependence, decentering nation-state teleologies and recovering marginalised voices (Beinin and Lockman 1989; Peters and Newman 2013).

The Cold War, with its ideological divides, left a durable imprint on the writing of history. Contending East and

West not only shaped contemporary politics but also infiltrated historians' accounts of the past, compelling scholars to confront the legacy of partisan compression and to piece together a past fragmented by competing certainties.

The subsequent decades, following the geopolitical fracture of 1945, saw the rise of movements pressing claims of human rights and social equity. In response, historians directed their attention to the reverberations of civil rights campaigns, struggles for women's liberation, and the assertion of minority rights, recovering voices that earlier accounts had silenced and advancing a version of the past that now insists on the co-constitution of society and polity.

Finally, the later 20th century's accelerating globalisation required a critical reassessment of historical causation. Historians turned to the mutual constitution of distant societies, examining how circulations of people, commodities, and ideas exceeded inherited national frames and revealing how localised developments were inextricably shaped by broader transnational currents.

The intersection of these global developments broadened the field of historical study and obliged historians to develop more nuanced and inclusive methodologies for interpreting the past. As the disruptive processes of the twentieth century refashioned the international order, they also refashioned the archival and conceptual tools of the discipline, clearing the way for the rise of new historiographical models that interrogated and, often, redefined long-dominant orthodoxies.

Public Reaction and Initial Resistance

The eruption of the New Historians provoked a stormy reaction that affected multiple social and political strata in Israel. Their revisionist readings, which confronted the nation's foundational myths with newly marshalled documentary and oral evidence, pierced the protective membrane of consensus that had long insulated collective memory. The result was a collective unease that rippled outward, manifesting in partisan debates, institutional retrenchment, and the reconstitution of popular memory. Established textbooks, once sacrosanct bearers of heroism and innocence, were subjected to a level of methodological auditing previously reserved for foreign scholarship. The reaction thus crystallised not only in political polemic but also in the anxious refashioning of educational syllabi and public memorials.

The most pronounced reaction came in the form of blanket rejection from defenders of the accepted historiography. The established political cohort, senior military leaders, and scholars rallied against any lapse from the older consensus. Critics in politics, the military, and academia challenged their methods and motives, arguing that revisionism distorted history and imperiled national legitimacy (Teveth 1989; Karsh 1997). The New Historians encountered slander and ultimately branded as traitors for attempting to foreground neglected, often painful, episodes in Israel's past. Detractors intensified their assault out of fear that the disclosures might tarnish the country's image abroad and undermine its relentless quest for legitimacy in the diplomatic arena.

A second, no less important, current of public sentiment arose from groups whose collective memory and civic virtue were explicitly anchored in the older chronicle. For these audiences the inherited stories—ritualised in textbooks and holiday oratory—constituted the emotive core of both nationalism and political conscience. The new analysis thus arrived as an unwelcome rupture, capable of unseating convictions upon which civic and private identity rested. Further compounding this sensitivity was the possibility, articulated in both taverns and parliament, that the entire edifice of memory might be rendered unsound, provoking an immediate, visceral and unyielding refusal to engage.

In scholarly quarters, where the confrontation between entrenched establishments and the generation of innovative historians unfolded with remarkable intensity, the atmosphere remained charged. Guardians of the prevailing paradigms directed their efforts to delegitimize, to isolate, and, when possible, to silence the counter-approaches, employing personal discredit as freely as refusal to publish alternative interpretations. The initial phase of this intellectual contest, therefore, unfolded under a pervasive sense of aggression, deepening rifts and fostering animosities within the research community itself.

Yet to record this acrimony alone would fail to note the discreet islands of enquiry and encouragement that arose alongside. Younger historians and critics, having inherited neither loyalty to predecessors nor the baggage of sectarian disputes, approached the New Historians' publications with genuine interest and a demand for reconsidered evidence. Their readiness to interrogate venerable certainties indicated not mere curiosity, but a wider institutional preparedness to engage with complexity. Supporters and younger scholars welcomed renewed scrutiny of foundational narratives and encouraged rigorous evidentiary standards (Shapira 1995; Shlaim 1995). The result was a contentious but generative public debate that pressed textbooks, commemorations, and curricula to confront complexity (Silberstein 1999; Kimmerling 2001).

When these tentative but insistent tremors of intellectual readiness reached broader social consciousness, it became increasingly plain that a decisive shift in the collective Israeli understanding of the past was already in the making.

Laying the Groundwork for Further Inquiries into 1948

After the initial shock, a more reflective phase opened, encouraging continued investigation into 1948 via sustained archival work, oral history, and digitisation (Morris 2008; Israel State Archives n.d.; AUB Libraries—POHA n.d.). Oral history initiatives preserved eyewitness accounts and everyday experiences often absent from diplomatic and military records, enriching the mosaic of perspectives (Beinin and Lockman 1989; AUB Libraries—POHA n.d.

). Digitised catalogues and online repositories lowered barriers of language and proximity, catalysing transnational collaboration and interdisciplinarity (Israel State Archives n.d.; Peters and Newman 2013; Akevot Institute n.d.). This widening aperture helped situate 1948 within broader constellations of imperial legacies, Cold War imperatives, and local agency (Shlaim 1988; Segev 2000; Morris 2008). Historians, emboldened rather than cowed, began to map the archive trails the critics had suggested were worth traversing, and to ask questions the standard curricula had kept at bay. Land settlement schemes, patterns of enforced migration, and the evolving Arab-Israeli conflict were subjected to sustained methodological cross-examination, leading to a substantial and cumulative re-evaluation of the period.

Central to this foundation-building phase has been a renewed, systematic effort to unearth long-neglected archival materials and eyewitness accounts. Historians have, therefore, constructed a dense mosaic of vantage points that together illuminate the complex reality of the events of 1948. Oral history initiatives, now firmly institutionalised, have ensured that the recollections of individuals who lived through the crises are recorded, catalogued, and made accessible; such testimonies introduce subtleties that even the most comprehensive political and diplomatic records can obscure, recounting the everyday fears, rituals of displacement, and moments of insistence that composite the lives of the uprooted.

Alongside these archival recoveries, recent developments in digitisation have enlarged the aperture through which the past can be scrutinised. Digitised catalogues, full-text searches, and vast online repositories of campus and national libraries now allow a semester's worth of primary records to be retrieved from a laptop, thereby lowering barriers both of language and of proximity. This openness has, in turn, catalysed a transnational and trans-civilisational dialogue among researchers, whose variegated disciplinary habits have interwoven legal, visual, and spatial analyses into the 1948 historiography; the result is an increasingly textured and reflexive account that refuses both reductive singularity and anachronism.

As foundational work on 1948 began to cohere, the New Historians' impact reached well beyond the boundaries of Israel and Palestine. Transnational collaborations incubated, as historians, archivists, and area specialists pooled findings and insights to reveal the entanglement of metropolitan policies, Cold War imperatives, and local agency that jointly choreographed the Middle East's post-war calibrations. Conferences, mobile research teams, and jointly edited volumes became occasions for sustained and sometimes contentious dialogue, integrating New Historical approaches into debates already framed by post-colonial, transnational, and micro-historical vectors within the global meta-history.

This transnational scholarly circulation encouraged a layered re-examination of 1948, inviting methods drawn from oral history, diplomatic history, and micro-sociology. The emergent empirical reconfiguration underscored the temporality and location of memory, the ideological slippages of archival silencing, and the agency of peripheral actors. In this context, the character of the past itself appeared politicised and pluralised, prompting historians to wrestle with the 'event' as an unresolved contest rather than a reductive closure, and thus widening the disciplinary aperture onto the seminal conflicts that still animate the contemporary Middle East.

References

- Akevot Institute for Israeli-Palestinian Conflict Research. n.d. https://www.akevot.org.il/en/

- American University of Beirut (AUB) Libraries. Palestinian Oral History Archive (POHA). n.d. https://libraries.aub.edu.lb/poha

- Beinin, Joel, and Zachary Lockman, eds. 1989. Intifada: The Palestinian Uprising Against Israeli Occupation. Boston: South End Press.

- Flapan, Simha. 1987. The Birth of Israel: Myths and Realities. New York: Pantheon Books.

- Gelber, Yoav. 2004. Nation and History: Israeli Historiography between Zionism and Post-Zionism. London: Vallentine Mitchell.

- Israel State Archives. n.d. English site. https://www.archives.gov.il/en/

- Karsh, Efraim. 1997. Fabricating Israeli History: The "New Historians." London: Frank Cass.

- Kimmerling, Baruch. 2001. The Invention and Decline of Israeliness: State, Society, and the Military. Berkeley: University of California Press.

- Masalha, Nur. 1992. Expulsion of the Palestinians: The Concept of "Transfer" in Zionist Political Thought, 1882–1948. Washington, DC: Institute for Palestine Studies.

- Morris, Benny. 1986a. "The Causes of the Palestinian Refugee Problem, 1947–49." Middle Eastern Studies 22 (1): 5–19.

- ———. 1986b. "Operation Dani and the Palestinian Exodus from Lydda and Ramle in 1948." Middle East Journal 40 (1): 82–109.

- ———. 1988. The Birth of the Palestinian Refugee Problem, 1947–1949. Cambridge: Cambridge University Press.

- ———. 2004. The Birth of the Palestinian Refugee Problem Revisited. Cambridge: Cambridge University Press.

- ———. 2008. 1948: A History of the First Arab–Israeli War. New Haven: Yale University Press.

- Pappé, Ilan. 1988. Britain and the Arab–Israeli Conflict, 1948–51. London: Macmillan.

- ———. 2006. The Ethnic Cleansing of Palestine. Oxford: Oneworld Publications.

- Peters, Joel, and David Newman, eds. 2013. Routledge Handbook on the Israeli–Palestinian Conflict. London: Routledge.

- Said, Edward W. 1978. Orientalism. New York: Pantheon Books.

- Schiff, Ze'ev, and Ehud Ya'ari. 1984. Israel's Lebanon War. New York: Simon & Schuster.

- Segev, Tom. 1986. 1949: The First Israelis. New York: Free Press.

- ———. 2000. One Palestine, Complete: Jews and Arabs under the British Mandate. New York: Metropolitan Books.

- Shafir, Gershon. 1989. Land, Labor and the Origins of the Israeli–Palestinian Conflict, 1882–1914. Cambridge: Cambridge University Press.

- Shapira, Anita. 1995. "Politics and Collective Memory: The Debate over the 'New Historians' in Israel." History & Memory 7 (1): 9–40.

- Shlaim, Avi. 1988. Collusion Across the Jordan: King Abdullah, the Zionist Movement, and the Partition of Palestine. New York: Columbia University Press.

- ———. 1995. "The Debate about 1948." International Journal of Middle East Studies 27 (3): 287–304.

- ———. 2000. The Iron Wall: Israel and the Arab World. New York: W. W. Norton.

- Silberstein, Laurence J., ed. 1999. The Postzionism Debates: Knowledge and Power in Israeli Culture. New York: Routledge.

- Teveth, Shabtai. 1989. "Charging Israel with Original Sin." Commentary 88 (3). https://www.commentary.org/articles/shabtai-teveth/charging-israel-with-original-sin/

- The National Archives (UK). n.d. "The 20-year rule." https://www.nationalarchives.gov.uk/information-management/manage-information/planning/20-year-rule/

2
Benny Morris and the Reconsideration of 1948

An Introduction to Benny Morris and His Academic Journey

Benny Morris became a central voice in the New Historians, the cadre of Israeli scholars who interrogated the dominant historiography of the emergence of the Israeli state. His birth in 1948, the decisive year of the British retrenchment and the Palestinian exodus, positioned him, symbolically and autobiographically, at the intersection of biography and event. Morris, whose intellectual formation unfolded both at the Hebrew University of Jerusalem and in the archival labyrinths of Cambridge, derived his historiographical method from the incisive, empiricist tradition of Raphael Patai and the normative scepticism encouraged by Moshe Ma'oz. Surgical archival scrutiny, a consciousness of the moral stakes of evidence, and a refusal to accept the teleological designs of the existing narratives coalesced in his first monograph, which revealed the continuity of expulsion and settlement in 1948. By the late 1970s, the first Israeli civil war had morphed into a protracted national conflict, and the broader wave of late-imperial scepticism in the West reverberated in Israeli universities. The intersection of Morris's methodological innovativeness and the volatile conjuncture of intifada diplomacy, the collapse of the Soviet mandate of Arabs, and postmodern appropriations of testimony animated his continuing re-examination of the birth of a polity whose official historiography still accrued triumphalist sediment.

Positioned uniquely as an Israeli historian free from the disciplines that usually govern the field, he was able to interrogate the dominant myths and presuppositions without reservation, thereby catalysing an expansive re-evaluation of the historiographical terrain. Merging disciplined research with an uncompromising commitment to evidence, Morris unsettled fixed narratives and beckoned the international community to revise its perception of one of the 20th century's decisive eras. The following discussion traces the intellectual currents that directed Morris's early development, identifies the key publications that secured his place among leading historians, and reflects upon the lasting effect of his investigations upon the discipline as a whole.

The Intellectual Climate of the Late 20th Century: A Historical Context

Across the converging currents of the late twentieth-century discipline, the academy was animated, and sometimes paralysed, by debates over the nature of historical explanation and the interplay of power and memory. Historians long anchored in positivist techniques felt themselves at once emboldened and endangered by the rise of the so-called cultural turn, which urged analysts to look beyond documents and toward the indeterminacies of language, spectacle, and the subject positioned at the margin of the nation. The buoyant, reconstructive optimism of the immediate post-war period was corrosively tested by the Vietnam debacle, the spectres of authoritarian liberalism, and the vertiginous return of once-critical nationalist ideologies. No facet of the human past remained exempt, even the archives of democracy, and the twin spectres of trauma and late capitalism forced a reconfiguration of the archive itself. The critique of teleology, long a scholarly topos, morphed into an urgent imperative: historians found themselves re-writing not merely episodes, but the very temporality of contestation. It was at this tensile juncture, when the interdependence of self and other, liberator and colonised, was theorised with renewed ferocity, that Benny Morris's interrogative texts penetrated disciplinary reflexes, provoking both scholarly rebuttals and popular outcry, and thereby accelerating a world-historical appraisal of nationalist conflicts in the Levant and beyond.

Armed with emergent methodologies and previously inaccessible archival material, contemporary historians have acquired the means to dismantle the bulwarks of officially sanctioned accounts, revealing the inherent precariousness of purported historical certainties.

A Revolutionary Lens: Reevaluating the Founding Myths

Benny Morris, celebrated for both the rigour of his archival practice and the contentiousness of his conclusions, has reshaped the scholarship on the myths that accompanied the birth of the State of Israel. His pioneering analysis invites the scholar and general reader alike to re-question the premises of rival historical schools by exposing the temporal slippages and evidential gaps that were hidden within earlier patriotic synthesis. Morris interrogates primary documentation alongside diplomatic correspondence, contemporary press accounts and military records, permitting him to reconstruct episodes long sealed within ideological outcome. The result is a disaggregation of the mythologised moment of statehood from the contingencies, violence and property displacements that accompanied it, yielding a clearer picture of what contemporary observers deemed both public achievement and private tragedy. His work therefore compels a sustained critical re-examination of the collective memories that continue to inform the historiography of Israel-Palestine.

Morris's investigation reveals the dense interlacing of political circumstance, ideological commitment, and the factual past. By painstakingly tracing decisive junctures—most notably the 1948 Arab-Israeli War and the ensuing Palestinian flight—he advances a sequence of events that unsettles standard historiography. Figures once enfranchised as emblematic of singular motives are instead reconstituted within a matrix of layered imperatives, strategic calculations, and human agency. Such an expansive treatment undermines reductive schemata, exposing the labyrinthine aggregation of determinants that ultimately reoriented the region's trajectory.

Morris's confrontation of mythic foundations further disturbs presupposed certainties, pressing audiences to entertain painful realities that long resisted reconsideration. His fearless examination of intercommunal exchanges and the dialectic of violence acknowledges the bereavement sustained on both sides while dismantling commemorative fictions. In departing from settled folklore, his work bids readers—whether singularly or collectively—to undertake the awkward dialectic of recognizing an unsettled past that both ethical and political futures continue to demand that people bear.

Through his critical reexamination of foundational narratives, Morris invites a transnational and trans-temporal conversation that addresses the practice of historical interpretation and its bearing on present deliberations. His method foregrounds the necessity of treating the past as an active site, in which rigorous scrutiny and open exchange may reconfigure inherited understandings. Morris's project thus assumes the role of an incitement, encouraging confrontation with uncomfortable verities and, in so doing, opening avenues for empathic engagement and reconciliatory politics across the often fractious landscape of collective memory.

Morris's Methodology: Archival Revelations and Challenges

Benny Morris's influential studies of the 1948 war are characterised not only by incisive theoretical contributions, but by a methodical deployment of archival evidence capable of dissolving dominant historiographical sediment. His research programme was predicated on a scrupulous immersion in previously withheld records, including the hold of the Israel State Archives, the Military Intelligence Directorate, and assorted private collections, augmented by personal correspondence within the Higher Command and Jewish Agency circles. Through a triangulated reading of these heterogeneous and hierarchically structured dossiers, Morris was able to expose contradictions, rearguing incidents previously overwritten by the political or ideological imperatives of earlier narrators. His recovery of marginal documents—captain's diaries, operational orders, and absorbed epistolary asides—permitted a dimensional shift, revealing the war as a theatre dense with contingency and precarious human choice. Nevertheless, the pursuit of these documents was circumscribed by significant resistance. His intrusion into politically saturated archives encountered both bureaucratic obstruction and interpretive pushback from guardians of the Zionist historiographical tradition, while the disclosure of sensitive intelligence material provoked ethical scrutiny regarding the terms of confidentiality and the implications for contemporary national security. The labour of archival reconstruction thus compelled Morris to sustain a discipline of distanced critique, yet debates regarding selection and contextual weighting thus entered the disciplinary arena. Critics questioned whether the emphasis placed on certain documents indicated an excessively deterministic interpretation, while the disclosure of troubling operational decisions necessitated, according to various observers, a heightened moral accountability from the historian.

This chapter examines the intellectual tenacity with which Morris confronted formidable obstacles in both the Semitic and Western archives, and traces the long-term ramifications of this engagement on subsequent historical practice. Attention is focused on the disjunction between archival organism and historiographic organism, weighing the historiographical incentives, practical impediments, and conceptual fallout of Morris's method in the layered arena of modern historical enquiry. His methodological reformulations remain operative, prompting a subsequent cohort of scholars to embrace the intellectual and ethical intricacies that define the craft of reconstructing a past in which one's own contemporaneity is irrevocably entangled.

1948 Reconsidered: Key Events and Contested Narratives

The year 1948 registered a decisive inflection in the Map of the Middle East, culminating in the proclamation of the State of Israel. Since that moment, the chronological junction has generated a superfluity of rival accounts, each competing for epistemic and mnemonic dominance. This segment will methodically reassemble the chronological skeleton of 1948 as historiographically reformulated since Morris's original study, foregrounding those disputed nodes of interpretation that refuse closure and that animate both scholarly debate and broader public consciousness.

Analyses of the constitutional moment surrounding the founding of the State of Israel continue to reveal irreconcilable narratives concerning the interplay of domestic and external forces. Scholars remain divided over the agency of the Jewish and Arab polities, the role of imperial and post-imperial states, and the interpretative status of the mass population dislocation that accompanied the military confrontation of 1948. As a consequence, historians confront a corpus of evidence that simultaneously reproduces and contradicts itself, thereby embedding the polarised accounts of 1948 in a historiographical impasse.

The critical reassessment of the year involves a renewed focus on the interplay of military operations, refugee movements, and the reconfiguration of regional power equilibria. Previously dominant historiographies that privileged singular narratives are now being supplemented by extensive collation of archival materials, oral testimonies, and diplomatic correspondences, thereby disclosing a complexity that transcends the reductive binaries of victim and victimiser. Such a methodological pivot invites a more cautious calibration of causality, while underscoring the contingent and interactively produced character of the decade's decisive settlements.

The debates surrounding the events of 1948 transcend geopolitical disputes, penetrating social, cultural, and ethical domains. Accounts of individuals and communities displaced and traumatized during the year have emerged as indispensable portals into the lived realities that exceed the abstraction of statecraft. When historians return to the flashpoints of 1948, they foreground the volatile interaction between shifting power structures, collective grief, and the clashing aspirations of national projects—forces that continue to haunt the territory of contemporary conflict.

The discord over how to narrate 1948 also compels scholars to scrutinise the vocabulary employed to characterise the unfolding crises. Terms such as "exodus," "transfer," and "displacement" evoke radically different moral landscapes and positional stances, imprinting themselves upon collective memory and identity formation. Any reexamination of decisive episodes therefore demands a sensibility to the mutually constitutive relation between language, persuasion, and historical representation.

What follows is a systematic disaggregation of these contending narratives, a study directed toward the historiographical reassessment of 1948. By confronting the plural interpretations and the vantage points from which they emanate, we endeavour to chart the multilayered continuities that the year has created across the Middle East and their reverberations in global debates about nationalism, memory, and justice.

Critiques and Counterarguments: Responses from Peers and Public

Benny Morris's reexamination of the circumstances surrounding the establishment of the State of Israel in 1948 has elicited a range of critiques from historians and laypersons alike, confirming that any radical alteration of the scholarly consensus will galvanise extended, cross-disciplinary enquiry. Among the recurrent objections, the first centres on the interplay between scholarly neutrality and interpretive judgement. Detractors contend that Morris's rearguard of archival evidence may conceal latent ideological commitment, thereby damaging the neutrality that the discipline demands. Equally, several reviewers caution that the limited chronological and administrative frame of reference adopted by Morris obscures the longer trajectories of Ottoman, Mandate, and regional history, thereby impoverishing any attempt to situate the 1948 outcomes within a generation's worth of Palestinian and Zionist processes.

Thomas N. Fryer, for instance, has argued that Morris unevenly weighs evidence in a way that accentuates military deliberations harming sociopolitical, cultural, and transnational factors; other reviewers insist that the selective citation of military orders, diplomatic reports, and survivors' testimonies risk constructing a linear explanation whose explanatory power diminishes in more fragmented and contradictory datasets. The critiques extend to the archival material itself, where Morris's critics have challenged the interpretive frames he applies to Israeli Defence Forces documents. Some observers have questioned the manner in which Morris calibrates the evidentiary contours of the Israel State Archives against Lebanese, British, and UN files, arguing that the equilibrium of judgement wobbles on details whose incommensurability the conventional historiography on 1948 long ago suppressed. Collectively, these arguments insist that any monographic revaluation of 1948 must remain self-aware of both its evidentiary scope and its epistemic reflexivity, lest it be construed not as a correction of the past but as a reformatting of its memory that resets rather than resolves the historiographical impasse.

Critics of the objections to Benny Morris argue that the author's documented archival practice and reflective testimony legitimacy constitute a compelling corrective to the historiographical consensus pertaining to the summer of 1948. Supporters commend his readiness to interrogate empirically the disquieting dimensions of the period, reading this as a guarantee of intellectual honesty that cannot be ignored. They further insist that every historiographical position, including the orthodoxy that Morris once surveyed, is likewise constructed upon specific epistemic decisions, rendering his eventual conclusions an equally rigorous—if dissenting—articulation of evidence and interpretation. Public reception confirms the archival debate's traction: Morris's willingness to question quasi-sacrosanct units of collective remembrance has catalysed widespread affect, inhering both overt accolades and vitriolic rejection. Those who commend his articulation regard it as a precondition for an unobscured and potentially conciliatory confrontation with the past; conversely, defenders of the earlier consensus construe his findings as an assault upon the narratives that consolidate national unity and retributive memory. Resonances thus issued, the controversy now threads through contemporary political advocacy, media articulation, and the mnemonic formation of both Israeli and Palestinian societies. The sharp division of reception, whether through scholarly critique or civilian mobilisation, attests to Morris's reexamination as a fulcrum upon which present and future understandings of the Palestinian question and of historical conscience are precariously balanced.

The Balance of Objectivity and Controversy in Morris's Work

Benny Morris's pioneering studies of the 1948 events have won both acclaim and fierce opposition, igniting fervent exchanges in academic forums and popular discourse alike. Motivated by a distinctive quest for verifiable evidence, Morris repeatedly confronted dominant historical paradigms, supplementing the archive with interrogated documentation, statistics, and comparative contextualisation. This chapter examines the equilibrium, fragile yet consequential, between neutral appraisal and incendiary claim that suffuses Morris's oeuvre. By exposing the precise manner in which his revelations reframed the discourse, it becomes apparent that the historian's decisions not only reopened the evidential record but also redefined the ethical and epistemological obligations of the profession vis-à-vis unresolved trauma and contested memory.

A central tenet of Morris's scholarship is his persistent reliance on primary sources and archival holdings. His disciplined study of official documents, survivor depositions, and diplomatic exchanges has yielded an evidentiary basis without which his conclusions would lack cogency. By painstakingly charting event sequences and interrogating received interpretations, Morris has obliged the scholarly world to reckon with disquieting realities embedded in the 1948 moment of Israel's statehood. Yet, his determination to meet the canons of empirical enquiry has not immunised him from reproach; the reconstruction he offers has incited fervent backlash from guardians of conventional national chronologies. Morris's provocative reconceptualisation has highlighted the porous boundary separating historiography from ongoing political contests. By reassessing decisive junctures in the state's genesis, he has compelled audiences to engage the fraught convergence of archival veracity and contemporary polemics. The fallout from his writings ripples outward beyond historiographical fora, fuelling debate over collective identity, equitable redress, and the politics of memory. The blending of scholarly enquiry with wider societal controversies has in turn magnified scrutiny of Morris's archival practice, generating a polarized reception characterised by equal measures of esteem and reproach.

In negotiating the tension between objectivity and controversy, Morris's scholarship has decisively broadened the frontiers of historical analysis. By confronting politically charged and emotionally freighted subjects, he has urged the discipline to confront difficult realities and to cultivate more layered interpretations. The vehement disagreement his arguments have stirred, however, reminds us of the multilayered character of the past and of historians' moral duties to their sources and audiences. The lasting influence of Morris's oeuvre, therefore, may be measured not by consensus but by its insistence that historical scholarship remain open to relentless re-examination, thereby illustrating the shifting interplay between objective methodology, the inevitability of dispute, and the ongoing pursuit of historiographical accuracy.

Implications for the Palestinian Narrative: A Shift in Perspective

Morris's revised examination of 1948 has obliged scholars and activists alike to rethink the trajectory and framing of the Palestinian narrative itself, generating consequences that extend well beyond academic debate into the arenas of public memory and policy. By meticulously tracing the military and civil governance decisions that accompanied the birth of the State of Israel, Morris complicates the earlier schema of a triumphant, morally unambiguous national rebirth. In place of the notion of a largely self-chosen exodus, he documents a catalogue of coercive expulsions, massacres, and psychological warfare that refutes the principle of voluntary migration assumed by the earlier historiography. These findings, drawn from archival military correspondence, minute books of the newly formed state, and contemporaneous testimonies, do not elide the fact that the Zionist movement acted, rhetorically and strategically, to secure the Jewish population against existential threats. Yet, they demonstrate that this legitimacy cannot silence the resultant fabric of

Palestinian pain and dispossession. Morris's work thus expands the historiographical aperture by situating the conflict within the ordinary dynamics of colonial and civil war imperatives, urging scholars to confront the past's ethical compounding of suffering on all sides. The result is a narrative that invites, rather than precludes, the articulation of Palestinian agency while acknowledging that this agency has itself been produced by, and yet has been rendered intelligible only against, a constellated experience of loss.

Benny Morris's pioneering reconsideration of the 1948 conflict remains an indispensable touchstone for today's discussions on the Israeli-Palestinian conflict. His relentless archival investigation and merciless commitment to evidential rigour produced revelations whose influence endures, generating ongoing contestation of historicity, pathways to reconciliation, and the fragile interweaving of rival collective memory. Central among the legacies Morris bequeaths the discipline is the incisive critique of sedimented historiography. By documenting systematic displacement, dispossession, and lethal violence that attended the emergence of the Jewish state, he compelled a critical reassessment of earlier Zionist "heroic" models while thereby granting the Palestinian experience an overdue and critical contemporaneity. In tandem, his scholarship dismantles the conceit of Israeli exceptionalism by laying bare the moral and operational ambiguities that shadow the polity's inception. The resulting realisation obliges students of the conflict to reconsider the state's internal organism and its contractual obligations to a circumspect international order. Within current exchanges, Morris's conclusions function as an accelerant, energising stringent demands that unacknowledged historical injustices be openly confronted lest their effects perpetuate. His conclusions have moreover bequeathed a historical stage upon which previously excluded testimonies now resonate; the voices of the 1948 uprooted and their diasporic progeny no longer occupy the margin but inhabit the temporal centre of debate.

Furthermore, Morris has played a decisive role in promoting a transparent modality of historical investigation. He insists that confronting difficult truths and revising dominant narratives are not optional, and his disciplined analytical frame, allied to an unwavering dedication to verifiable evidence, has established a standard that historians and policymakers alike must now meet whenever they address the legacies of contentious pasts. The consequences of his scholarship ripple well beyond the university: they now inform popular conversation, diplomatic negotiations, and schemes of reconciliation. His discoveries have precipitated a more expansive interrogation of the foundational myths that sustain modern nation-states, pressing communities to confront the darker chapters of their past and to reckon with the human expenses of nation-building. Consequently, Morris's interventions persist in shaping current discussions, remaining a reference point for those who advocate for transparency, restorative justice, and a historiography that seeks to incorporate the widest possible range of human experience.

Concluding Observations on Truth, Reconciliation, and Historiography

In bringing this enquiry to its close, we must weigh yet further the repercussions of Benny Morris's pioneering historiography for the understanding of 1948 and for the practice of history as a field of moral witness. Although his conclusions elicit both fierce contestation and intellectual disquiet, they have irreversibly altered the terms of the debate. The affirmation of Morris's habilitation by succeeding generations of scholars guarantees the capacity of disciplined enquiry to displace older slogans and confront societies with the necessity of confronting, rather than suppressing, the discord between memory and document.

Equally, Morris's archive-based reexamination compels a rethinking of Israel's founding tales and simultaneously reopens the hermeneutical fault-line between history and memory. His detailed reconstructions expose the entangled ambiguities, elisions, and counter-factual trajectories that any historical event harbours, thus warning that the designation of a fixed historical truth is necessarily provisional and contingent upon the perpetually renewed act of scholarly interrogation.

Finally, Morris's study stands as an admonitory emblem of the historian's ethical vocation. The statistical demonstration of violence, the demographic correlates of exile, the circumscription of commemorative innocence—all oblige the discipline to assist, however indirectly, the protracted work of reconciliation by charting the sequences that futures must acknowledge if they will not repeat. Historians, when they confront the weights of remembrance and denial, participate in the slow nursing of a collective memory that is simultaneously just and liveable.

Through a meticulous analysis of the events of 1948, Morris has successfully opened up space for a more layered and inclusive comprehension of a fractured past. His work highlights that any future reconciliation between Israelis and Palestinians demands a candid confrontation with painful historical facts—including the collective traumas of both groups—rather than a selective memory that seeks to minimise discomfort. Morris's insistence on placing competing narratives side-by-side does not seek equivalence of suffering, but rather asks for equal attention to the reality that both peoples carry unresolved legacies of violence.

When situated within the larger field of historiography, the enduring import of Morris's conclusions points to the capacity of relentless, transparent scholarship to reshape political and cultural discourse. His example confirms that confronting contentious and polarising material does not delay peace, but rather lays the groundwork for it. The duty of historians, therefore, extends beyond documentation; it requires them to cultivate environments where difficult conversations can occur without the decay of scholarly objectivity. In this light, accepting the evidence Morris produces becomes a condition for fostering a culture not only of intellectual integrity but also of shared moral responsibility.

Re-consideration of 1948, then, exemplifies how historiography can operate as a constructive, rather than a destructive, force in societies divided by memory. By refusing to grant one version of the past a monopoly on legitimacy, scholarship creates openings for mutual recognition, and, in so doing, it does more than record; it actively contributes to the slow, layered work of reconciliation.

Morris's scrupulous scholarship, coupled with a steadfast commitment to fidelity to the evidence, reveals the layered structure of competing accounts that constitute our shared past. By compellingly situating these accounts within their full historical context, he compels us to confront the disquieting truths that are often submerged beneath the more celebratory layers of memory. It is precisely this fearless confrontation with the contradictions and uncertainties of history that enables a more charitable, discerning, and ultimately reconciliatory orientation toward the future.

References For Further Reading

- Akevot Institute for Israeli-Palestinian Conflict Research. n.d. https://www.akevot.org.il/en/

- American University of Beirut (AUB) Libraries. Palestinian Oral History Archive (POHA). n.d. https://libraries.aub.edu.lb/poha

- Beinin, Joel, and Zachary Lockman, eds. 1989. Intifada: The Palestinian Uprising Against Israeli Occupation.

Boston: South End Press.

- Flapan, Simha. 1987. The Birth of Israel: Myths and Realities. New York: Pantheon Books.

- Gelber, Yoav. 2004. Nation and History: Israeli Historiography between Zionism and Post-Zionism. London: Vallentine Mitchell.

- Israel State Archives. n.d. English site. https://www.archives.gov.il/en/

- Karsh, Efraim. 1997. Fabricating Israeli History: The "New Historians." London: Frank Cass.

- Kimmerling, Baruch. 2001. The Invention and Decline of Israeliness: State, Society, and the Military. Berkeley: University of California Press.

- Masalha, Nur. 1992. Expulsion of the Palestinians: The Concept of "Transfer" in Zionist Political Thought, 1882–1948. Washington, DC: Institute for Palestine Studies.

- Morris, Benny. 1986a. "The Causes of the Palestinian Refugee Problem, 1947–49." Middle Eastern Studies 22 (1): 5–19.

- ———. 1986b. "Operation Dani and the Palestinian Exodus from Lydda and Ramle in 1948." Middle East Journal 40 (1): 82–109.

- ———. 1988. The Birth of the Palestinian Refugee Problem, 1947–1949. Cambridge: Cambridge Universi-

- ———. 2004. The Birth of the Palestinian Refugee Problem Revisited. Cambridge: Cambridge University Press.

- ———. 2008. 1948: A History of the First Arab–Israeli War. New Haven: Yale University Press.

- Pappé, Ilan. 1988. Britain and the Arab–Israeli Conflict, 1948–51. London: Macmillan.

- ———. 2006. The Ethnic Cleansing of Palestine. Oxford: Oneworld Publications.

- Peters, Joel, and David Newman, eds. 2013. Routledge Handbook on the Israeli–Palestinian Conflict. London: Routledge.

- Said, Edward W. 1978. Orientalism. New York: Pantheon Books.

- Schiff, Ze'ev, and Ehud Ya'ari. 1984. Israel's Lebanon War. New York: Simon & Schuster.

- Segev, Tom. 1986. 1949: The First Israelis. New York: Free Press.

- ———. 2000. One Palestine, Complete: Jews and Arabs under the British Mandate. New York: Metropolitan Books.

- Shafir, Gershon. 1989. Land, Labor and the Origins of the Israeli–Palestinian Conflict, 1882–1914. Cambridge: Cambridge University Press.

- Shapira, Anita. 1995. "Politics and Collective Memory: The Debate over the 'New Historians' in Israel." History & Memory 7 (1): 9–40.

- Shlaim, Avi. 1988. Collusion Across the Jordan: King Abdullah, the Zionist Movement, and the Partition of Palestine. New York: Columbia University Press.

- ———. 1995. "The Debate about 1948." International Journal of Middle East Studies 27 (3): 287–304.

- ———. 2000. The Iron Wall: Israel and the Arab World. New York: W. W. Norton.

- Silberstein, Laurence J., ed. 1999. The Postzionism Debates: Knowledge and Power in Israeli Culture. New York: Routledge.

- Teveth, Shabtai. 1989. "Charging Israel with Original Sin." Commentary 88 (3). https://www.commentary.org/articles/shabtai-teveth/charging-israel-with-original-sin/

- The National Archives (UK). n.d. "The 20-year rule." https://www.nationalarchives.gov.uk/information-management/manage-information/planning/20-year-rule/

3
Ilan Pappé
Unveiling the Ethnic Cleansing Argument

Ilan Pappé's Work and Influence

Ilan Pappé is widely regarded as a leading scholar within the New Historians movement, instrumental in reframing the historiography of the Palestinian catastrophe and the founding of the State of Israel. Hailing from Haifa and completing his graduate studies in Israel and the United Kingdom, Pappé gained prominence for his refusal to accept the traditional Zionist consensus and, more provocatively, for his insistence that the evidence supports a diagnosis of premeditated ethnic cleansing during the critical years of 1947 to 1949. His impact on the discipline proceeds from a methodological rigour tempered by a moral imperative to bear witness to the silences in the archives, and his writings continue to prompt both scholarly debate and civil condemnation.

Pappé's investigations begin where most earlier historians hesitated: in the classified documents of the Israeli military and internal political correspondence that reveal the systematic expulsion of Palestinian communities. By triangulating these sources with Palestinian oral histories, refugee testimonies, and previously neglected British and Arab archives, he reconstructs a chronology that displaces the heroic myth of a spontaneous and voluntary barren land welcoming a persecuted Jewish population. Instead, Pappé portrays the founding moment as a calculated campaign in which population transfer became a military objective, thereby compelling readers to reconsider the continuity of that founding logic in subsequent Israeli state policies.

As a prominent historian, Ilan Pappé has systematically insisted on the imperative of recognising the suffering of the Palestinian population, thereby inaugurating critical inquiries into collective historical responsibility. Through both empirical research and public advocacy, he has demonstrated the scholarly obligation to construct layered and inclusive narratives that centre the experiences of those who, historically, have been rendered peripheral to dominant accounts of the Israeli state and its formation.

Pappé's impact, however, extends well beyond the lecture hall. His publications, media engagements, and public lectures have shifted the terms of debate among journalists, policymakers, and civil society, encouraging a collective re-examination of long-accepted truths. By systematically interrogating received narratives and exposing the operations of state-sponsored violence, he has fostered a discipline of self-questioning among both historians and lay audiences, thereby expanding the interpretive field to include previously suppressed data and testimonies.

Internationally, recognition of Pappé's scholarly innovations has encouraged a wider acceptance of competing historical testimonies and has underscored the necessity of a historiography that refuses closure on the suffering that is willing to engage with enduring human rights claims. His steadfast commitment to empirical accuracy, ethical responsibility, and the recovery of subjugated voices has, consequently, imprinted upon the discipline a model of historical enquiry that is inseparable from the pursuit of collective reparative justice.

Historical Context: The Academic Environment of the New Historians

The rise of scholars such as Ilan Pappé under the New Historians banner has indelibly transformed discourse on the Israeli-Palestinian conflict, yet any appraisal of their contribution must begin with the institutional conditions that framed their work. By the late twentieth century, Israeli historiography had consolidated a dominant narrative that recast the founding of the State of Israel as a paragon of national survival. Within this dispensary of memory, the uprooting of the Palestinian population was either extenuated as wartime necessity or relegated to the collateral of heroism, thereby locating the legitimacy of the Zionist project within the arc of a redemptive, forward-looking hero's journey.

Within this intellectual frame, a new generation of historians emerged, systematically interrogating the epistemic borders that had long insulated Zionist state-building from critical scrutiny. Their projects served as interventions in literal and figurative archives, revealing the contingency of triumphalism and recovering analytics that had, at best, been relegated to footnotes or were expunged from the public sphere. The New Historians' resolute orientation toward the archives of dissent and the demographics of the disempowered not only unsettled the monologic character of Israeli scholarship but also coaxed the university into a reflective practice long subsumed by national canon. Consequently, the Israeli academy was obliged to confront the antinomic character of its own self-understanding and to debate the epistemic costs of narrative sedimentation.

In addition, it remains crucial to situate the New Historians against the wider contours of the global postcolonial moment. The latter decades of the twentieth century witnessed mounting interrogations of the legacies of empire, prompting historians to expand their methodological and epistemological horizons. Such an environment rewarded scholars who interrogated received orthodoxies, who refused the luxury of moral evasion, and who sought to render the voices and experiences rendered peripheral by colonial governance audible. The emergence of the New Historians can therefore be understood not as an autonomously triggered event, but as a moment crystallising within a transnational wave of critical historiographical revision.

These wider historiographical pressures prepared the field

for the methodological rupture signalled by scholars like Ilan Pappé. Their determination to engage the most incendiary topics—expulsion, ethnic cleansing, and colonial-era state violence—provided the field with a historiographical pivot that unsettled long-rehearsed narratives. Yet, the institutional environment for such enquiry was, and remains, fraught. Pappé contended with a disciplinary matrix that prized consensus, and with a public culture that clung to national myths as forms of social cohesion. The collision of rigorous enquiry and cultural resistance thereby reveals not only the scholarly significance of Pappé and his fellow travellers, but also the threshold Socratic lesson that critical historiography is inseparable from the politics of its production.

Ethnic Cleansing or Unfortunate Exodus? A New Perspective

The historiography of the Palestinian 1948 exodus remains deeply polarised, yet recent scholarship invites a reframing more attentive to the contingent and contingent-seeming character of state-making. In his latest volume, Ilan Pappé reconsiders the movement of nearly 700,000 Palestinian Arab refugees as the cumulative outcome of both wartime disruption and a concerted policy of removal sanctioned by state authorities. While earlier interpretations have situated the exodus within the logic of interstate war and refugee crisis, Pappé redirects focus toward deliberate policy choices and tactical violence aimed at ethnically consolidated territorial control.

To advance this reading, Pappé integrates newly accessed archival records with a corpus of exiled Palestinian testimonies that testify to the temporality and sequenced implementation of displacement. He traces the systematic destruction of over four hundred Palestinian villages at the hands of Israel Defence Forces, documenting the spatiotemporal logic that guided demolitions and the concurrent political announcements promising land reclamation for Jewish settlement. The cumulative weight of the evidence – from contemporaneous military reports to the charting of newly emptied tracts on official maps – compels a reassessment of the exodus not as a regrettable by-product of war but as a condition foreseen and energetically operationalised by the Jewish state.

Pappé's central claim hinges upon a deliberate re-interpretation of the terms that frame the exile itself. He argues that the Arabic noun Nakba, signifying catastrophe, properly embraces both the widespread trauma and the scale of human loss endured by the Palestinian people. By re-centering the analytic lens upon this term, he insists that recognition of the event itself must give priority to the human toll and to the long-term consequences of the forced dispersal.

In addition, the historian interrogates the guiding rationales of both the Zionist armed formations and the emerging Israeli Defence Forces across the years immediately preceding and following 1948. He conducts a close reading of Plan Dalet, the operational design for territorial consolidation, arguing that the plan's contours reveal a systematic goal of popu-

BREAKING THE WALL OF SILENCE 83

lation removal. This disclosure, he contends, re-orients the discussion toward the ethical and legal dimensions of state creation, obliging the audience to confront the disquieting realities embedded in the original geopolitical formation of present-day Israel.

Pappé's intervention thereby placed under rigorous scrutiny the accepted understanding of the events of 1948, insisting that a transparent and evidence-based reckoning with the data requires scholars and the public to confront the intertwinement of violence and legacies of political intent. By repositioning the Palestinian expulsion as a calculated ethnic-cleansing campaign, he obliges historiography to address openly the differential bearing of power, to assess the moral implications of state formation and to acknowledge how these foundational choices continue to configure daily existence in both communities. Such a reframing invites a methodological extension that neither theologises historical rupture nor normalises diplomatic silence, but rather insists that the historian remain accountable to those past agents whose displacement still reverberates in the contemporary conjuncture.

Key Publications and Their Impact on Historical Discourse

Ilan Pappé has emerged as an influential voice in the historiography of the Israeli-Palestinian conflict, and his oeuvre has decisively altered how both scholars and the broader public engage with this fraught past. In his 2006 monograph, *The

Ethnic Cleansing of Palestine*, Pappé assembles an extensive array of archival, military, and oral sources to argue that the mass expulsion of Palestinians during the 1948 war was premeditated and systemic, rather than an accidental consequence of hostilities. By re-categorising the 1948 exodus as ethnic cleansing, Pappé rejects the prevailing post-Zionist insistence on moral ambiguity and re-establishes the moral and political urgency of the Palestinian catastrophe. The book provoked immediate and polarising debate, forcing historians and educators alike to confront the limitations of previously dominant apologetic and narrativist paradigms. In 2014, Pappé continued this critical trajectory with *The Idea of Israel: A History of Power and Knowledge*, in which he excavates the symbiotic relationship between historiography, statecraft, and forms of colonial governance. Mapping how Zionist scholars employed Eurocentric categories of race and culture, he demonstrates that Israeli identity was forged through both territorial control and the strategic subsumption of Palestinian place within Jewish space. Together, these studies have not only functioned as analytical provocations but have also provided an openly partisan framework within which contemporary anti-colonial scholarship on the Levant continues to evolve.

The breadth of empirical enquiry and the unequivocal claims advanced in these works have positioned Pappé at the forefront of historiographical scholarship, affecting the perceptions of academics, the training of students, and the calculations of policymakers. Close analysis of these texts reveals not only the modification of historiographical paradigms but also the intangible yet potent effects of Pappé's interventions upon the collective comprehension of the Israeli-Palestinian dispute.

Critics of Pappé: Voices of Dissent from Traditionalist Scholars

Opposition to Ilan Pappé's revisionist historiography of the Israeli-Palestinian conflict continues to emanate from scholars who uphold the prevailing scholarly consensus. These traditionalists contend that Pappé's conclusions rest upon a selective reading of archival material, insufficient substantiation in primary sources, and an openly avowed political commitment that, they allege, compromises the neutrality expected of the historian. While they acknowledge the occurrence of civilian flight in 1948, they contend that framing the entire episode as 'ethnic cleansing' distorts temporally and spatially heterogeneous realities of warfare, voluntary migration, and expulsion that characterised the period. Moreover, they assert that his method of reading canonical sources through a predetermined theoretical lens neglects countervailing evidence, thereby reifying an alternative narrative that displaces, rather than integrates, the scholarly consensus. Their avowed commitment to a stringent evidentiary standard underlines a more general reluctance to permit historiographical revisionism to supplant established interpretations that rest on decades of archival cross-verification. Scholars further warn that Pappé's reading risks migrating unmediated from the academic to the political arena, where they believe it could harden partisan narratives, diminish empathy for competing national narratives, and ultimately impede the practical pathways to reconciliation they deem nevertheless open to negotiation.

Moreover, critics have suggested that Pappé's reconfiguration of the past may lend itself to instrumental use in political contexts, thereby perpetuating existing ideological schisms. The collision between his revisionist framework and the established, predominant historiographical paradigms has produced a vigorous, layered exchange among scholars, mirroring larger contestations over the nature of historical truth, the formation of competing narratives, and the partisan anchoring of interpretation. The animated resistance that Pappé's scholarship elicits serves to reaffirm the continuing relevance of sustained historical enquiry and its power to regulate collective memory, inform political rhetoric, and structure the legitimating narratives of societies.

Methodology: Revisiting Sources with a Critical Lens

Ilan Pappé's research reconfigures prevailing historiographical frameworks by employing a resolutely critical methodology that has irreversibly recalibrated scholarship on the Israeli-Palestinian conflict. Central to his intervention is the re-examination of extant historiography through a rigorously sceptical optic that interrogates archival records, bureaucratic documents, and oral testimonies, thereby bringing to the fore the voices that dominant accounts have long overlooked. By dismantling hegemonic narratives and reassembling them from the vantage of those rendered peripheral, Pappé exposes the ideological lacunae and historiographical silences that conventional scholarship has elided. Such a procedure not only entails methodological discipline but demands a principled engagement with the ethics of representation, acknowledging the profound stakes that attach to the historical record. Pappé's enterprise thus surpasses customary disciplinary delineations, insisting that the practice of reconstructing the past is inseparable from a politically attuned ethical responsibility. Each revisited source is coupled with a recognitional imperative to integrate Palestinian testimonies, archival traces, and lived experience that have habitually been deployed as marginal not only to the historical narrative but to the political consciousness of the archive itself. Through this twin procedure of critical disaggregation and ethical reconstitution, Pappé illuminates the repressed violence of the past while simultaneously compelling the discipline to reflect on the criteria by which historical knowledge is authorised. The method challenges the reader to interrogate the sedimented certainties of prior scholarship, thereby fostering a hermeneutic space wherein a more reflexive and empathetic apprehension of the past can emerge.

Pappé's pioneering methodology compels us to explore the inseparable bond between history and collective memory, reformulating debates surrounding the Israeli-Palestinian conflict while illuminating the multilayered nature of historical interpretation. By interrogating unexamined assumptions and deeply rooted ideologies, his scholarship demonstrates the capacity of rigorously applied historiography to modify our understanding of the past, affirming the enduring significance of critical enquiry in shaping our communal memory.

The Interdependence of Politics and Historical Narrative

The fields of politics and historical narration are irreducibly intertwined, particularly in relation to conflicts marked by competing identities and grievances, such as the Israeli-Palestinian dispute. Ilan Pappé's argument for the ethnic cleansing of the Palestinian population has, perhaps more than any other single claim, crystallized the reciprocal relation between scholarly research and political discourse.

His scholarship illustrates the manner in which political imperatives can distort the construction of memory, persuading historians to recalibrate the past to buttress nationalist or ideological projects. In the Israeli case, the historical account of the state's emergence and the continuous contestation of its borders have become prisms through which the legitimacy of Israeli sovereignty is adjudicated, affecting electoral platforms, foreign interventions, and the formulation of norms for international discourse. Consequently, historical representation is neither neutral nor incidental; it is the battleground upon which the legitimacy of competing political claims is won or lost.

Moreover, the instrumentalisation of the past may hinder the disinterested practice of history, compelling practitioners to align with sanctioned doctrines under threat of retribution. Pappé has himself confronted academic ostracism and official censure, revealing the considerable obstacles confronting any historian who seeks to disentangle empirical judgement from partisan priorities upon disputed sites of memory.

At the same time, the consequences of historiographical reappraisal for present-day governance cannot be ignored. Pappé's re-reading of the formative years of the Israeli state has catalysed internal argumentation over collective memory, collective guilt, and the feasible broadening of peacemaking horizons. Outside Israel, the same scholarship has framed international commentaries and recalibrated diplomatic stances, thereby revealing the transnational trajectory of historiographical persuasion.

The interplay between politics and historiography, therefore, demands sustained scholarly attention, for it reveals how narratives once marginal may crystallise into determinants of state action. Acknowledging this reciprocal motion permits both historians and practitioners to deepen the precision with which the past is correlated to present policy. At the same time, such awareness imposes upon them an ongoing obligation to resist the use of history as a stratagem of political mobilisation, reinforcing the necessity of academic impartiality and institutional autonomy.

In summary, the interdependence of political motives and the interpretation of history comes into sharp relief in Ilan Pappé's writings, illuminating the layered difficulties of confronting disputed historical episodes. Moving forward to analyse the varied responses to his scholarship both within Israel and in international circles, we ought to pay careful attention to the persistent capacity of political lenses to shape historiographic debates and to the ongoing, if often complicated, search for a disinterested apprehension of earlier events.

Reception in Israel and Beyond: A Global Scholarly Debate

Outside Israel, Pappé's findings have been met with both interest and critical examination. His scholarship has enriched the transnational academic discourse not only on the 1948 events but on their continuing relevance to the enduring conflict. In university seminars, peer-reviewed journals, and public lecture circuits, scholars have adopted, dissected, and dangerously recontextualised Pappé's archival discoveries. Some observers hail the work as a courageous, if painful, confrontation with the archival record; others caution against the blending of empirical evidence with imperatives of political correction. This polarised international discourse illustrates how the act of historicisation remains entangled with the logics of current politics, diplomatic positioning, and popular memory.

Influence on Contemporary Understanding of the Israeli-Palestinian Conflict

Pappé's scholarship has reshaped the prevailing frame through which the Israeli-Palestinian conflict is dissected in both academic and public circles. By meticulously cataloguing and reordering the documentary evidence of 1948, he has unsettled the conventional chronological and causal schemas that have secured disciplinary assent for decades. His insistence on articulating the displacement of Palestinians not merely as collateral damage but as a constitutive logic of the Israeli state projects a much darker and, for many, a more compelling theory of colonial temporality. Scholars now confront the challenging implication that the conflict, rather than evolving through a series of geopolitical contingencies, may have been instantiated as the reproduction of a certain colonial modernity. Such a reframing forces the field to negotiate not merely its archival apparatus but its ethical and political assignments to the past.

Pappé's scholarship has elicited sustained reflection and vigorous debate across academic forums, policymaking environments, activist networks, and among wider public audiences. His careful exposition of the Palestinian experience and his challenge to the dominant Zionist narrative have together deepened awareness of the intricate and often asymmetrical dynamics that shape the conflict.

Pappé's work most notably excels in rendering the historical past legible in human terms, thereby retrieving voices and experiences frequently relegated to the margins. By emancipating the chronicles of uprooting, loss, and determined survival, he has illuminated the variegated human toll inflicted upon Palestinian communities, cultivating a richer and more compassionate consciousness among those weighing the conflict's enduring costs.

In parallel, Pappé's steadfast advocacy for historical accuracy and for justice has emboldened a burgeoning cohort of researchers and movement organisers to interrogate critically the legacies that the Israeli-Palestinian conflict has bequeathed. His readiness to engage with distressing realities and to interrogate asymmetrical power has reinvigorated campaigns aimed at fostering accountability and reconciliation, thereby fortifying the intellectual and moral foundations required for a just and durable settlement.

Within contemporary intellectual circles, Pappé's work has systematically disrupted prevailing paradigms, compelling scholars and citizens alike to reassess what is considered credible and what debates can be legitimately entertained regarding the Israeli-Palestinian impasse. By meticulously exposing the colonial stratagems that crystallised in the late nineteenth and twentieth centuries, he has made space for previously marginalised perspectives, thus enriching the interpretative repertoire with voices that had long been adjudicated as extraneous. Consequently, the public and scholarly imagination is now oriented toward a more textured and accurate comprehension of the multilayered animosities and aspirations that continue to animate the region.

Pappé has, moreover, redefined the vocation of the historian by insisting that enquiry cannot be dissociated from moral accountability. The historiographical innovations he has bequeathed—disaggregating the concept of "memory" from that of "fact," and placing intentional displacement at the centre of the Israeli state narrative—resist the temptation to normalise documented injustices under the guise of detached analysis. The reach of his propositions is not confined to professional journals; they reverberate in civil society, media debates, and legislative enquiry, galvanising activists and prompting institutional reflection. In these ways, Pappé has elevated the standard for what scholarly work can and, by ethical requirement, must engage, thus insisting that the bar for intellectual integrity is set only as high as the moral stakes of the subject permit.

Conclusion: Legacy and Future Directions in Historiography

The pioneering interventions of the New Historians—foremost among them Ilan Pappé—have permanently reframed the historiography of the Israeli-Palestinian conflict. Their disciplined reassessment of key moments has not merely contested dominant interpretations; it has also inaugurated fresh trajectories for scholarly research and public engagement. By subjecting canonical accounts to rigorous scrutiny, the New Historians have uncovered the region's past in all its layered complexity, compelling scholars and lay observers alike to reconsider long-held beliefs. This endeavour has produced a legacy that circulates well beyond the university, shaping national conversations and activist movements alike.

Yet historiography can never rest, and the path that now lies ahead is marked as much by tension as by promise. The reverberations of the New Historians demand that later generations continue to interrogate their questions and methods, probing both the evidentiary bases and the theoretical frames they employed. At the same time, the discipline's expanding methodological arsenal invites the incorporation of archives, oral histories, and digital resources that once lay beyond reach, while also amplifying the recordings of those who have long stood at the margins of dominant narratives. Thus, the next phase of research must not only sustain the critical spirit of the past thirty years but actively engage with its plural legacies, in the pursuit of a history that is, at long last, as variegated and contested as the societies it attempts to understand.

An essential point of scholarly focus is the dynamic interplay between history and collective memory, which decisively informs present-day perceptions and attitudes. Continued archival and interpretative efforts uncover previously silenced realities, yet these enterprises must reckon, simultaneously, with the sedimented memories that forge national imaginaries. The historian's task of reconciling divergent memories while honouring the injuries inscribed in the past becomes, therefore, a defining and delicate obligation of coming historiographical ventures.

At the same time, developments in archival digitisation and the increasing availability of multilingual source material create rare openings for the refinement of historical practice. Online repositories, systematic oral history initiatives, and expansive transnational research constellations invite a reconsideration of the Israeli-Palestinian conflict that remains capacious and reflective. If scholars harness these resources in concert, they risk neither the occlusion of marginalised voices nor the entrenchment of unilateral perspectives, thus enlarging the historiographical field and enabling a more intricate comprehension of a still-contested past.

The direction of the historiography of the Israeli-Palestinian conflict will rest, in the final analysis, on ongoing adherence to strict scholarly standards, on the imperatives of ethical scholarship, and on an unwavering effort to parse the layered intricacies of the past. Those who will take the field in coming decades will accept the dual burden and the honour of producing accounts that reflect precision and compassion, thus empowering perspectives that may yet foster reconciliation, mutual comprehension, and, in the best of outcomes, enduring peace.

References For Further Reading

1. Ilan Pappé, The Ethnic Cleansing of Palestine. Oxford: Oneworld Publications, 2006.

2. Ilan Pappé, *A History of Modern Palestine* (Cambridge University Press, 2003).

3. Ilan Pappé, *The Idea of Israel: A History of Power and Knowledge* (Verso, 2014).

4. Shlaim, Avi. "The Debate about 1948." International Journal of Middle East Studies 27, no. 3 (1995): 287–304. Cambridge University Press.

5. Pappé, Ilan. The Idea of Israel: A History of Power and Knowledge. London: Verso, 2014.

6. Khalidi, Walid. "Plan Dalet: Master Plan for the Conquest of Palestine?" Journal of Palestine Studies 18, no. 1 (1988): 4–33. University of California Press/Institute

for Palestine Studies.

7. Morris, Benny. The Birth of the Palestinian Refugee Problem Revisited. Cambridge: Cambridge University Press, 2004.

8. Morris, Benny. 1948: A History of the First Arab-Israeli War. New Haven: Yale University Press, 2008.

9. Khalidi, Walid, ed. All That Remains: The Palestinian Villages Occupied and Depopulated by Israel in 1948. Washington, DC: Institute for Palestine Studies, 1992.

10. Sa'di, Ahmad H., and Lila Abu-Lughod, eds. Nakba: Palestine, 1948, and the Claims of Memory. New York: Columbia University Press, 2007.

11. Abu Sitta, Salman. The Atlas of Palestine 1948. London: Palestine Land Society, 2004.

12. Karsh, Efraim. Fabricating Israeli History: The "New Historians." London: Frank Cass, 1997; updated ed., 2000.

13. Gelber, Yoav. Palestine 1948: War, Escape and the Emergence of the Palestinian Refugee Problem. Brighton: Sussex Academic Press, 2001.

14. Penslar, Derek J. Israeli History and the Jewish Past. Oxford: Oxford University Press, 2018.

15. Said, Edward W. Orientalism. New York: Pantheon, 1978.

Additional verifiable resources and primary/official materials

1. University of Exeter, Department of History. "Professor Ilan Pappé." Staff profile page with biographical and publication details. https://www.exeter.ac.uk (navigate: Faculty of Humanities, Arts and Social Sciences → History).

2. United Nations General Assembly Resolution 194 (III), "Palestine—Progress Report of the United Nations Mediator." 11 December 1948. Official UN Documents System: https://www.un.org/en/about-us/un-charter (search: Resolution 194 (III)).

4
Avi Shlaim
Critique on Israeli Diplomacy and Military Strategy

Introduction to Avi Shlaim and His Historical Significance

Avi Shlaim occupies a central position in contemporary scholarship on Israeli diplomacy and military policy, and his contributions have fundamentally shifted the parameters within which historians and analysts interpret the evolution of the state of Israel. His rigorous re-examination of archival material, combined with a commitment to situating Israeli actions within the wider geopolitical field, has rendered traditional readings of Israeli statecraft not merely inadequate, but historically misleading. Shlaim's intellectual journey—from a Baghdadi Jewish family to a childhood in Israel—imbues his scholarship with an often understated but acute awareness of the intersections between state narratives and diaspora experiences. After undergraduate training at the Hebrew University of Jerusalem, he completed his doctorate at the University of Oxford, where he crafted an analytical framework capable of interrogating the interplay of military decision-making, international sponsorship, and domestic political imperatives. The publication of his landmark volume, *The Iron Wall: Israel and the Arab World*, marked a critical point in the historiography, in which he argues that Israeli security policy has, since its inception, depended on the conviction that force could insulate Israel from the Arab world while simultaneously fuelling the very hostility it purported to quench. Through meticulous archival excavation and sustained engagement with previously inaccessible primary sources, Shlaim has successfully illuminated the hidden mechanisms that, he argues, have periodically disrupted prospects for political settlement and entrenched a cycle of repression and resistance in the region.

This section will examine Shlaim's intellectual legacy by demonstrating how his work has decisively informed current global assessments of Israeli policy across both the scholarly community and broader public discourse. It will further show how his archival rigour has created space for a wider and more interrogative re-assessment of established historical accounts, presenting new interpretative angles that systematically interrogate and, often, unsettle dominant historiographical paradigms.

The Making of a Critic: Academic Foundations and Influences

Avi Shlaim, born in Baghdad and educated in Israel, embodies a convergence of experiences that have decisively shaped his scholarly contributions. His studies at Tel Aviv University and the University of Paris exposed him to a wide spectrum of historiographical and philosophical currents, while the tumultuous politics of the Middle East—particularly his family's forced exodus from Iraq—impressed upon him a dynamic sense of temporal and spatial discontinuity. The very experience of forced migration turned the scholarly pursuit, for him, into a mode of critical recollection and procedural enquiry, underlying his later demand for rigorous archival substantiation and for a reflective historiography attentive to displaced voices.

Shlaim's early intellectual trajectory gravitated toward the politics of diplomacy, with Israeli foreign policy and military doctrine the principal objects of his investigation. His inaugural studies dissected the strategic logics that have animated the state's external conduct, but they also interrogated the underlying assumptions that have, in his view, too often passed for common-sense explanations. The influence of distinguished mentors, coupled with a wide readership of archival memoirs and critical theory, fostered a scholarly habit of excavating contradictions and lacunae neglected by dominant discourses. Shlaim's oeuvre typifies a deliberate refusal to let empirical data slide into apologetic narrative: every assertion of causality is attended by acknowledgment of the contingency that historical actors, from political office-holders to common soldiers, themselves faced.

Beyond archival engagement, Shlaim's development was animated by key texts in diplomatic history and political theory. The works of A. J. P. Taylor, Kenneth Waltz, and Hans Morgenthau, among others, supplied methodological and ethical touchstones, while the writings of Israeli and Arab historians demonstrated the productivity of a multi-archival and multi-perspectival approach. The resultant method privileges complexity, refuses thematic simplification, and insists that the politics of memory in the Middle East, volatile though it remains, must be measured against the rigorous apparatus of scholarly evidence.

His immersive confrontation with foundational literature alongside emergent, frontier scholarship endowed him with an arsenal of analytical concepts necessary to disentangle the kaleidoscopic interrelationship of governance, armed conflict, and societal metamorphosis. Such intellectual scaffolding was not peripheral but catalytic, moulding Shlaim into a critic of rare reach, whose mastery of archival minutiae is never eclipsed by a penetrating strategic vision and by sophisticated contextual calibration.

In this intellectual foundry, whose flames were kindled by variegated academic heritages, testimonial memory, and devoted mentorship, Avi Shlaim's singular voice first crystallised. Traversing venerable institutional corridors while engaging the slippery margins of historiographical difference, he found his intellectual patrimony coalescing into an unwavering purpose: to unearth the occluded layers of

Israeli statecraft and of the operational logics that underpin it. The disciplined apprenticeship, conjoined with a visceral immersion in the Middle Eastern labyrinth, sharpened his instruments of archival excavation and refined his commentary. The furnace of his scholarly odyssey eventually yielded a breathtaking critique of consensual chronicle, in which finely chiselled nuance is brandished to unsettling received wisdom and to disclose the subterranean verities it has sought to repress.

Revisiting the Birth of Israel: Shlaim's Diplomatic enquiry

Avi Shlaim's thorough reassessment of Israeli diplomatic and military conduct mandates a renewed consideration of the negotiations that ushered the state of Israel into being. His calibrated dissection of competing historiographies directs renewed scholarly focus to the formative diplomatic chronicle that continues to influence the contemporary politics of the Levant. Central to Shlaim's enquiry is the dense accumulation of negotiations, conflict-management efforts, and pattern-shifting power relations that jointly constituted the moment of nationhood. In so doing, he exposes the compromises and tactical ambiguities that sovereignty invariably demanded. Through a disciplined archival gaze he traces the concerted engagement of international organisations, foremost among them a departing British mandate, the United Nations, and several great powers, each of which materially shaped the parameters of statehood. Shlaim further situates diplomatic choices within the calculus of individual leaders, and he dissects the tactical adjustments and long-range orientations that crystallised the diplomatic agenda of the formative state. His account thus recovers the fraught agency of early Israel, and it reconstitutes the moment not simply as a triumph of military will, but as a negotiated outcome conditioned by competing sovereignties.

In his incisive enquiry, Shlaim dissects the far-reaching consequences of the diplomatic undertakings surrounding the establishment of Israel, illuminating their multilayered effects that resonate across both the Middle East and the wider international context. His analytical rigour foregrounds the negotiation and compromise that, far from being peripheral, proved indispensable to the state's inception, thereby destabilising reductive narratives that portray the process as a deterministic or unilateral progression. Reassessing this pivotal moment through a diplomatic lens, Shlaim entices his audience to confront the disquieting subtleties of policy and power that informed each decisive step, thereby fostering a historiography that balances moral rigour with empirical nuance. The result is a reflective expedition that not only revises settled understandings of a foundational episode, but simultaneously compels consideration of how the legacies of diplomatic choices continue to adjudicate the balance of power in an unquiet region.

Ariel Sharon and the Crossing of Borders: Military Strategy Unveiled

Sharon, an architect of both military doctrine and political direction in the State of Israel, transcended the locus of the battlefield to shape regional configurations irreversibly. His career, marked by layered involvements from the Palestine Campaign of 1948 to the premiership, crystallised a mode of governance in which operational choices were imbued with diplomatic intent. Simultaneously embraced and contested within Israeli and foreign circles, his decisions concerning frontiers, population movements, and counterinsurgency methods prompt continuous re-examination by historians and security specialists.

The 1956 Suez Crisis crystallised Sharon's comprehension of the intersection between warfare and diplomacy. Tasked as the commander of the southern front, he executed the assault on the Sinai that, while framed as a limited confrontation, served to both neutralise the immediate threat from Egyptian forces and re-position the Sinai as a stage on which superpower dialogue would be contested. The coordination with France and Britain, although ultimately a diplomatic miscalculation, illustrated Sharon's readiness to employ military risk as a currency in the negotiation of Israel's strategic space.

His operational signature achieved its zenith in the Six-Day War of 1967, when the assault he directed through the elevated routes of the Sinai Peninsula epitomised the combination of intelligence, mobility, and tactical misdirection that characterised the Israel Defence Forces of the age. The rapid encirclement of Egyptian formations shattered front-line unity and expanded the latency of Arab military capability for the decades that followed. The seamless transition from battlefield victory to the political seizure of the Golan Heights, the West Bank, and the Sinai region altered the cartography of the Levant and rendered Sharon a central architect of Israel's post-colonial territorial calculus.

His focus on preemptive action coupled with rapid, synchronized offensives reinforced his readiness to redefine conventional limits. In addition, Sharon's pivotal involvement in consolidating Israeli control over the West Bank and Gaza Strip during the conflict layered an abiding complexity onto the region's geopolitical matrix, a complexity that still influences policy and conflict trajectory.

The Lebanon War of 1982 delineated a further hinge of Sharon's career, bringing his operational choices and contested conduct into conspicuous relief. Serving as Defence Minister, he directed the Lebanon incursion conceived to neutralise the Palestinian armed presence that had gained refuge in Lebanese hinterlands. The campaign's aftermath, particularly the Sabra and Shatila killings, invited widespread domestic and international censure, reframing the discourse on Sharon's military doctrine and the accompanying moral calculus.

A careful appraisal of Sharon's border policy discloses an integrative calculus wherein coercive power and diplomacy interlaced. His commitment to fortified, elongated perimeters translated into programmes that incorporated the establishment of civilian blocs in OCI-held terrain, a policy that kindled acute controversy and augmented intercommunal frictions. The continuing ramifications of these decisions permeate contemporary debates on the interplay of security imperatives, claims to sovereignty, and the coherence of territorial configuration in the Levant.

Ariel Sharon's military strategy invites scrutiny that reaches beyond tactical engagements and situates itself at the confluence of Israeli history and enduring geopolitical currents. Whether characterised as an unorthodox commander or an emblem of ideological division, Sharon emerges as a decisive actor whose choices shaped not only the landscapes of battle but also the institutional and moral foundations of the state. His legacy, simultaneously celebrated and contested, thus functions as a revealing prism through which to interrogate the interwoven motifs of statecraft, personal ambition, and the relentless pursuit of security amid persistent and layered regional instability.

Pivotal Moments: Key Conflicts and Their Consequences

The Israeli-Arab conflict is a dense braid of intersecting historical occurrences, each charged with its own weight and each producing reverberations far beyond its immediate decade. Avi Shlaim, in his scholarship distinctive for its unsparing examination of Israeli statecraft and armed doctrine, invites us to specify the flashpoints that have carved the region's long groove. Among these, the Suez Crisis of 1956 stands as a decisive fracture. Israel, together with Britain and France, authorised a clandestine strike framed as reprisal for Egypt's nationalisation of the canal; what was a tactical objective quickly matured into a theatre of multinational imperial calculation. The enterprise collapsed under American and Soviet pressure, yet its centrifugal force was unmistakable: Washington's courting of the Cairo regime, the reallocation of Western subsidies to burgeoning military establishments, and a multiplied Arab sense of strategic encirclement. The crisis, therefore, did not terminate with a diplomatic settlement; it reorganised the whole political-institutional architecture of the region, reinforcing the paradox that every military initiative for Israeli security ended by multiplying the number and cohesion of adversarial polities.

The Six-Day War of 1967 represented a pivotal inflection point in the Arab-Israeli conflict, as Israel's swift, asymmetrical victory redrew the map and reconstituted the very critical geopolitical balance in the Levant. The resultant occupation of the West Bank, Golan Heights, Sinai Peninsula, and Gaza Strip introduced a form of territorial governance that, anchored in asymmetrical power, bred enduring irredentism and territorial contention that, decades later, remain constitutive of both regional diplomacy and cyclical military confrontations.

The subsequent Yom Kippur War of 1973 reaffirmed the inherent volatility of Arab-Israeli relations. Egypt's and Syria's coordinated, albeit strategically limited, assault, executed on the holiest day of the Jewish calendar, shattered the prevailing illusion of immunity that the earlier victory had inspired. The conflict not only bared the fallibility of Israel's intelligence apparatus and the centralised decision-making that had assumed prolonged quiet, but it also incentivised both sides to recalibrate military doctrines and diplomatic postures, embedding a new logic of deterrence that recognised the centrality of surprise.

The intifadas that followed, especially the First Intifada (1987-1993) and the Second Intifada (2000-2005), complicated the signage of both resistance and militarised governance. Each uprising, catalysed by distinct social and economic substrates, placed the quotidian nature of occupation on the diplomatic agenda, compelling a re-evaluation of the conflict's moral, legal, and strategic registers on domestic and international stages. The first unleashed civil disobedience, stone-throwing, and mass mobilisation that undermined the occupation's opacity, while the latter introduced lethal asymmetry and counterinsurgency that hardened institutional and ideological intransigence on both sides.

The decisive events of that era should not be regarded purely as the remnants of history; rather, they function as the structural constituents of the present-day intricacies characterising the Israeli-Arab conflict. A careful examination of their aftermath is therefore indispensable for grasping the layered sophistication of Avi Shlaim's analytical intervention and for recognising its wider influence on the evolving discourses of diplomacy and military strategy within this persistently disputed milieu.

Secret Conversations: The Diplomacy Behind Closed Doors

In the intricate lattice of contemporary international relations, diplomacy frequently unfolds beyond the gaze of the public sphere. Avi Shlaim examines the concealed negotiations and informal deliberations that have sculpted the contours of Israeli statecraft. These undisclosed exchanges are not peripheral appendages to the paler, more accessible confrontations: they are constitutive elements for any rigorous appraisal of the region's political subtleties. Immersing himself in a prodigious body of newly available archival material, Shlaim reconstructs the contours of concealed meet-ups, discreet shuttle diplomacy, and low-profile understandings that have quietly calibrated the vector of Israeli diplomacy. Removed from the glare of publicity, these occult dialogues disclose the calibrated choreography of leverage, persuasion, and trade-off that transpires among guarded walls. Through a blend of scrupulous archival excavation and nuanced interpretive commentary, Shlaim dissects the concealed ambitions and concealed scripts of principal actors in this diplomatic mini-opera, thereby placing writer and reader alike in fresh possession of the determinants that have, quarter by quarter, redirected the arc of history. He discloses the tactical sorting, the tempered exchanges, and the concealed constellations that have shaped Israel's rapport with proximate states and with metropolitan capitals alike. In the same breath, Shlaim clarifies the frictional choreography between political ideology and prudential statecraft in these hushed arenas. The study of this subterranean diplomatic sphere unsettles prevailing historiographic orthodoxies and invites scholars and practitioners to confront the layered complexities that punctuate contemporary international order.

Shlaim's excavation of concealed exchanges directs our attention to the seldom-visible channels of coercion and concession that lie between the ritualised performances of statecraft. Such revelations signal that diplomatic history encompasses far more than the ceremonial signing of accords or the public posturing of summits. The narrative of these classified deliberations exposes a continuous furling and unfurling of hidden ambition, experimental candour, and calculated betrayal, illustrating how the broad contours of Israel's international posture have been shaped by transient balances of confidence and duplicity. In doing so, it lays bare the operational matrices of power and anxiety that undergird the ongoing pursuit of state security and diplomatic recognition.

Collaborative vs Aggressive Tactics in Regional Politics

The contrast between collaborative and aggressive tactics remains a fixture of strategic thinking and policy design in regional politics. In the Israeli diplomatic and military calculus, the distinction is particularly consequential, informing both the management of foreign relations and the pursuit of security. Collaborative tactics—centred on diplomacy, treaties, and joint initiatives—are regarded as indispensable for crafting stability and nurturing partnerships with proximate states and the wider international community. Such tactics involve sustained dialogue, alliance-building, and the identification of shared interests, all directed at fostering coexistence and mitigating friction. In contrast, aggressive tactics encompass a spectrum of confrontational actions intended to project strength, protect perceived vital interests, and reshape geopolitical contests. Military incursions, clandestine operations, and resolute posturing characterise this approach, which prioritises deterrence and coercive success. Evaluating the efficacy and moral ramifications of either track demands a rigorous survey of historical case studies, current manifestations, and prospective outcomes. The dialogue between these modes is further complicated by shifting regional power distributions, competing ideological visions, and the perpetual possibility of armed conflict.

The moral contours of employing coercive force and diplomatic dialogues, alongside mediation practices, generate ceaseless ethical scrutiny, compelling states and scholars to reckon transparently with their moral agency in the region. Sustained deliberation regarding the strategic integration of cooperative and coercive approaches thus emerges as both pragmatic necessity and normative obligation. It necessitates discerning the porous boundaries separating military capacity and diplomatic influence, the public clang of militaristic doctrine and the subterranean precision of diplomatic overtures, the sanctity of state autonomy, and the collective aspiration for durable peace. This section will therefore historicise the emergence of these tactics, identify their present-day manifestations, and survey the principal contributions of the scholarly literature that illuminate the reciprocal reinforcement of cooperative and coercive strategies in the political evolution of Israel within the broader regional milieu.

Reactions and Repercussions: Scholarly Engagement and Public Discourse

Avi Shlaim's interrogation of Israeli statecraft and military policy has produced pronounced consequences both within academia and the court of public opinion. His reconstruction of pivotal episodes in Israeli history, wedded to a relentless critique of diplomatic choices and operational doctrines, has ignited both vigorous endorsement and formidable rebuttal. Historians, political scientists, and international relations specialists have, in turn, published articles, symposia, and monographs that either reinforce or contest Shlaim's interpretations, thus generating a scholarly conversation of considerable multidisciplinarity and depth. Concurrently, the wider public—within Israeli society and the transnational discourse surrounding the Israeli-Palestinian conflict—has engaged with the substance of his claims, according them a discursive weight that surpasses conventional academic reach. Shlaim's archival rigour and his calibrated, sometimes unsettling, commentary have obliged analysts and practitioners alike to subject conventional chronologies to a renewed critical lens, risking the destabilisation of long-settled explanatory prisms. Such recalibrations, both in published commentary and in policy fora, have in turn influenced media representations, educational curricula, and activist rhetoric. The cumulative effect has been a discernible increase in reflective interrogation of Israeli diplomatic and operational comportment, thereby reconfiguring the parameters within which citizens and scholars alike deliberate the determinants of Israeli state behaviour in a strategically contested region.

Moreover, controversies surrounding Shlaim's scholarship now reach beyond university presses, influencing op-ed pages, broadcast commentary, and civic debate. Consequently, his intellectual legacy extends well beyond the lecture hall, guiding public conversation on Israel's past and its present place in the Middle East. The persistence of Shlaim's critique illustrates how disciplined historical research can become a catalyst for both scholarly advance and public reassessment. The fervour of the responses his arguments have elicited reveals the essential contribution of rigorous historical enquiry in making opaque geopolitical processes transparent and in encouraging nuanced, informed discourse.

Critique as Legacy: Shlaim's Influence on Contemporary Discourse

Avi Shlaim's incisive critique of Israeli statecraft has indelibly shaped the terms of contemporary conversation on the Israeli-Palestinian conflict. Through painstaking dissection of governmental records, diplomatic correspondence, and military records, Shlaim has grounded both scholarly and public debate in the rigours of empirical evidence while simultaneously interrogating the moral and political foundations of the Zionist project. His writings are now synonymous with the virtues of archival diligence, theoretical sophistication, and an unwavering commitment to interrogating the complacencies of received wisdom. Shlaim is particularly astute in situating Israeli actions within a wider international-relations context, illuminating how shifting great-power agendas and regional alignments have conditioned, and constrained, Zionist statecraft. By exposing the layered calculus that underpins political and military decisions—and by demonstrating how civilian and military spheres are ineluctably fused—he has undercut the reductive binaries that habitually polarise commentators. His unrelenting quest for precision and measured judgement has thus elevated the argument beyond partisan rhetoric, prompting even sceptics of his conclusions to reckon with the empirical foundation on which they rest. The reach of Shlaim's writings, however, is not limited to the scholarly journals; his analyses have entered the popular press, informed diplomatic roundtables, and shaped the curriculum in a generation of undergraduate and graduate programmes.

By detailing key historical episodes and tracing their prolonged aftershocks, Shlaim has stimulated both self-reflection and analytical scrutiny of dominant accounts, culminating in a revision of beliefs once regarded as settled. At the same time, his insistence on ethical imperatives and human-rights considerations has injected indispensable moral content into deliberations on diplomacy and conflict settlement, compelling decision-makers to face painful realities and to champion principled governance and international engagement. The influence of his work outlives its author, encouraging emerging scholars, activists, and statecraft circles to pursue thorough enquiry, to challenge established orthodoxies, and to demand a just and lasting settlement within the region. In so doing, he has established a durable corridor for sustained deliberation, for reconciliation efforts, and for the relentless quest for verifiable historical record. Shlaim's lasting relevancy affirmatively positions the critical interrogation of historical narratives as essential to disentangling the interwoven strands of influence, rhetoric, and the sustained endeavour for durable peace.

Conclusion: Navigating Complex Legacies of Power and Persuasion

Navigating the layered legacies of power and persuasion calls for sustained critical vigilance and methodical analysis. Avi Shlaim's incisive revision of Israeli statecraft and military doctrine permits scholars to discern the knots of interest and ideology that bind the present to the century-long contest for Palestine. Faced with divergent and often contradictory memories, we recognise that the interplay of statecraft, balance-of-power calculations, and the formative narratives of collective identity has left sedimentary traces that historians and decision-makers alike must sift.

Shlaim's patient dissection of the diplomatic choreography that underlay Israeli statehood reveals the hidden conversations and tactical placements that once passed for realpolitik. These archival findings have not settled; rather, they intervene in present geopolitics through the persistence of decisions taken in the shadow of war and the calculated ambiguity of "waiting games" that disavow transparency. The diplomatic residue, therefore, does not belong exclusively to the past; it rejuvenates the present, constraining the vocabulary of peace and entrenching the positional certainties that still govern the analysis of every ceasefire, election, and foreign mediation.

Shlaim's rigorous interrogation exposes the complex interrelation of military doctrine and nation-building in Israel's

BREAKING THE WALL OF SILENCE

past. He traces the decisive moments of policymaking, from Sharon's bold operations to the coercive logics that governed successive wars, illustrating how the convergence of immediate military judgement and broader geopolitical necessity forged an enduring strategic framework. The consequences of this framework have structured the post-conflict territorial and political calculus, producing effects that extend well beyond the immediate battle lines.

Reflecting on the durability of Shlaim's contribution, we must recognise its transformative effect on current historiographical disputes. The analytical conversations he provoked have matured into a dynamic field of contestation, where scholars test and refine his interventions in turn. These sustained debates, far from fading, preserve the immediacy of his questions and invite successive generations to interrogate accepted wisdom. Shlaim's writing, therefore, does not merely belong to the past; it actively catalyses a reflexive, trans-century dialogue that reshapes our understanding of the Israeli state and its multiple legacies.

Through engagement with Avi Shlaim's foundational contributions, one is compelled to acknowledge how historical enquiry itself governs both our retrospective and prospective imaginaries. Shlaim unravels the intricate braid wherein diplomacy is inseparable from military calculus and critical historiography, thereby situating the intellectual labour of the scholar within the same fraught terrain that statesmen occupy. This synthesis does more than catalogue past entanglements; it illumines the epistemic assumptions that distort present debate and prescribes the scholarly counsel of synthetical, reflexive, and disaggregated analyses when confronting the generative crises of our era.

5
Simha Flapan
Rethinking National Myths

Simha Flapan and His Pioneering Work

Simha Flapan stands as a formidable intellectual in Israeli-Palestinian historiography, whose foundational research permanently altered the scholarly landscape. Born in 1911, his formative years as a political activist, coupled with his involvement in the pre-state Yishuv, endowed him with a distinctive, reflexive perspective from which to interrogate the legends undergirding the Israeli state.

A tireless champion of peace and binational cooperation, Flapan devoted his career to dismantling the dominant historiographic edifice that enshrined exclusive national memories. He earned a reputation for cerebral integrity and for confronting evidence on its own terms, irrespective of the political fallout. Mobilising archival documents and situating evidence within carefully delimited contexts, he unravelled the layered myths that had come to masquerade as immutable pillars of Israeli identity.

Flapan's pioneering volume, *The Birth of Israel: Myths and Realities*, endures as an emblem of scholarly audacity and a relentless commitment to evidentiary rigour. In this pivotal study, he dismantled the revered narratives that had crystallised around the birth of the state, revealing the less-discussed, often disquieting dimensions concealed beneath triumphant accounts. His exposition of the diplomatic, military, and demographic vicissitudes of those formative months provided a reconstituted interpretive matrix, setting aside celebratory clichés and substituting a more textured and variegated understanding of the convergence of local and imperial forces.

Flapan, in the tradition of the dispassionate investigator, eschewed simple refutation in favour of a pedagogy that invited interrogation and reflective re-examination. His exegesis pressed the collective conscience of Israeli society to acknowledge the disjunction between ethos and praxis, prompting both scholars and the public to re-evaluate inherited convictions. The moral acuity that suffused his enquiry, paired with an unwavering commitment to human rights, conferred upon Flapan a singular, and in the end transformative, originality within the evolving corpus of Israeli historiography.

Simha Flapan's enduring influence reaches well beyond his publications. His commitment to fostering a candid and pluralistic historiography still energises current discussions about the Israeli-Palestinian conflict. Examining Flapan's intellectual trajectory and his corpus invites a trajectory that exceeds customary historical study, carrying the investigator into spheres of social consciousness and ethical obligation.

Deconstructing the Foundational Myths of Israel

Myth has a persistent magnetic pull, weaving tales that forge a common identity. Within the domain of national history, ritual myth making tightens the bonds of collective memory and shapes the prevailing moral sensibility. Yet Simha Flapan, historian of the Israeli polity, exposes the explanatory weakness of the established founding myths, peeling away sedimented legend to reveal a more layered picture of the nation's emergence. His critical dissection does not rest on polemic alone; rather, Flapan marshals archival traces and completed chronological accounts, letting contradicting evidence mask no essential fissure, and thus reframes the entire explanatory frame. Consequently, the intellectual field is unsettled; once-settled convictions are placed under forensic scrutiny and the contours of the birth of Israel are redrawn. Such an enquiry not only clarifies the relative contours of historical truth, but obliges observers to reconsider the authoritative tales which, through repetition, have colonised public perception. Unravelling the myths, Flapan fosters the disciplined detachment necessary for an unembellished appraisal of the coercive, accidental, and purposeful acts that inaugurated the polity, and distinguishes verifiable sequences from the emblematic sources that have animated national memory. In sequel, his work invites renewed reflection upon how public imaginings of the past continue to structure moral and political commitments in the present.

In addition, it cultivates an atmosphere of reflective examination, pressing societies to reconsider the ethical dimensions woven into the national story. Within this space of rigorous intellectual questioning, the lasting relevance of Flapan's scholarship becomes unmistakable, exceeding the limits of universities to reach the shared moral imagination. The effects of reclaiming, revising, and, when necessary, dismantling myths of origin are profound, requiring an unflinching evaluation of episodes now freed from partisan frames. While we traverse the intellectual path flanked by Flapan, we are obliged to face disquieting realities and to engage the braided texture of the past. The refusal to shelter foundational fables instead becomes an invitation to a philosophical journey whose trajectory alters not only our grasp of history but our very conceptions of identity.

Analysing 'The Birth of Israel: Myths and Realities'

In The Birth of Israel: Myths and Realities, Simha Flapan rigorously interrogates the formative processes that led to the state of Israel, determined to separate verifiable evidence from mythological embellishment. Providing a dense and rewarding synthesis of diplomatic papers, military orders, and personal testimonies, the author invites readers to reconsider every pillar of the conventional account. Flapan directs sustained analytical attention to the period surrounding the 1948 Arab-Israeli War, rigorously countering the glorified mythos that permeates both popular and academic treatments. He observes that decisively measured tactics, rather than naive heroism, underlay both Haganah strategy and the response of the Arab military forces, and he documents the strategic miscalculations that, contrary to expected Arab military dominance, permitted the Israeli forces to secure territorial gains that were initially deemed improbable. The interpretative ground shifts when Flapan interrogates the emerging Palestinian refugee crisis, revealing a far more circumspect and deliberate strategy than the popular reconstruction of spontaneous flight and disorder. Continuing the line of critique, the volume lays bare inconsistent Western diplomatic pressures that shaped refugee dispersal, emphasising administrative decisions often obscured by polemic. In every chapter, Flapan combines archival decisiveness with historiographical fairness, permitting neither vindication nor vilification to colour the presentation of evidence and arriving, at each conclusion, at a sobering and indelible assessment of the human and political costs embedded in nation-building.

Flapan's insistence on the conflict's variegated dimensions allows him to move beyond the reductive binaries that often truncate public debate, thereby encouraging a more granular apprehension of the converging political, military, social, and ideological currents. We will therefore attend to his incisive dismantling of dominant explanatory frameworks, demonstrating that his painstaking archival reconstruction has reframed both the chronology and the interpretive terrain of the period and continues to orient subsequent enquiry. By subjecting his procedure and inferences to sustained critique, we thereby appreciate the resilient afterlife of *The Birth of Israel: Myths and Realities* and its ongoing challenge to historians and policy analysts alike as they confront the persistent reverberations of July 1949 on subsequent phases of the Arab-Israeli conflict.

Evaluating the Impact on Israeli Historical Narrative

Simha Flapan's influential volume, The Birth of Israel: Myths and Realities, poses a decisive intervention within the evolving Israeli historical narrative, whose commemoration and contestation Flapan now compels historians to interrogate. Through the disciplined dismantling of sedimented nationalist varnish that shields foundational events, the author activates a historiographical fault-line, inviting new categories of doubt and enquiry that previous scholarship had largely deferred. Flapan's forensic reading of documents, together with a calculus of ambitions and coercive relationships, has thereby redrawn the contours of the pre-state and immediate post-state eras, fracturing the celebratory cartography that long resisted fracturing.

By tracing policy, correspondence, and non-disclosures in an unbroken chain between intent and consequence, Flapan vectors attention toward vainly suppressed inconsistencies that the grand narrative had bracketed as momentary uncertainties. To the dismay of myth guardians, the frankness of his reconstructions realigns the legacies of important people and choices, redefining foundation conflicts as multi-layered, contingent, and morally monitored rather than heroic and predetermined. Where once consensus historical memory deferred to the patriotic mythos, Flapan's patient excavation compels a restless re-evaluation of memory's foundational documents, situating the origins of the state within a broader dialectic of conquest, expulsion, and re-skinned civilisational narrative.

In addition, Flapan's scholarship has initiated a more expansive conversation within both academic and civic domains regarding how collective memory and national identity are narrated and enforced. By obliging historians to confront the mechanisms by which myths are originally contrived and thereafter naturalised, Flapan has prompted a reconsideration of previously unassailable assumptions and tropes, thereby promoting a deeper, more textured understanding of Israeli society and its evolving historical contingencies.

The impact of Flapan's inquiries has travelled well beyond the confines of the academy. His documentation has contested dominant interpretations and provoked a collective reflection on how historical imaginaries shape present attitudes and policy decisions. As a result, Flapan's critical disclosure of the mythical underpinnings of national memory has catalysed a necessary, albeit often fraught, collective exercise in re-evaluating settled accounts, advocating a more candid and reflexive grappling with the multi-layered legacies that constitute Israel's past.

In summation, Flapan's scholarship wields an exceptional force upon the historiography of Israel: its effects are neither ephemeral nor limited to the classroom, and its reverberations are already visible in the historiographical methodologies of the next generation. By subjecting closely guarded beliefs to rigorous empirical scrutiny and exposing the contingent character of foundational images, he has not only revised the content of the period but also altered the questions that scholars and public audiences now quote and pursue. The resonance of his inquiries survives the successive publication of competing accounts, and ensures that any future attempt to account for Israel's early decade must now reckon with the criteria he insisted upon. Flapan's work, therefore, operates not as a terminal critique but as a lasting impetus, inviting further revision and sustained attention to the politics of memory that shape the very production of the past.

Flapan's Methodological Approach to Unearthing Truth

Simha Flapan, a foundational figure in Israeli historiography, adopted a systematic and disciplined methodology to expose the underlying truths masked by the national myths of Israel's birth. His procedure exemplified a profound commitment to scholarly objectivity and to establishing the chronological record upon empirical grounds. Flapan sifted through the national and colonial archives, evaluated contemporaneous documents, and constructed a synthetic account that consistently contested the dominant historiographical consensus. The luminosity of his enterprise resided in his sustained critical reading and discriminating employment of his evidence. By refusing ideological predispositions and by elevating documents above belief, he established a terminus status quo for historiographical integrity in the Israeli context. He navigated the intersecting networks of party representation, bureaucratic secrecy, and personal commitment that frequently distort the production of memory, maintaining a disciplined distance between the scholar and the politics of the moment. His meticulous concern for verification and his practice of inter-source triangulation fortified the verification of his conclusions. The methodological rigour he exemplified illuminated not only the conditionality of the events themselves, but also operated as a powerful vehicle for the dissection of received falsehoods and for the disaggregation of durable legends. Flapan's unswerving insistence upon systematic documentation and persistent cross-examination established the horizon for a more analytically refined and chronically precise comprehension of Israel's formative period.

As scholars confront diverging interpretations of Israel's founding, Simha Flapan's disciplined enquiry provides an exemplary commitment to truth, guiding the discipline toward an unflinching confrontation with the past. His model encourages historians to prioritise archival rigour and moral candour, thus preserving the integrity of the craft for coming practitioners.

Key Myths Challenged by Flapan: A Closer Look

Flapan's key interventions, delivered with surgical precision, unsettle several cornerstone myths. In The Birth of Israel: Myths and Realities, he first interrogates the image of a monolithic, amicable Jewish society in mandate Palestine. Through a meticulous sifting of archival correspondence and journals, he highlights tensions among Zionist elites, settlement leaders, and long-standing Palestinian Jews, revealing a society marked by ideological rifts and mutual suspicions. The harmony, Flapan concludes, is a retrospective fabrication.

Equally rigorous is his critique of the 1948 Zionist military narrative. Opposing the portrayal of the Haganah and Irgun as impromptu guardians responding to external siege, Flapan excavates orders and strategy papers that show deliberate preparation, arms procurement, and immediate post-war expansion. The distinction between defence and expansion is thus the product of conscious choice rather than external compulsion. Lastly, he contests the framing of the 1948 war as an Arab assault, arguing that Zionist military operations and border skirmishes catalysed rather than suppressed Palestinian resistance. Crying Arab aggression, Flapan contends, obscures the domestic and international asymmetries that shaped the conflict's trajectory.

Flapan systematically dispels the notion of a voluntary Palestinian flight during the 1948 war by marshalling empirical evidence that counters the long-circulated belief that Palestinians departed their villages of their own accord. His detailed enquiry into patterns of population displacement alongside documented Zionist expulsion policies produces a starkly reverse portrayal, revealing that coercion, rather than choice, governed much of the Palestinian exodus.

Simultaneously, Flapan's scrupulous exploration of governmental practice undermines the utopian image of Israeli democracy that circulates in diplomatic circles. His examination of legal frameworks that subordinate non-Jewish citizens, coupled with the enforcement of military rule against Palestinians within the 1948 borders, reveals a persistent incompatibility between the founding Zionist imperative and the normative tenets of democratic governance.

In sum, Flapan's exhaustive documentation and penetrating critique obligate an interrogation of the historiographical underpinnings of the Israeli state. He invites a revision of settled assumptions by unmasking the sedimented fictions that underwrite national memory. Through a scholarship marked by both depth and precision, Flapan disassembles the romanticised meta-narrative, exposing the braided complexities and unresolved contradictions that continue to condition the historiography of Israel's emergence.

Reactions from Scholars and the Wider Public Sphere

Simha Flapan's intervention in the historiography of the Israeli state, most critically articulated in his study 'The Birth of Israel: Myths and Realities', provoked sustained and multifaceted reactions among both specialised historians and the wider populace concerned with the nation's formative past. The book's frank examination of the ideological underpinnings of the Israeli mythography disrupted scholarly consensus, compelling historians—whether situated within Israeli universities, the diaspora, or neutral archival spaces—to reassess the documentary record of the 1948 period against the counter-narrative Flapan elaborated. Employing both archival material and a methodical dissection of legend, Flapan invited historians to acknowledge the dissonance between myth and evidence, thereby precipitating a wave of self-scrutiny and methodologically rigorous counter-reading. Outside the lecture hall, Flapan's text circulated among practitioners of civic history, educators, and politically engaged citizens, such that the book quickly transcended its academic origin. Public seminars, journalistic reviews, and later radio and television features catalysed a wider civic enquiry into the provenance of the Hebrew Republic. The observable intensification of media comment, civic panel deliberation and counter-text publication established a reciprocal dynamic: scholarly debate nourished public debate, and vice versa, thus framing the historiography itself as a domain of contemporary civic relevance. The resultant exchanges identified the foundational myth as a live political and pedagogical issue, and the scale of the engagement—both specialised and public—confirmed the enduring power of Flapan's critical reappraisal.

While his conclusions attracted many supporters, a formidable cadre refused to abandon convictions painstakingly fortified over decades. This stark polarisation magnified the debate's intensity. Accusations and rebuttals crystallised around what historians and reporters described as the emotional bedrock of differing collective memories. Furthermore, Flapan's capacity to provoke such a range of indignation, enthusiasm, and doubt suggested his research intercepted the vital arteries of national identity and shared remembrance. Wherever the reverberations of his argument reached, historians rediscovered the value of testing inherited assertions and the public adopted a new, and sometimes passionately, sceptical spirit. Thus, a single, decidedly courageous publication unwittingly compelled readers to practise history as truth-seeking rather than myth-reinforcement. In sum, the variegated responses within university seminars, editorial columns, and articulate crowds confirmed, long before the centennial elegies, the lasting importance of an enquiry that exposed the cost and necessity of confronting received wisdom.

The Ripple Effect: Influence on Subsequent Historiography

Simha Flapan's landmark study has left an indelible mark on later historiography, reconfiguring the intellectual terrain and challenging the settled narratives that once suffused Israeli history. Following Flapan's incisive dissection of the myths that have long consecrated the origins of Israel, succeeding historians have felt an urgent obligation to re-examine both their explanatory frameworks and their epistemological presuppositions. The consequences of Flapan's work thus exceed the confines of the scholarly archive; they have effectively inaugurated a research-strategy metamorphosis and have reopened the politics of memory surrounding national identity. Among the most decisive corollaries of Flapan's conclusions has been the articulation of a more sophisticated, multivalent account of the 1948 environment.

By interrogating the mythical substrata that once passed unexamined, Flapan has imposed a stricter hermeneutical discipline on both primary and secondary materials, thereby exposing the latent biases that historiographic study must now account for. This imperative for critical interrogation has, in consequence, escalated the demand for a corroborative evidentiary matrix and has negotiated the alleged self-evidence of previously dominant explanatory models. Flapan's intellectual legacy has further migrated into forms of collective memory; the publication of his work has catalysed impassioned debates and a sustained self-reflexivity within Israeli civil society and within the wider diasporic awareness.

It is the discipline demonstrated in his careful dismantling of the myths that define the nation which has compelled both intellectual and public spheres to reconsider the design of collective memory itself and the role such memory plays in reconciliation and the longstanding project of peace-building. Each subsequent cohort of historians now finds in Flapan's analyses the necessary ballast for critical work that continues to confront multilayered pasts. His oeuvre remains a vital, if not defining, measure for a historiography that insists upon balance, inclusivity, and a moral sine qua non. The intellectual aftershock of his arguments continues to shape disciplinary currents, permitting and indeed requiring younger scholars to confront, rather than deflect, the uncomfortable segments of both documents and legacies. In his persistent willingness to confront the unvarnished evidence, Simha Flapan has, in turn, determined the formal and ethical orientation of Israeli historiography itself and, in the broader sense, reconfigured the terms upon which the pursuit of understanding may be pursued.

Integrating Flapan's Insights into Contemporary Discourse

Simha Flapan's pioneering studies occupy an indispensable space in present-day conversations spanning scholarship, media, and policy formation. His unflinching critique of national mythologies compelled a re-examination of the formative years of the Israeli state, forcing a fresh confrontation with sources previously relegated to the margins. Flapan's patient, archival-based scholarship punctured the idealised narrative of national rebirth, revealing the processes and decisions that, though uncomfortable, had sustained state formation. With the steady accrual of new readers, this interrogation is no longer confined to specialists; politicians, civil society leaders, and concerned citizens now deliberate its findings. A principal pathway for more in-depth engagement with Flapan's work is the pedagogical sector. When instructors introduce his arguments in secondary and higher-education syllabi, students acquire a readiness to entertain conflictual and plural understandings of the past, nurturing the critical capacity expected of informed citizens. Concurrently, his interpretive orientations have reconfigured modern historiography, encouraging scholars to interrogate accepted periodisations, to excavate ambiguous sources, and to appreciate the interplay between ideology and contingency. The cumulative effect is a historiographic turn that feeds more transparent public conversations and gradually recalibrates collective memory across varied arenas of Israeli and transnational society.

Flapan's scholarship thus constitutes an indispensable

touchstone for the formulation of diplomatic frameworks and the orchestration of conflict resolution initiatives. Recognising the rigorous verity of his investigations, states persons and mediators may confront historical grievances—traditionally the axis of animosities—within a matrix of empathy and comprehension, thereby inaugurating dialogues that are both expansive and substantively anchored. In tandem, the work prompts a systemic re-conceptualisation of national identity and collective memory, obliging polities to examine the fissured subtexts of their past and to pursue the difficult labour of collective self-examination. Such programmes of reflection enable societies to confront that which had long been repressed, and to synthesise a composite memory that deliberately integrates plural voices. The abiding impact of Flapan's interpretations thereby illustrates the perennial utility of rigorous historical scholarship in the choreography of present-day discourse. When his conclusions are diffused across pedagogical, diplomatic, and civic domains, the prospect of a polity capable of sustaining historical consciousness without succumbing to its divisive potential is appreciably augmented.

Conclusion: The Legacy of Rethinking National Narratives

In societies where collective memory informs identity and policy, the re-examination of national narratives remains an imperative intellectual and ethical priority. Professional historians bear responsibility for recalibrating the lens through which past events are judged, thereby conditioning the moral measures by which present and future are evaluated. Simha Flapan's scrupulous dissection of Israel's founding myths has thereby reconfigured the terrain of historical scholarship. By dislodging the sedimented myths that sedimented into the national psyche, Flapan invited both scholars and citizens into an arena of sustained critical re-deliberation. The consequences of his enquiry have radiated well beyond the seminar room, altering the lexicon of public debate and the calculus of policy-makers. The enduring contribution of his scholarship, and of the enterprise of interrogating national narratives generally, resides in its ability to render the collective memory both pliant and interrogative, thereby encouraging a memory that is both compassionate and reflective.

In altering the discipline's self-understanding, Flapan's findings have destabilised broader societal habits of thought. They have compelled Israeli society to reckon openly with the paradoxes concealed by then-dominant historic frames, nudging citizens to interrogate the circumstances that shaped their polity. The communal effect has been an enriched appreciation for the variegated texture of memory, and an ethical recognition of the moral imperatives that attend competing recollections. Through such awareness, the polity has moved, however incrementally, toward a memory that remains in conversation with the past rather than entirely consenting to its myths.

The practice of re-evaluating national narratives has thus generated a more inclusive and empathetic societal discourse, one that integrates multiple experiences and continues to confront historical wrongs. Flapan's scholarship has articulated the contours of that practice and has bequeathed to successive scholars a methodological prototype combining rigorous research, systematic enquiry, and moral bravery. His analysis demonstrates the durable relevance of historical research in unpacking the variegated forces that have moulded national identities. By excavating strata of myth and misconception, Flapan has underlined the necessity of verifiable narratives in any project of genuine reconciliation and durable public progress. The experiential insight gained from rethinking national narratives knows no local or temporal borders; its effects radiate as a continent-wide mandate, attesting to the transformative agency of historiographical labour.

To conclude: the historiographical revolution sketched in the lifetime work of Simha Flapan stands as an enduring index of research's power to breach chronological confines and to elicit profound civic self-analysis. In an era marked by intricate geopolitical disputes and layered intra-societal tensions, Flapan's memory continues to function as an analytical and moral lodestar, steering enquiry toward a more enlightened reconciliation with the shared past and a more equitable collective future.

References For Further Reading

Works by Simha Flapan
- Flapan, Simha. The Birth of Israel: Myths and Realities. New York: Pantheon, 1987.

    — The cornerstone of Flapan's challenge to Israel's founding narratives; combines archival work with pointed myth-deconstruction.

The "New Historians" and Adjacent Revisionist Scholarship
- Morris, Benny. The Birth of the Palestinian Refugee Problem, 1947–1949. Cambridge: Cambridge University Press, 1987; rev. as The Birth of the Palestinian Refugee Problem Revisited, 2004.

  — Foundational for debates on the causes of the 1948 exodus; heavily archival, frequently engaged by supporters and critics alike.

- Morris, Benny. 1948: A History of the First Arab–Israeli War. New Haven: Yale University Press, 2008.

  — Strategic-military synthesis of the war with extensive primary documentation.

- Morris, Benny. Israel's Border Wars, 1949–1956. Oxford: Clarendon Press, 1993.

  — Key for understanding postwar dynamics and cross-border raids.

- Shlaim, Avi. Collusion Across the Jordan: King Abdullah, the Zionist Movement, and the Partition of Palestine. New York: Columbia University Press, 1988.

  — Reassesses diplomacy and alleged Zionist–Jordanian understandings during 1947–49.

- Shlaim, Avi. The Iron Wall: Israel and the Arab World. New York: W. W. Norton, 2000 (updated eds.).

— Long-view diplomatic history using the "Iron Wall" concept to frame Israeli strategy.

- Pappé, Ilan. The Ethnic Cleansing of Palestine. Oxford: Oneworld, 2006.

  — Forceful thesis on 1948 expulsions; widely cited and contested.

- Pappé, Ilan. The Idea of Israel: A History of Power and Knowledge. London: Verso, 2014.

  — On Israeli historiography, ideology, and the politics of knowledge production.

- Segev, Tom. 1949: The First Israelis. New York: Free Press, 1986.

  — Social history of Israel's first year; complicates heroic nation-building narratives.

- Segev, Tom. One Palestine, Complete: Jews and Arabs Under the British Mandate. New York: Metropolitan Books, 2000.

  — Rich portrait of the Mandate period that reframes the pre-1948 context.

Critical Counter-Arguments and Mainstream Perspectives
- Karsh, Efraim. Fabricating Israeli History: The "New Historians." London: Frank Cass, 1997; 2nd ed., 2000.

- The most sustained critique of the "New Historians," questioning method and inference.

- Karsh, Efraim. Palestine Betrayed. New Haven: Yale University Press, 2010.

  — Emphasizes Arab leadership decisions in explaining 1948 outcomes.

- Gelber, Yoav. Palestine 1948: War, Escape and the Emergence of the Palestinian Refugee Problem. Brighton: Sussex Academic Press, 2006.

  — Military and political analysis challenging expulsion-centered accounts.

- Shapira, Anita. Israel: A History. Waltham, MA: Brandeis University Press, 2012.

  — A leading Israeli historian's synthetic narrative; useful as a mainstream counterpoint.

- Teveth, Shabtai. Ben-Gurion and the Palestinian Arabs: From Peace to War. Oxford: Oxford University Press, 1985.

  — Reassesses Ben-Gurion's policies and intentions toward Palestinian Arabs.

Palestinian Scholarship on 1948, Memory, and Displacement

- Khalidi, Walid, ed. From Haven to Conquest: Readings in Zionism and the Palestine Problem until 1948.

Washington, DC: Institute for Palestine Studies, 1971; updated eds.

— Comprehensive documentary anthology placing Zionist and Palestinian texts in dialogue.

- Khalidi, Walid. All That Remains: The Palestinian Villages Occupied and Depopulated by Israel in 1948. Washington, DC: Institute for Palestine Studies, 1992.

— Definitive reference on depopulated villages; essential for microhistory.

- Khalidi, Walid. "Plan Dalet: Master Plan for the Conquest of Palestine." Journal of Palestine Studies 18, no. 1 (1988): 4–33.

— Text and analysis of Plan Dalet; pivotal to arguments about intent and expulsion.

- Khalidi, Rashid. Palestinian Identity: The Construction of Modern National Consciousness. New York: Columbia University Press, 1997.

— Classic work on the formation of modern Palestinian identity.

- Khalidi, Rashid. The Iron Cage: The Story of the Palestinian Struggle for Statehood. Boston: Beacon Press, 2006.

— Structural constraints and leadership dilemmas in Palestinian politics.

- Masalha, Nur. Expulsion of the Palestinians: The Concept of "Transfer" in Zionist Political Thought, 1882–1948. Washington, DC: Institute for Palestine Studies, 1992.

  — Traces "transfer" ideas in Zionist discourse; often read alongside Morris and Pappé.

- Masalha, Nur. The Palestine Nakba: Decolonising History, Narrating the Subaltern, Reclaiming Memory. London: Zed Books, 2012.

  — Memory, narrative, and decolonial framing of 1948.

- Sa'di, Ahmad H., and Lila Abu-Lughod, eds. Nakba: Palestine, 1948, and the Claims of Memory. New York: Columbia University Press, 2007.

  — Essays linking memory to politics and historical narration.

Memory, Myth, and Historiographical Method (Conceptual Tools)

- Zerubavel, Yael. Recovered Roots: Collective Memory and the Making of Israeli National Tradition. Chicago: University of Chicago Press, 1995.

  — Seminal study on myth, commemoration, and Israeli national tradition.

- Sternhell, Zeev, with Mario Sznajder and Maia Asheri. The Founding Myths of Israel: Nationalism, Socialism, and the Making of the Jewish State. Princeton: Princeton University Press, 1998.

— Interrogates ideological myth-making in Zionist society.

- Kimmerling, Baruch. The Invention and Decline of Israeliness: State, Society, and the Military. Berkeley: University of California Press, 2001.

— State-society-military triangle and identity formation.

- Shafir, Gershon. Land, Labor and the Origins of the Israeli–Palestinian Conflict, 1882–1914. Cambridge: Cambridge University Press, 1989.

— Structural analysis of Zionist settlement and labor policy.

- Anderson, Benedict. Imagined Communities: Reflections on the Origin and Spread of Nationalism. London: Verso, 1983 (rev. ed. 1991).

— The classic on nations and narratives; useful framing for "founding myths."

- Hobsbawm, Eric, and Terence Ranger, eds. The Invention of Tradition. Cambridge: Cambridge University Press, 1983.

— How "traditions" are constructed; a toolkit for myth analysis.

- Halbwachs, Maurice. On Collective Memory. Chicago: University of Chicago Press, 1992.

  — Foundational theory of social memory relevant to national narratives.

- Nora, Pierre. Realms of Memory: Rethinking the French Past. New York: Columbia University Press, 1996–1998.

  — Case-study model for sites of memory; methodologically comparable.

Document Readers, Archives, and Primary Sources
- Rogan, Eugene L., and Avi Shlaim, eds. The War for Palestine: Rewriting the History of 1948. Cambridge: Cambridge University Press, 2001; 2nd ed., 2007.

  — Essay collection that crystallized post-Flapan debates; pairs well with his themes.

- Laqueur, Walter, and Barry Rubin, eds. The Israel–Arab Reader: A Documentary History of the Middle East Conflict. New York: Penguin, various editions.

  — Broad documentary sampler (UN, speeches, accords) for quick reference.

- United Nations General Assembly. Resolution 181 (II): Future Government of Palestine (1947); Resolution 194 (III) (1948).

  — Core diplomatic texts commanding central place in

narratives and disputes.

- United Nations Special Committee on Palestine (UNSCOP). Report to the General Assembly (31 August 1947).

    — Baseline Mandate-era primary document.

- Israel State Archives (ISA); IDF and Defense Establishment Archives (IDFA); Central Zionist Archives (CZA); British National Archives (FO 371 series).

    — Where much of the archival backbone of the historiography resides.

Broader Surveys and Textbooks for Orientation

- Morris, Benny. *Righteous Victims: A History of the Zionist–Arab Conflict, 1881–2001*. New York: Knopf, 1999.

    — Wide-ranging synthesis engaging political, military, and social dimensions.

- Gelvin, James L. *The Israel–Palestine Conflict: One Hundred Years of War*. Cambridge: Cambridge University Press, 2005; 4th ed., 2021.

    — Concise, balanced overview with strong pedagogy.

- Smith, Charles D. *Palestine and the Arab–Israeli Conflict*. Boston: Bedford/St. Martin's, multiple eds.

    — Standard teaching text with documents and historiographic signposts.

- Tessler, Mark. A History of the Israeli–Palestinian Conflict. Bloomington: Indiana University Press, 1994; 2nd ed., 2009.

    — Comprehensive and even-handed; helpful for readers new to the field.

Pedagogy and Dual-Narrative Approaches
- Adwan, Sami, Dan Bar-On, and Eyal Naveh, eds. Side by Side: Parallel Histories of Israel/Palestine. New York: The New Press, 2012.

    — Juxtaposes Israeli and Palestinian narratives; a practical extension of Flapan's call for reflexive, plural historiography.

Historical Method (for Flapan's evidentiary ethos)
- Bloch, Marc. The Historian's Craft. New York: Vintage, 1953.

    — A classic reflection on evidence, context, and critical method.

- Howell, Martha, and Walter Prevenier. From Reliable Sources: An Introduction to Historical Methods. Ithaca: Cornell University Press, 2001.

    — Nuts-and-bolts of source criticism and archival practice.

- Gaddis, John Lewis. The Landscape of History: How

Historians Map the Past. Oxford: Oxford University Press, 2002.

— Clear guide to inference, causation, and narrative in historical analysis.

- Ginzburg, Carlo. Clues, Myths, and the Historical Method. Baltimore: Johns Hopkins University Press, 1989.

— On reading traces and building arguments—apt for Flapan's documentary style.

6
Revisiting the 'David vs. Goliath' Paradigm

Introduction to the David vs. Goliath Narrative

The storied origins and enduring resonance of the David and Goliath motif are inextricably linked to the layered history of the Israeli-Palestinian conflict. Emerging from the biblical recounting of the shepherd youth who, armed with a mere sling, overcame the Philistine champion, the image has migrated into contemporary parlance as shorthand for the little guy's improbable victory over a heftier foe. Within the Israeli-Palestinian context, the allegory has been repurposed to crystallise the prevailing imbalance of forces perceived to characterise the struggle.

This motif's staying power owes not only to its vividness, but to its capacity to condense the conflict's geopolitics into a moral parable. Political leaders invoke it, analysts quote it, and the public readily grasps its import. The analogy's durability can be traced to its biblical provenance and the subsequent exegetical traditions that have granted it traction far beyond the original text, embedding the image in the imaginaries and argumentations that continue to animate the region.

The conflict has often been framed as a lonely nation besieged by vast enmity, a framing that has resonated deeply across public consciousness. This motif has transcended Israel and Palestine, affecting international interpretations of the continuing upheaval in the Eastern Mediterranean. Each actor has adopted the image strategically, casting itself alternately as the oppressed David or the moral avenger.

Yet, a dispassionate appraisal discloses a landscape more layered than the motif allows. Attention to the longue durée of empire, population displacement, and institutional stratification indicates that the metaphor, while illuminating in limited respects, conceals as much as it reveals. It flattens the array of agencies, the variations in power, and the heterogeneous sufferings that the dispute produces.

To arrive at a more adequate comprehension. Therefore, we must interrogate the narrative's genealogy and transformation. Such an enquiry will illuminate how this compelling comparison has structured perceptions, guided policy, and crystallised in the collective memory of both societies, thereby shaping the prolonged and intractable nature of the disagreement.

The Genesis of a Mythical Analogy

The centuries-old story of David and Goliath, inherited from the biblical corpus, has long been a magnet for both popular and scholarly imagination. Visualising the diminutive shepherd confronting the armoured colossus magnifies the drama of the asymmetrical combat, securing for the episode an enduring licence as the quintessential underdog narrative. Such potency has encouraged its repeated invocation whenever the asymmetry of strength has been deemed salient, especially regarding the discourse on the Israeli-Palestinian conflict. The familiar formula of 'David' meeting 'Goliath' has colonised historical and rhetorical space, shaping commentary from parliaments to popular media and thereby consolidating its file on the mental archives of the public. Within this paradigm, the compact of the towering, state-backed opponent against the besieged, fragmentary community directs the analyst's gaze toward the binaries of oppression and resistance. Yet, the persistence of the David-Goliath figuration itself begs a rigorous exploration of its origins and migrations, for, rather than an objective mirror of geopolitics, it represents the sedimentation of selective memory and narrative streamlining. The narrative's traction stems from the human impulse to compress multivalent forces into a single legible image, thereby eclipsing the stratifications and resistances that an ethnographic gaze would otherwise uncover.

The abiding fascination with binary oppositions and archetypal figures within narrative constructs yields a potent lens through which politically charged confrontations can be illuminated. Simultaneously, the perennial attraction of the underdog motif penetrates the cultural psyche, thus serving as an effective medium for the transmission of ethical imperatives. A lesser, outwardly vulnerable protagonist defying a larger, apparently dominant antagonist evokes a widespread yearning for hope, endurance, and moral rectitude. Consequently, the mythic pattern of David and Goliath becomes deeply embedded in collective memory, modulating public interpretations of a given struggle. Yet, within this captivating narrative, one must rigorously unwind the reductive framing of historical encounters. A sustained enquiry into the precise geopolitical configurations, historical trajectories, and sociocultural textures framing each conflict yields a graduated perception of the distribution and exercise of power. An adequate comprehension of the Israeli-Palestinian dispute therefore requires one to move beyond static oppositions and to engage with the layered realities of the past. Though the David and Goliath motif retains an archetypal energy, its deployment in this instance warrants a disciplined critique to disclose the intricate weave of historical condition and causal agency.

An Uneven Battlefield: Rethinking Power Dynamics

Traditional analyses of the Israeli-Palestinian conflict frequently portray the situation as a stark binary: a militarily omnipotent Israel arrayed against a politically and militarily impotent Palestine. Such a depiction has permeated elite and popular discourse alike, generating policy assumptions and humanitarian interpretations alike that treat the conflict as a moral equation rather than a political process. A more scrupulous enquiry, however, exposes the limitations of this framing and urges a re-examination of the underlying power configurations.

A re-evaluation of the power axes at work exposes a battlefield profoundly more heterogeneous than the binary permits. Israel, while exhibiting conspicuous advantages in military technology and economic resources, faces a Palestinian society that has, against the odds, mobilised formidable capacities of endurance, popular mobilisation, and transnational advocacy. Furthermore, power is multidimensional; the absence of territorial sovereignty for the Palestinian polity does not negate other forms of agency, including cultural persistence, social networks, and transnational diasporic support that shape the event, memory, and politics of the conflict.

A calibrated analysis must therefore attend to the historical legacies of colonial displacement, the variable engagements of great powers in the region, the tactical peculiarities of asymmetric conflict, and the evolving micro-dynamics of everyday security governance. Only by contextualising the power differentials within this broader kaleidoscope can scholars and policymakers alike transcend the reductionist impulse and cultivate a more accurate, empathetic, and politically actionable grasp of this enduring rupture.

Power imbalances permeate everyday life in the region, shaping access to resources, freedom of movement, and prospects for socioeconomic advancement. These inequities are not limited to explicit displays of control; rather, they infiltrate routine social exchanges, colour public perceptions, and entrench enduring structural inequalities. The result is a persistent hierarchical ordering that shapes individual choices and collective life chances.

The global geopolitical environment further complicates intra-regional power relations. Major states, multilateral institutions, and transnational actors routinely intervene, applying diplomatic, economic, and military instruments that recalibrate the balance of forces on the ground. The overlapping vital interests of external sides, the convergence and divergence of alliances, and the conditionality of aid and recognition weave the local conflict into a larger geopolitical mosaic, highlighting the impossibility of isolating the Israeli-Palestinian question from global patterns of power.

A rigorous re-examination of these asymmetries is imperative for any dialogue that seeks durability rather than momentary cease-fires. Recognising that power is not merely a question of momentary military advantage, but a layered, territorial and social phenomenon that is actively reproduced, allows negotiators to conceive of interventions that address the underlying processes of domination rather than superficial symptoms. Only through such calibrated engagement can the stakeholders begin to constitute conditions for an equitable and just coexistence of Israelis and Palestinians.

David's Slingshot: The Role of International Politics

The metaphor of David confronting Goliath applied to the Israeli-Palestinian conflict serves to complicate rather than to clarify the distribution of power, revealing instead the multilayered influence of global politics on the enduring animosities. The image allows analysts to foreground the asymmetry of military capabilities, while also revealing how external actors continually recalibrate the balance of power through formal and informal networks of support. The Israeli state, conventionalised as the contemporary Goliath, has acquired from several Western states, most conspicuously the United States, military hardware, intelligence-sharing, and diplomatic cover, thus entrenching its military superiority and smoothing the political costs of its operations. Western advocacy at the United Nations and other forums has also muted formal sanctions and legal accountability, consolidating this advantage.

The Palestinian cause, construed as David, has in turn oriented its political and diplomatic efforts toward obtaining recognition within multilateral institutions, courting support from a spectrum of states and organisations whose motives range from solidarity to geopolitical chess. Multilateral entities, including the Arab League and now expanded to a constellation of global south states, have granted symbolic and political heft, while conditional aid packages from the European Union and others have paradoxically reinforced systemic vulnerabilities. The intricate choreography of recognition, state-building rhetoric, and international legal strategies demonstrates how global political structures recalibrate the weight of force with the weight of formal legitimacy, complicating any linear reading of the conflict's trajectories.

Furthermore, the involvement of major international actors—most prominently the European Union and the Russian Federation—adds another layer of complexity to the prevailing power structures. Their engagement alters the geopolitical landscape and simultaneously shapes how the leadership of Israel and the Palestinian territories interpret each other's intentions and recalibrate their strategic choices. Manoeuvring among global powers exerts a tangible influence on core questions of territorial demarcation, access to scarce resources, and the practical application of international legal norms, each of which remains pivotal to any sustainable resolution.

The notion of a 'David's Slingshot' that recurs in the multilateral diplomatic theatre signifies the dual dimensions of reinforcements that each actor acquires on the global stage. This backing comprises not only military and humanitarian consignments and formal diplomatic ostentation, but also systematic lobbying, purposeful advocacy campaigns, and the legitimisation of competing historical narratives. Such international endorsements are capable of altering domestic and international public perceptions, guiding governmental choices, and reframing the hegemonic narratives that surround the conflict, each of which constitutes a decisive vector in determining the conflict's future evolution.

The complex interaction between worldwide strategic concerns and the Israeli-Palestinian conflict illustrates how global power arrangements permeate localised circumstances. The results of international diplomacy ripple through the ordinary lives of individuals enduring years of discord. This convergence of influences cannot be relegated to the periphery of analysis; rather, it demands that any enquiry into the quest for justice or sustainable settlement situate local grievances within the larger matrix of international decision-making and strategic calculation.

Goliath's Armour: Military Strength and Perception

The familiar 'David versus Goliath' imagery articulates how perceptions of military power shape prevailing conflict trajectories, and, applied to the Israeli-Palestinian struggle, the metaphor attains considerable weight. Goliath's encumbering armour emerges as a proxy for military superiority, evoking Israeli Defence Forces doctrine and technology, while David embodies the Palestinian recourse to asymmetric resistance. Stationed in a unified, technologically enhanced operational structure, the IDF frequently dominates external analytic portraits as the seemingly indomitable Leviathan. Such portrayals crystallise not only among international audiences, but penetrate the marrow of Israeli public and security discourse. The metaphor of Goliath's battered, insulated shell, however, exceeds kitschy imagery; it embeds itself in collective perceptions regarding the psychological burden of assumed, prevailing dominance. The resulting ambience compels Israeli planners to iterate a suite of measures calibrated by—rather than merely reacting to—putative omnipotence. Goliath's psychological footprint thus becomes a hidden variable in the calculus of deterrence, preemption, and a persistent expectation that Israel alone enjoys the upper hand for the preservation of national objectives. At each echelon of Israeli governance, the conviction that the armoured behemoth of resource, training, and intelligence obliviously dwarfs its rival steers the formulation of policies that, while militarily sophisticated, remain layered by the chimeric necessity of securing total superiority over a dispersed and contested civilian populace.

The metaphor of Goliath's armour continues to saturate public consciousness, cultivating a sense of historical entitlement and invulnerability within certain circles of Israeli society; this, in turn, reverberates through the evolution of national identity and collective memory. By visually and rhetorically amplifying the image of Israel as an indomitable military force, the metaphor effectively eclipses the structural asymmetries of power and the pervasive, daily realities of occupation confronting Palestinian communities. Such framing exercises a determinative influence on diplomatic currents, strategic alliances, and the formulation of foreign policy vis-à-vis the Israeli-Palestinian conflict. Goliath's armour thereby colours international calculations regarding humanitarian assistance, commercial exchange, and military cooperation, complicating the intricate geopolitical fabric of the region. Yet, a critical exploration must transcend the ostensible spectacle of military supremacy to interrogate the deeper, protracted asymmetries that animate the conflict. Disentangling the subtleties of the power relations involved and reconsidering the ramifications of the Goliath metaphor will yield a more analytically robust framework for apprehending the multilayered realities that continuously shape relations between Israelis and Palestinians.

Media's Portrayal and the Reproduction of Myth

Media institutions invariably shape both collective memory and political subjectivity through selective reporting and strategic imagery. In relation to the Israeli-Palestinian conflict, the diffusion of the 'David versus Goliath' motif invites persistent examination and critique. Televised news segments, newspaper headlines, and digital commentaries routinely reduce the conflict to a grand theatrical binary of the small, valiant David besieged by a titanically disproportionate Goliath.

The endurance of this myth derives, in large measure, from synchronization of framing and editorial inhibition. Leading news organisations tend to illustrate the Israeli polity as a besieged underdog encountering quasi-superhuman odds, while Palestinian agency, whether in activism or victimhood, is either criminalised or relegated to the margins of the visual and textual frame. Such unequal weighting gravely distorts the historical scale and asymmetries of the conflict, allowing the heroic micro-macro parable to settle into conventional wisdom.

Visuality, too, retains a disproportionate weight in myth installation. Iconic stills and circulating footage seize flashpoints—rockets, protests, demolished homes—that simplify and hypermobilise the polarity of muscular might versus fragile human life. Supplemented by polemical captions and emotive soundtracks, these images archive a heroic narrative that commemorative institutions later mobilise to justify political positions, locking historical experience into a fast, emotive lexicon.

Furthermore, the role of editorial policy and concentration of media ownership in sustaining this simplified and misleading myth is an aspect that demands sustained critical attention. The selective editorial practices of news organisations, frequently calibrated to reflect their underlying commercial imperatives or partisan affiliations, dictate the contours of reporting that relate to the confrontation. Simultaneously, the merger of political loyalty with media capital corrupts the presentation of the conflict itself, magnifying the rhetorical force of the 'David and Goliath' dichotomy.

One must acknowledge the wide and durable consequences of this journalistic myth-making. The broad acceptance and subconscious appropriation of these reductive images mask the conflict's multiple layers and inhibit the cultivation of an informed and sympathetic comprehension of both parties. The continued circulation of the 'David and Goliath' motif consequently abstracts the historical and geopolitical specificities, enforcing a stark and polarised interpretive framework that obstructs the sincere dialogues that precede any durable resolution.

In responding to the deleterious effects of media perpetuation, it is imperative to interrogate and contest the dominant imaginaries that shape public consciousness. Cultivating a more discerning and layered practice of media consumption permits constituencies to detach the sediment of myth that has long veiled the conflict's protracted trajectory. Concurrently, amplifying heterogeneous, and especially marginalised, voices that elude dominant circuits of representation can disrupt sedimented narratives and produce a more textured comprehension of the tensions involved.

Tragedy & Travesty in the "David and Goliath" Trope

The oft-cited "David and Goliath" schema, circulated in Western media and political rhetoric, has occasioned vigorous contestation precisely because it encapsulates events in a manner that neutralises the conflict's historical and social complexities. The alluring image of a beleaguered underdog confronting a colossus is media-friendly yet chronically reductive; it glosses over colonial legacies, geopolitical asymmetries, and the variegated forms of violence deployed across years. Such narrative economy is alluring, yet it misrepresents prevailing power relations and compresses plurality into caricature.

The ensuing distortion simplifies complexity and calcifies a discursive formation that obfuscates what the conflict actually entails. To transform understanding. Therefore, one must trace the concept's genealogical emergence, interrogate its strategic deployment, and expose what the metaphor suppresses—a constellation of actors, technologies, and historical legacies that defy binary fate.

At the centre of this argument lies the rejection of the binary framing that casts David as the virtuous, beleaguered champion and Goliath as the ruthless tormentor. Disassembling this pomposity reveals that each party possesses its own capacity for action, its own points of frailty, and its own historical depth—elements that the familiar story renders mute.

Turning now to the wider geopolitical consequences of allowing this binary to circulate unexamined, one can trace the distortion the dyad works upon global perception. The reductive framing compresses a multifaceted reality into a neat, heroic tableau, thereby foreclosing possibilities for genuine comprehension and, in turn, for durable remedial action.

Images of the confrontation filtered through the 'David versus Goliath' motif further occlude the quieter yet decisive critiques that refuse to be captivated by its poetry. These alternative discourses, frequently marginalised by the compelling imagery, illuminate the attendant ethical and political quandaries confronting each party, thereby loosening the grip of fixed assumptions and cultivating a more solicitous apprehension of the entire confrontation.

The well-known 'David versus Goliath' trope ultimately restricts rather than illuminates our analysis of the Israeli-Palestinian conflict. Subjecting the analogy to rigorous examination and giving voice to critical counterarguments enables us to exceed the confining assumptions it propagates. In so doing, we open the intellectual space necessary for dialogue grounded in empirical realities and moral complexity, dialogue that any viable and equitable settlement must entice and sustain.

Critical Voices: Dissenting Perspectives

Within the ongoing discourse over the so-called 'David versus Goliath' frame, organised dissent has gained sufficient traction to unsettle dominant interpretations of the Israeli-Palestinian conflict. Academics and policy analysts aligned with these dissenting positions question the binary scheme in its entirety, insisting instead upon a repertoire of historic and structural inequalities that a mere underdog mythology obscures. Among the most consistent objections to the dominant narrative is the insistence that the Israeli polity, while facing conflictual provocations, simultaneously enjoys an array of military, technological, and diplomatic edges that the 'underdog' paradigm cannot adequately incorporate.

Beyond the structural critique, these dissenting voices place historic memory at the centre of their analysis. The sustained invocation of the Holocaust, reinforced by the memorial cultures of contemporary Israel and global Jewish diaspora communities, has helped to configure Israel as a perpetual victim in the court of world opinion. This memorial frame, in their view, conflates historic vulnerability with contemporary power and thereby sanctions repressive practices under the aegis of self-defence. The critique thereby extends beyond empirical falsification to the psychosocial domain, interrogating how memory, symbolism, and affect mutually constitute the effectiveness of the 'David versus Goliath' trope over successive decades.

Additionally, heterodox voices emerging within both Israeli and Palestinian constituencies interrogate the prevailing binary framing of the conflict, contending that it effaces the stratified and disputed character of the struggle. By interrogating asymmetries of power, intra-societal fractures, and variegated national aspirations, these interlocutors illuminate the imperative of transgressing reductionist storylines.

Critically, a number of dissidents aver that the 'David versus Goliath' trope yields consequences both for historiography and for the plausibility of a durable peace. By sustaining a narrative of ceaseless victimisation on one side and unassailable might on the other, the trope inhibits the cultivation of reciprocal empathy and the willingness to barter concessions, thereby obstructing the trajectory toward resolution.

When these dissident analyses are brought to the foreground, their contribution to a rounded comprehension of the Israeli-Palestinian conflict becomes unmistakable. They compel scholars and practitioners alike to forgo binary shortcuts, to reckon with the sedimented complexities of the historical record, and to interrogate the durable consequences of deep-rooted myths and figurative discourse. To omit these critical voices is to impoverish the dialogue; to integrate them is to advance the pursuit of a more inclusive and analytically robust framework for engaging the ongoing conjuncture.

Impact on Israeli and Palestinian Identity

The enduring 'David versus Goliath' metaphor has penetrated the core of Israeli and Palestinian self-understanding, embedding itself in collective memories and enduring worldviews. For Israelis, the trajectory of the small, beleaguered nation defeating larger adversaries has become a mythic register in which they articulate nationhood, consecrating perceived historical miracles into a doctrine of inevitable survival. Within this frame, success against the odds fortifies a self-image of moral and historical vindication, simultaneously acting as a social glue that reasserts the justification for sovereign self-determination. Conversely, the same metaphor, when reinterpreted by Palestinians, crystallises experiences of exile and structural injury into a clear-cut but tragic portrait of continuous martyrdom. The asymmetric power relationships implicit in 'David versus Goliath' sanction a rhetoric of dispossession that galvanises Palestinian narratives of inalienable land and of rights denied by a juggernaut viewed as irredeemably coercive.

The artistic, literary, and educational channels through which the metaphor circulates have, in each society, deepened the entrenchment of irreconcilable memorial registers. Curricula, public commemorations, novels, films, and graffiti double as instruments of identification and estrangement, locking each community into a portrait of the other that eludes empathic translation. Within this dialectic, mistrust crystallises into identity, and the metaphor transforms from a rhetorical strategy into a structuring principle of collective remembrance, persistently frustrating initiatives geared toward negotiated coexistence.

The reverberations of this figurative edifice, however, are not confined to chronicles and declarations of power; they also saturate the unconscious registers through which each group negotiates the social world.

For Israelis, the narrative sustains an unwavering sense of vigilance and moral permission in the face of what they perceive as existential peril, perpetuating a mental landscape akin to a perpetually fortified enclave that colours decisions, speech, and the rhythm of everyday life. For Palestinians, in tandem, the same narrative reinforces an indomitable ethos of steadfastness, framing every setback as a rehearsal for eventual restitution and every concession as a call to intensified assertion of what they regard as inalienable rights.

Yet, the intractable character of these interlocked beliefs constitutes a formidable barrier to resolution. Identification with dated heroic scripts leaves little cognitive space to imagine futures that pivot not on heroic durability but on shared human vulnerability. Were Israelis to lose the sense of the existential siege, the symbolic structure of their state would alter; were Palestinians to concede the certainty of historical loss, their collective memory would feel violated. Breaking from the gravitational pull of the 'David vs. Goliath' trope toward a horizon of dialogue that prioritises interdependence rather than adversarial narrative demands that the sedimented wounds be reinterpreted within a framework that privileges empathy and recognition over zero-sum vindication. Only an unflinching yet compassionate examination of how past narrative mutes rather than metabolises lived experience can open the trajectory toward reconciliation that neither heroic suffering nor victimised steadfastness can resolve alone.

Conclusion: Transcending Reductionist Analogies

The enquiry into the 'David versus Goliath' analogy has demonstrated the remarkable resilience of this historical motif in shaping the cognitive frames of Israeli and Palestinian populations alike. Our critique reveals that the metaphor operates on several registers: it reinterprets the past, stylises the present, and solidifies the symbolic repositories through which national collectives narrate their identities.

Decoupling the metaphor from political rhetoric thus permits the articulation of the Israeli-Palestinian conflict in terms that do justice to its inherent stratification and permutation. When scholars and practitioners place the canon of simplistic oppositions under interrogation, they invite an examination of how asymmetries of power, identity, and narrative coalesce in contingent, rather than predetermined, ways. This orientation fosters a departure from the rigid, moralised cylinder of victim and perpetrator, allowing a refracted view in which agency and suffering are unequally yet reciprocally distributed.

Transcending reductionist imagery requires rigorous attention to the layered contingencies that history entails. Recognition of divergent, overlapping, and sometimes commensurable memories is not an optional addendum but the methodological point of departure. Such recognition may, in a future yet undetermined, create the epistemic and emotional space in which dialogue, recognition, and, potentially, durable peace may germinate.

Moreover, rejecting the reductive David versus Goliath lens is indispensable for advancing a just and sustainable peace. By moving beyond such a polarised frame, we permit the emergence of narratives that honour the humanity, suffering, and endurance of all who bear the conflict's scars. This, in turn, cultivates the empathy, conversation, and promise of authentic reconciliation that the present moment demands.

We must acknowledge that, although the David versus Goliath imagery has energised both sides and briefly animated their narratives, its distortion of reality has crystallised hardened positions and obstructed genuine rapprochement. A commitment to a richly contextualised historical understanding, in contrast, opens the present to a time in which cooperative discourse, compassion, and a collectively envisioned future of coexistence can replace antagonistic posturing.

The analysis pursued here makes clear that moving beyond such simplistic metaphors is not merely advisable, but imperative for surmounting historical resentments and for the deliberative construction of a future anchored in mutual respect, and in the reciprocal recognition of each other's memories. Only by interrogating historical simplifications and daring to dwell in the past's complexities can we responsibly chart a route to lasting peace and reconciliation within the region.

References For Further Reading

Core Theoretical & Critical Frameworks

Said, Edward W. The Question of Palestine. Vintage, 1992.
Gladwell, Malcolm. David and Goliath: Underdogs, Misfits, and the Art of Battling Giants. Little, Brown, 2013.
Gregory, Derek. The Colonial Present: Afghanistan, Palestine, Iraq. Wiley-Blackwell, 2004.

Mamdani, Mahmood. Neither Settler nor Native: The Making and Unmaking of Permanent Minorities. Harvard UP, 2020.
Why relevant: Traces how colonial conflicts are narrated as "ancient hatreds"; critiques the moral binaries that sustain the David/Goliath trope. Connects to the text's call for "graduated perception of power."
Historical Genealogy & Power Asymmetry

5. Khalidi, Rashid. The Hundred Years' War on Palestine: A History of Settler Colonialism and Resistance, 1917–2017. Metropolitan Books, 2020.
6. Shlaim, Avi. The Iron Wall: Israel and the Arab World. W.W. Norton, 2014 (revised ed.).
7. Pappe, Ilan. The Idea of Israel: A History of Power and Knowledge. Verso, 2014.

8. Farsakh, Leila. Palestinian Labour Migration to Israel: Labour, Land and Occupation. Routledge, 2005.

Media, Myth-Making & Representation

9. Philo, Greg, et al. The Israel-Palestine Conflict: Mapping News Media Bias. Pluto Press, 2013.
10. Matar, Dina. What It Means to Be Palestinian: Stories of Palestinian Peoplehood. I.B. Tauris, 2010.
11. Khalidi, Rashid. Brokers of Power: The U.S. Role in Palestine and the Arab-Israeli Conflict. Haymarket Books, 2023.

Identity, Memory & Dissenting Voices

12. Bar-Tal, Daniel, and Izhak Schnell. The Impacts of Lasting Occupation: Lessons from Israeli Society. Oxford UP, 2013.
13. Swedenburg, Ted. Memories of Revolt: The 1936–1939 Rebellion and the Palestinian National Past. Univ. of Arkansas Press, 2003.
14. Lentin, Ronit. Traces of Racial Exception: Racializing Israeli Settler Colonialism. Bloomsbury, 2023.
15. Abu-Lughod, Lila. Do Muslim Women Need Saving? Harvard UP, 2013.

Alternative Paradigms for Resolution
16. Abu-Nimer, Mohammed. Nonviolence and Peace Building in Islam: Theory and Practice. Univ. Press of Florida, 2003.

17. Peteet, Julie. Lamentation and Land: Palestinian Mourning and the Israeli Occupation. Stanford UP, 2023.

18. Gunning, Jeroen, and Ilan Pappé. Trials of the Resistance: The Future of the Israeli-Palestinian Conflict. Pluto Press, 2021.

7

The Palestinian Exodus
Causes and Controversies

Setting the Historical Context

Understanding the 1948 Palestinian exodus—commonly referred to as the Nakba—requires immersion in a historical continuum whose fracture lines were already deep before the decisive rupture. This rupture severed communal ties and crystallised divergent nationalist historiographies that continue to shape the political lexicon of the Middle East. The decades preceding the exodus were themselves a period of reconfigured power, in which the Ottoman imperial apparatus succumbed to European colonial reordering and the British Mandate established a fragile equilibrium that was progressively undermined by mutually exclusive nationalist projects. Concurrently, Jewish immigration, bolstered by the Balfour Declaration and international sanction, reinforced the demographic and territorial ambitions articulated in political Zionist discourse. The territorial compromise envisaged by the United Nations in 1947—entailing partition of the Mandate into a Jewish and an Arab state—was met with Arab diplomatic and military rejection. The internment of this partition initiated renewed civil violence, and the post-announcement period witnessed a systematic escalation of military operations. The resultant hostilities, pitting Jewish paramilitary formations against Arab volunteer forces and local militia, invalidated the protective framework that had previously confined communal skirmishes, precipitating the organised and, in some instances, coercive evacuation of Palestinian civilian populations whose collective memory would thereafter crystallise as the defining event of 20th-century dispossession.

The trajectory that culminated in the mass expulsion of Palestinians was informed by a confluence of historical injustices, nationalist aspirations, and competing ideological commitments that situated the Nakba decisively within the larger Arab-Israeli confrontation. The operative effects of these layered antecedents materialised in a turbulent confluence of armed conflict, pervasive anxiety, and dislocation that shattered the intricate social and communal networks of Palestinian life. Within that volatility, the experience of those who were rendered homeless attained disproportionate salience, coming to emblemise the persistent, transgenerational resonances of the Nakba and to govern the collective psyche of those who followed. In consequence, a rigorous study of the Palestinian diaspora must begin by embedding the rupture in its comprehensive historical framework, so that the confluence of causative variables that produced this watershed in modern Middle Eastern history may be fully apprehended.

Narratives of Displacement: A Dual Perspective

The flight of Palestinian refugees in 1948 remains a flashpoint of historiographical contention, eliciting sharply disparate interpretations that crystallise the enduring schism in the Arab-Israeli conflict. This chapter scrutinises the constellation of events surrounding the displacement, foregrounding a bifocal analytic lens that simultaneously respects the antithetical frameworks in which each side recounts the trauma. Within Zionist historiography, the flight typically emerges framed as an operational necessity, circumstantially justified by wartime conditions and the overriding commitment to the consolidation of a sovereign Jewish polity. Advocates of this interpretation underscore the individual and collective decisions to evacuate, reject the premise of a coordinated expulsion, and parse the phenomena of flight as an artifact of troop movements, psychological bombardment, and regional fragility.

Palestinian chronicles, in sharp rebuttal, portray the same movements as a calculated campaign of ethnic displacement, systematically directed by paramilitary and governmental organs alike. Descriptions of forcible evacuations, summary executions, and threats of reputational annihilation recur in these testimonies, each inscribed into the collective memory of villages and neighbourhoods shredded by the offensive. The confrontation of these mutually exclusive readings does more than signal clashing legacies of grief; it exposes an intractable dilemma of the historian, for every analytic gesture finds itself recomposed by the competing moral imperatives that animate memory, identity, and the struggle for narrative hegemony in the modern Middle East.

Through a comparative reading of these opposing testimonies, this section strives to reveal the layered complexity of the Palestinian exodus and the plural character of lived experience in war and exile. The mutual reinforcement of survivor accounts, military orders, and political calculations generates a palimpsest of interpretations, compelling scholars to engage with the conflicting and frequently adversarial stories that have crystallised around this episode. The argument thus moves beyond historiography to the politics of memory, encouraging scrutiny of how these contesting accounts are produced, legitimised, and rewritten. The broader implication is a critical reappraisal of how divergent memorial frames shape present political dialogue and how they enable, or in some cases foreclose, the possibility of genuine reconciliation in a context still marked by asymmetrical power and persistent violence.

Zionist Strategy or Circumstantial Tragedy?

The nature of the Palestinian exodus of 1948 elicits sharply contrasting interpretations regarding whether the outcome stemmed from premeditated Zionist design or from the fortuitous and violent oscillations of wartime dynamics. Advocates of the former position cite a multidimensional corpus of correspondence, military plans—most critically Plan Dalet—and inaugural declarations by Zionist spokesmen that, they assert, lend a semblance of systematic intent underlying the expropriation of Arab inhabitants in strategic corridors. They further contend that the resultant demographic pattern reflected the ultimate goal of establishing a stable Jewish hegemonic majority. Conversely, proponents of the latter thesis underscore the incoherence of military and civil order, the tumult of competing armies, and the atmosphere of apprehension, suggesting that the movement stemmed from momentary decisions and extemporised evacuations rather than a single strategic architect. They regard the liquidity of the moment—fear of massacre, impending military advances, and the disintegration of social fabric—as formative causal factors conditioning collective flight. Such adversarial frameworks not only reflect the difficulty of establishing a single explanatory paradigm in a conjuncture marked by convergent and overlapping logics, they also serve modern agitations, since the legitimacy of competing interpretations influences the legitimacy ascribed to politically charged claims today.

The pursuit of profound comprehension necessitates a discriminating method, one that accounts for the varied determinants at work while remaining cognisant of the ways in which past occurrences intersect. An investigation of the Palestinian Exodus, fraught with dispute, obliges the scholar to subject both original documents and interpretive literature to rigorous scrutiny, while also remaining open to the divergent interpretations that have crystallised throughout successive eras. Such an engagement with the dense tiers of testimony and exegesis permits the extraction of a more integrated account of the forces that propelled the exiled population, illuminating a chapter of the twentieth century whose aftereffects continue to shape collective memory and geopolitical realities.

Arab Testimonies and Lived Realities

Following the cataclysm of 1948, the voices of displaced Palestinians have provided, and continue to provide, the primary vector of knowledge concerning the mass uprooting of the Arab population from the territory that became Israel. These oral histories, gathered by scholars, activists, and memory-project teams, deliver the affective texture of exile: the smell of smoke in the streets, the sound of the last door being slammed, the colour of the almond trees that were left behind. By privileging the subjective experience over administrative categories and military reports, the testimonies invite historians to confront the event in its material and ethical immediacy rather than through the clean abstractions of external analysis. The narratives refuse to be assimilated into the opposed ideological master-versions of the event; instead, they multiply the voices, the motives, and the contradictions that any comprehensive account must confront. Thus, they perform the necessary operation of decentering the state-sponsored recollections that have dominated the historiography since 1948.

The accounts recorded in refugee camps, exile circles, and diaspora gatherings reveal the contours of communal memory and the persistence of lived history. Respondents evoke the textures of their former villages: the particular knot in the olive tree, the courtyard that sheltered three weddings, the neighbourly rivalries that punctuated daily life. Such details carry, for the narrators, the force of testament; they

BREAKING THE WALL OF SILENCE 177

are not mere ornamentation but factual anchors of identity that are persistently negated by the terminology of normalization. The accounts also bear witness to the dialectical relationship between rupture and carry-on, between the currents of physical expulsion and the stubborn efforts to retain the memory of the original geography. Violence, though omnipresent, does not exhaust the frame; the accounts equally emphasize the acts of mutual care that characterised the shared experience of diaspora: the communal prosthetic memory built in small rooms, the coordinated efforts to safeguard the chain of names across borders, the transmission of dialect and dress from grandmothers to granddaughters. In narrating both uprooting and continuance, the testimonies provide the historian with the paradox of history as both wound and narrative architecture.

Arab testimonies further enrich our understanding of the socio-economic and cultural consequences of forced migration. They expose the profound obstacles Palestinian refugees confronted while attempting to reconstruct their lives in alien environments, frequently facing poverty, systemic discrimination, and socio-political marginalisation. The accounts reveal a communal will to survive and adapt, as displaced families mobilised scarce resources, created informal support networks, and insisted on the continuance of cultural practices that marked their communal and familial identity even in diaspora.

Beyond individual recollection, these testimonies constitute a communal archive of memory and identity for the Palestinian people. They capture the sustained sense of dispossession and the inextinguishable desire for return that has permeated Palestinian memory across generations. The narratives evoke an indelible attachment to the homeland and articulate an unyielding demand for justice and restoration. In this way, the testimonies surpass the role of objective historical record; they articulate a continuous chronicle of endurance, of clandestine resistance, and of an unbroken pledge to reclaim dignity and assert the right to self-determination.

Arab testimonies further contest existing historiographical frameworks by inserting rival narratives that resist the consolidation of the past into monolithic accounts. By foregrounding the recollections of those intimately shaped by the 1948 upheaval, such testimonies obligate historians to reconsider prevailing paradigms and to acknowledge the contradictory and contingent dimensions of the Palestinian exodus. They insist on the scholarly recognition of a plural past, one whose interpretation must incorporate the variegated, lived realities that characterise violent dislocation and prolonged contestation.

Ultimately, Arab testimonies provide an indispensable instrument for apprehending the quotidian effects of the Palestinian exodus. They document the endurance, anguish, and future-oriented projects of a society engulfed by forces exceeding their agency. In so doing, the accounts not only broaden the analytic horizon on the events of 1948, but also illustrate the sustained efficacy of oral documentation in safeguarding the memories of the politically subdued and structurally disempowered.

Testimonies from people who fled the Palestinian exodus weave together distinct personal encounters, illuminating the emotional undercurrents that undergird this multifaceted and politically loaded historical rupture. Those who bore the rupture recount the dread, disorientation, and excruciating choices that mingled the final moments inside abandoned homes. Kinship bonds shattered, neighbourhood geographies redrawn, and daily routines irreparably interrupted—these visceral traces persist in the survivors' speech. Some recollections convey desperate odysseys punctuated by rounds of gunfire and rumour, others describe the final hour spent seizing a single garment while the rest of a lifetime's artefacts slipped into the past. The feelings articulated in these fragments reveal the indelible scars that displacement inflicts on both the self and the communal memory.

Khadija's testimony powerfully conveys the panic and fear that enveloped whole villages as families were forced to abandon their homes and their pasts. Her recollections spotlight the cruel moment when the weight of tradition is replaced by the weight of a single suitcase, illustrating how the calendar of village life is suddenly and violently erased. Ibrahim, similarly, speaks of the fields and orchards that were woven into the very fabric of his identity, describing the unyielding ache of watching the land that his ancestors had farmed reduced to a shaking memory. Together, their accounts strip away the abstractions of policy and produce a palpably human record of uprooting, reminding the listener that each removed person carries a world that will never be reconstituted.

Documenting the Departures: Eyewitness Accounts

These eyewitness testimonies allow us to grasp the Palestinian exodus as a complex process rather than a singular historical event, forcing us to reckon with the irremediable human costs that simplify reductionist lenses omit.

Each voice penetrates the diffusion of statistics, re-animating loss as lived reality. Consequently, the analyst is beckoned to recognise that beyond structural forces—military strategies, diplomatic manoeuvres, territorial maps—personal fates were supplanting childhood, parentage, and ancestral connection. Such disclosures interrogate the historian's moral charter, insisting that scholarly enquiry must be vigilant to the resonances of suffering that linger long after camps are emptied and borders are redrawn. The narratives further compel us to examine the memorial obligations of settler and neighbour alike, arguing that the legitimacy of contemporary claims, whether on land or narrative, must engage the memory of the living and the dead. To turn away from these accounts is, therefore, an abdication not of memory alone, but of the ethical duty to situate our discourses within the granular, irreducible scale of the human subject.

Historians attempting to explain the causes of the Palestinian Exodus have—predictably—made the question a proving ground for competing methodological and ideological commitments. The present chapter highlights the assorted scholarly prisms through which the dislocation has been studied, revealing cavities in which opposing constructed pasts collide. Interpretative divergence has widened not only over the transaction of peoples in 1947–1948, but over the political preoccupations of the scholars themselves. The camp asserting an intentional expulsion of the Palestinian population by Zionist agencies selects evidence of military directives, operational records, and systemic violence, contending that their cumulative effect was to engineer a Jewish demographic majority over a territory in whose contours a Zionist state would be announced. Opponents of that reading reject the emphasis on a cohesive, top-down

BREAKING THE WALL OF SILENCE

taboo, reconstituting the same evidence in a narrative that foregrounds civil war, military procession, and the ordinary calculations of displaced communities—fear of massacre, rumour of advancing troops, and the wish to pre-empt oppression—inducing voluntary, albeit tragic, departures. Scholarly confrontation therefore escalates into calibrating the war's contingency against the evidence of premeditated policy. Careful auditors of primary records, historians in both camps catalogue, compare, and interrogate the provenance, audience, and inherent bias of their sources. The intensity of this archival stand-off has prompted reinterpretations of previously neglected official documents in which, they argue, marginalised voices and dissenting testimony might yet be fitted into or against the familiar narrative.

Moreover, the study of oral testimonies remains indispensable, as these accounts validate the memories of those who endured the upheaval. Researchers must, however, contend with competing national articulations of the exodus, whereby Israeli and Palestinian historians frequently converge on the same occurrence yet arrive at contradictory conclusions, revealing how the past is often refracted through various political prisms. This continuing scholarly contest invites a close inspection of the disciplinary techniques historians wield, prompting a more nuanced recognition of the uncertainties that condition the Palestinian exodus. Consequently, a reflective appraisal of historiographical strategies broadens critical conversation and illuminates the long-term repercussions of the exodus on collective memory and political identity.

Refugee hood and Its Aftermath: Human Dimensions

The reverberations of the Palestinian exodus, or al-Nakba, illuminate the human enduring dimensions of forced displacement. The flight of several hundred thousand Palestinians in 1948 generated an immediate and sweeping humanitarian calamity, the repercussions of which continue to contour the lives of refugees and their descendants in the present. In the moment of flight, individuals and families confronted not only the sudden absence of home, but the immediate burdens of bereavement, instability, and the fight to secure basic subsistence. This analysis attends to the emotional and psychological currencies of refugee hood, moving beyond quantitative enumeration to the human scale of the disaster. It surveys the collapse of social infrastructures, the dismantling of productive livelihoods, and the fracturing of familial and communal networks. Counter to the gravity of loss, the writing also attends to imaginative and resourceful modes of endurance: refugees in tents, former public squares, and fragmented diaspora nodes have, under sustained adversity, navigated economic, educational, and cultural imperatives. Their cultural memory, articulated through language, ritual, and education, emerges as a resilient counter-narrative to subsistence crisis. The piece further interrogates the dimensions of generational trauma and the search for identity among stateless descendants: memory, trauma, and cultural remembrance transmit across the generational divide, shaping psychological landscapes and social hierarchies. The lingering psychological wounds and sustained socio-economic impoverishment thus underscore the long-tail effects of refugee hood, extending its dimensions beyond immediate memory to the structuration of future lives.

This section further analyses the functions performed by humanitarian assistance and transnational bodies in immediately responding to the needs of the Palestinian refugee cohort, while probing the structural limitations and delayed consequences of such actions. It equally investigates the persistent endeavours of the refugee cadres to secure institutional acknowledgement of their entitlements and to achieve reparative justice, thereby highlighting the durable tenacity and collective agency that animate these societies. By centring the lived realities of refugee hood, the discussion conveys a refined comprehension of how the traumatic arch of al-Nakba continues to shape the conditions and aspirations of Palestinian refugees.

International Reactions and British Policy

The Palestinian exodus of 1948 prompted diverse international reactions that scrutinised British policy across the region. The flight and expulsion of hundreds of thousands of Palestinians placed sudden humanitarian and political pressures upon the global order. The emergent role of the United Nations, alongside major world capitals, defined immediate responses and layered the unfolding tragedy within a contested diplomatic history. Following the Second World War, the shifting global order and intensifying regional tensions posed daunting complications for London. British officials confronted the competing claims of neighbouring Arab states, the Jewish settlement enterprise, and the Palestinian population itself, within a policy matrix that grew ever more brittle. Amidst this triangulation, the British administration faced relentless examination, provoking critical debate regarding its moral and legal duties. An evaluation of the contemporary international climate alongside the responses articulated in London fosters a deeper apprehension of the longer-term ramifications that this singular displacement event would imprint upon the region and upon subsequent global policy.

Revisiting Established Myths: Academic Insights

The critical reassessment of entrenched narratives in historical memory necessitates grounding analyses in original documents and confronting dominant explanatory frameworks with scholarly rigour. Regarding the Palestinian Exodus of 1948, long-held certainties giving shape both to scholarly argument and to broader societal beliefs have now been subjected to sustained re-examination, yielding findings that complicate and qualify simpler readings. Researchers have catalogued an expanding archive of testimonies, military orders, and statistical records that document, in granular detail, the processes of flight and forcible removal, thereby questioning the consensus that previously homogenised the phenomenon of dispersion.

Central to the debate is the myth that Palestinian flight could be described, in moral and causal terms, as either voluntary retreat or the product of exhortation by the Arab leadership.

Multi-layered approaches to the evidence now underscore that both alleged explanations obscure the simultaneity of impulses and pressures faced by different localities. Unanticipated violence, aerial bombardments, evolving orders regarding civilian evacuation, and the psychological weight of rumours combined unevenly, with the cumulative effect manifesting as compulsory migration in many villages and urban quarters. Quantitative analysis of refugee populations, juxtaposed with contemporaneous humanitarian records, reaffirms that the scale of expulsion-like phenomena surpassed voluntary migration. Historians, therefore, situate the event in a continuum of coercive practices rather than in a binary of choice and influence, thereby foregrounding the asymmetries of power that structured individual outcomes.

Scholarly scholarship has significantly reconfigured the historiographical landscape surrounding the Palestinian Exodus, interrogating census datasets, colonial archives, and demographic records to produce revised figures that exceed earlier assumptions regarding the scale of flight. By foregrounding island-wide population loss and its uneven demographic consequences, researchers challenge persistent underestimation of the subsequent societal rupture and highlight the methodological biases that have obscured the Exodus's longer-term implications. This rigorous reappraisal corrects archival lacunae and reaffirms the imperative of confronting the full amplitude of the human suffering that the uprooting entailed.

In parallel to revising quantitative benchmarks, a growing body of work has disaggregated the temporal and spatial dimensions of the refugee experience, tracing the protracted and fractured nature of flight, settlement, and re-settlement. This emphasis on cumulative legacies foregrounds recurrent crises of statelessness, chronic disenfranchisement, and the protracted negotiation over restitution claims. By mapping these entangled dimensions, scholars document how communal, familial, and individual trajectories of survival continue to produce humanitarian exigencies that span several generations, thereby foregrounding the enduringness of the refugee condition.

Against this cumulative critique, the historiography renders obsolete earlier simplifications that framed the Exodus as a discrete episode. Instead, it urges a historiographical pivot toward an interpretive framework that synthesises quantitative reformation with qualitative attention to lived experience. Such a framework does justice to the multifaceted, long-term entrenchment of the Exodus's consequences, yielding a more accurate and ethically responsive lens through which to interrogate its place within the wider trajectories of colonial dispossession and post-colonial state formation.

Transition to the Intellectual Battles Ahead

As we move from a reconsideration of entrenched myths to an anticipation of the intellectual confrontations that lie ahead, we arrive at a decisive moment within the historiography of the Palestinian exodus. The ongoing reappraisal of the salient events of the exodus itself has already initiated a climate of vigorous scholarly contestation. Such contests, however, extend far beyond the seminar room: their outcomes are capable of reconfiguring popular beliefs, informing statecraft, and, over the long term, aiding efforts directed towards an authentic and just reconciliation. Here, the intricate overlays of divergent viewpoints and divergent evidentiary cultures must be engaged in a plane of sustained, rigorous, and mutual examination.

The debates to come will stage a confrontation of historiographical paradigms, whose adherents each claim the authority to frame the past. Revisionists, in this context, confront dominant paradigms by mobilising recently accessible archival, audio, and oral testimony, while simultaneously recuperating previously silenced agencies within the exodus. Such scholars seek, in principle, a historiography that recognises the sedimented, plural faces of memory and a past permanently in the making. The successful articulation of their agenda requires both an unsettling of received certainties and a willingness to reckon with the residues of state and communal trauma that constitute the record.

Conversely, conservative historians adamantly protect conventional accounts, regarding challenges to these stories as destabilising to the shared national identity, social unity, and collective memory. The opposition between these factions primes a succession of intellectual confrontations that spill far beyond the university seminar.

These same confrontations subsequently migrate into the arena of public consciousness. Scholarly exchanges, once confined to peer-reviewed pages, trickle into everyday conversation and, more crucially, into the production of popular histories. It is amid shifting public opinion and packaging by the media that the broader consequences of reinterpretation emerge. Contentious assessments of the origins and consequences of the Palestinian exodus migrate from digital footnotes to classroom syllabi, parliamentary debates, and civic discourse, demonstrating the porous boundary between scholarly and societal life.

The shift towards these upcoming intellectual skirmishes thus marks a decisive juncture in the unremitting quest for historical veracity. It obliges all participants to uphold disciplined criticism, to practise civil exchange, and to welcome antithetical positions. Such a shift is more than rhetorical; it is an audacious foray into previously unexplored archival and interpretative space, where venerable certainties are subjected to fresh scrutiny and established orthodoxies must justify themselves to a new generation of analysts.

This moment calls for intellectual courage, integrity, and humility—an admission that the pursuit of truth is both difficult and essential. The struggles that lie ahead may yet reveal the clearer, more shared history that could guide us all.

***

References For Further Reading on the 1948 Palestinian Exodus (al-Nakba)

Core Monographs

1. **Morris, Benny** – _1948: A History of the First Arab-Israeli War_ (Yale UP, 2008); _The Birth of the Palestinian Refugee Problem Revisited_ (Cambridge UP, 2003).

Still the most comprehensive archival reconstruction of military operations that produced mass displacement. Use the 2003 "Revisited" edition for revised casualty and expulsion figures.

2. **Khalidi, Walid (ed.)** – _All That Remains: The Palestinian Villages Occupied and Depopulated by Israel in 1948_ (Institute for Palestine Studies, 1992).

Encyclopedic gazetteer with maps, photographs, and oral snippets for every destroyed locality; indispensable for micro-level spatial analysis.

3. **Pappé, Ilan** – _The Ethnic Cleansing of Palestine_ (Oneworld, 2006).

Counter-narrative foregrounding Plan Dalet and early Zionist leadership minutes; engages in direct debate with Morris.

4. **Masalha, Nur** – _The Palestine Nakba: Decolonising History, Narrating the Subaltern, Reclaiming Memory_ (Zed, 2012); _Palestine: A Four Thousand Year History_ (Zed, 2018).

Theoretically frames the Nakba within settler-colonial studies and longue-durée Palestinian history.

5. **Khalidi, Rashid** - _The Hundred Years' War on Palestine: Settler-Colonialism and Resistance, 1917-2017_ (Metropolitan, 2020).
Situates 1948 inside a century of imperial policy and Palestinian political agency.

Regional & Local Studies
6. **Nazzal, Nafez** - _The Palestinian Exodus from Galilee, 1948_ (Institute for Palestine Studies, 1978).
Early oral-history collection documenting flight patterns from the northern front.

7. **Manna, Adel** - _Nakba and Survival: The Story of Palestinians Who Remained in Haifa and the Galilee, 1948-1956_ (UC Press, 2022).
Focuses on those who avoided expulsion yet faced martial law and property expropriation.

8. **Kadman, Noga** - _Erased from Space and Consciousness: Israel and the Depopulated Palestinian Villages of 1948_ (Indiana UP, 2015).
Examines how place-names, maps, and Israeli textbooks erased former Arab localities.

Memory, Testimony, and Narrative Politics
9. **Abu-Lughod, Lila & Sa'di, Ahmad H. (eds.)** - _Nakba: Palestine, 1948, and the Claims of Memory_ (Columbia UP, 2007).
Interdisciplinary essays on trauma, commemoration, and

competing historiographies.

10. **Lentin, Ronit** – _Co-memory and Melancholia: Israelis Memorialising the Palestinian Nakba_ (Manchester UP, 2010).
Analyses how Israeli NGOs and artists contest official amnesia.

11. **Sayigh, Rosemary** – _Palestinians: From Peasants to Revolutionaries_ (Zed, 2023).
Life histories collected in refugee camps that foreground gendered and generational memory.

12. **Davis, Rochelle** – _Palestinian Village Histories: Geographies of the Displaced_ (Stanford UP, 2011).
Tracks how refugees narrate lost villages through family manuscripts, embroidery, and social media.

Document Collections & Primary Sources

13. **Karmi, Ghada & Cotran, Eugene (eds.)** – _The Palestinian Exodus, 1948-1998_ (Ithaca, 1999).
Conference volume pairing UN, British, and Haganah cables with refugee testimonies.

14. **Flapan, Simha** – "The Palestinian Exodus of 1948," _Journal of Palestine Studies_ 16:4 (1987), 3-26.
Early synthesis declassified Israeli and Western diplomatic archives.

15. **Government of Palestine** – _A Survey of Palestine, 1945-46_ (reprinted by Institute for Palestine Studies).
Mandate-era socioeconomic data essential for pre-1948

demographic baselines.

Historiographical & Methodological Debates

16. **Partner, Nancy** – "The Linguistic Turn along Post-Postmodern Borders," _New Literary History_ 39:4 (2008), 823-845.

Dissects how language, narrative framing, and genre affect Israeli vs Palestinian historiography.

17. **Confino, Alon** – "The Nakba and the Zionist Dream of an Ethnonational State," _History Workshop Journal_ 95 (2023), 131-153.

Uses comparative genocide and memory studies to reassess "ethnic cleansing" debates.

18. **Weintraub, Roy & Gibson, Lindsay** – "The Nakba in Israeli History Education," _Theory & Research in Social Education_ 53 (2024), 90-121.

Classroom ethnography showing how curricular choices reproduce or contest dominant myths.

International & Legal Dimensions

19. **Rogan, Eugene** – _The Arabs: A History_ (Penguin, 2012).

Chapter on 1948 integrates British Foreign Office and Arab League minutes.

20. **Auron, Yair** – _The Holocaust, Rebirth, and the Nakba: Memory and Contemporary Israeli–Arab Relations_ (Lexington, 2017).

Comparative study of trauma politics and competing victimhood narratives.

Supplementary Digital & Archival Resources

- **Palestine Remembered** (https://www.palestineremembered.com): Interactive atlas of pre-1948 localities, refugee testimonies, and scanned Mandate maps.

- **UNISPAL** (https://unispal.un.org): Full searchable database of every UN document on Palestine, 1917-present.

- **Zochrot** (https://www.zochrot.org): Israeli NGO archives of "Nakba tours," filmed survivor interviews, and bilingual maps for field visits.

8
Fierce Backlash
Intellectual Battles and Public Debate

The Immediate Reaction: Academic Circles Respond

Following the early publications of the New Historians, both Israeli and international scholarship entered a phase of extraordinary transaction, marked at once by eager appraisal and animated critique. Domestic responses were laced with both caution and curiosity; empirically minded historians debated the evidentiary weight of newly archived material, while political historians worried aloud of precedents that might compel a reconsideration of the legitimacy of the state's formation. Allies and critics of the New Historians deployed the journals as arenas for methodological dissection: discussions of sampling, archival lacunae, and the politicisation of memory were rehearsed in symposia organised by institutions from the Hebrew University to the Ben-Gurion

Research Institute.

Global commentators, attentive to the intersection of historiography and public policy, recognised in the New Historians a methodological pivot that invited reinvention of the scholarly canon. Reviews in journals of comparative politics and memory studies pronounced the monographs occasion studies in the sociology of trauma as much as in the politics of historiography. Some observers welcomed the monographs as preliminary gestures toward trans-historical empathy; others argued, with concern, that the evidentiary realignment risked erasing earlier, politically sensitive, narratives of minority resistance. Across continents, members of the discipline affirmed a paradox: the historiographical audition that the New Historians inaugurated represented both an intellectual advance and a continuing gamble upon the openness of Israeli and Palestinian political-memorial discourse.

During this contest of interpretations, the media emerged as a crucial agent in configuring public attitudes toward the New Historians' enquiries. Coverage oscillated between passionate celebration and excoriating rejection, a testimony to the divisive character of the revised narratives. Eye-catching headlines competed for dominance over weighty methodological critiques, complicating the already charged public discussion. The capacity of journalistic framing to determine the stakes of the debate became starkly apparent, as the multi-layered studies of the New Historians were reduced to punchy quotations and digestible tropes, obscuring methodological subtleties and, occasionally, entrenching erroneous readings.

The subsequent scholarly reception, in turn, provided a revealing microcosm of the historiographical landscape. Reaction to the New Historians revealed a wide array of intellectual stances—some sympathetic, others scornful, and still others calibrated to invite re-examination of the evidentiary base and theoretical constructs. The reverberations of these exchanges were thus demonstrably both scholarly and public: for the preoccupations of historians were rapidly inscribed within broader civic debates, recalibrating how the past was remembered and narrated outside the lecture hall.

Public Perceptions and Media Representations

The circulation of the new historians' scholarly contributions provoked an immediate and heterogeneous public reaction. Different media sectors adopted divergent reporting strategies regarding the historiographical revisions, and in doing so, they sculpted competing public interpretations of the conflict. The circulation of these reconstituted narratives evoked significant intellectual and emotional reverberations in constituencies both inside and beyond Israel. While some groups welcomed the reconstruction of previously canonized narratives, others categorically repudiated the counter-accounts. Media outlets functioned as a crucial conduit for these opposed voices, thereby mirroring and magnifying the intricate tensions embedded within the Israeli-Palestinian conflict. Representations of the new historians and their enterprises diverged sharply, thereby reinforcing contending narratives and aggravating pre-existing societal polarities. The global press further accentuated the transnational exigency of historiographical enquiry in politically charged contexts. The affordances of social media platforms accelerated the circulation and examination of these discussions, permitting public evaluations to evolve in near-simultaneity with the scholarly production itself. Digital fora, argumentative threads, and editorial interventions enabled participatory engagement with the historiographical contests, recalibrating public consciousness regarding the enduring conflict.

Moreover, representations of the conflict and its historiography in literature, film, and visual art constitute a decisive factor in the formation of public attitudes. These domains afforded alternative pathways for audiences to confront the historiographical revisions, thereby recalibrating not only popular comprehension but also the discursive and aesthetic enterprises within cultural fields. The resultant polyphonic and often contradictory representations underscored the necessity of a reflexive engagement with historical narratives and their enduring influence on the constitution of collective memory. Ultimately, the dissemination of the new historians' findings across diverse media has not only directed public opinion but has also rendered the intractable fractures and loyalties of Israeli society, and of the diasporic spectators who receive its images, legible to one another and to themselves.

Governmental Critiques and Political Tensions

Following the rise of the New Historians and their provocative retellings of the past, the Israeli state confronted a challenge of unusual intensity. These revisionist accounts, counterpoised against the official commemorative recounting, disturbed the symbolic order that the government regarded as essential to Israeli self-understanding. Anxiety coursed through the electoral and ministerial arenas as the debates overlapped with impending national votes. Criticism from state representatives occurred not merely to invalidate empirical claims, but to shore up the traditional historical framework that had long constituted the civic religion of the state. Such efforts intensified intra party and interparty discord, as ideological and doctrinal camps rallied to champion mutually exclusive reconstructions.

The strategy of the cabinet and its agencies was layered, mixing frontal denunciation with licit and tacit interventions designed to erode the New Historians' standing. Press releases, reports, and curriculum directives declared the revised theses to be speculative and partisan, whilst reaffirming the canon of a heroic, defensive birth of the state as the one veritable record. The authoritative apparatus, enjoying access to resources, amenities, and public forums, vied with scholars seeking autonomy on the premises of discipline. Thus, an asymmetrical contest unfolded, with both sides manoeuvring to cultivate public allegiance and external non-governmental sponsorship.

The dispute was never confined to the domestic public sphere. As Israeli diplomats confronted a sceptical global community, the New Historians' findings were periodically presented as evidence of a moderated, self-critical polity and summoned to refute unilateral accusations of impenitent expansionism. The interplay of historiography and diplomacy, framed by the imperatives of legitimacy, thereby acquired an instructive salience both in the study of statecraft and in the sociology of knowledge.

Confronted by the global proliferation of disputed historiographical arguments, the Israeli administration endeavoured to limit the prospective diplomatic damage without alienating the increasingly vocal domestic proponents of rival interpretations. The need to sustain vital strategic partnerships while simultaneously navigating the fractious contest over the nation's past placed extraordinary pressure on policymakers.

Within this precarious milieu, the enduring clash over historical representation was elevated to the level of statecraft, shaping elite discourse and permeating grassroots communities alike. Each contesting faction politicised its reading of the past, turning historiographical debate into a surrogate for contemporary partisan rivalry. Paradoxically, the very polarisation generated by the struggle for memory revealed a deeper, collective confrontation with the unfinished legacy of Israel's formation and its enduring consequences for national and regional futures.

The Role of International Scholars and Institutions

The influence of the New Historians has diffused well beyond the confines of Israel and Palestine, sending tremors through global universities and think tanks that study the region. Their radical rereading of the historiography of the Israeli-Palestinian conflict has triggered a sequence of comparative projects and seminar series at major academic centres from Berkeley to Berlin. The polemical evidence and the revised chronology advanced by these scholars continually invite reflection, prompting senior scholars abroad to scrutinise the epistemological and ethical consequences of the New Historians' methodological innovations.

Leading universities, independent research institutes, and policy-oriented centres have, therefore, become crucibles for sustained transcontinental debate. Coordinated by faculty and visiting fellows, a sequence of resident workshops, colloquia, and international symposia has encouraged specialists from archival science, postcolonial studies, and international law to interrogate these new documents and to consider their ramifications for peace processes and memory politics. Consequently, the international scholarly community has assumed a proactive role in mapping the historiographical terrain, thereby elevating the study of the conflict's memory to a central concern of contemporary social analysis.

Scholars from widely dispersed regions and traditions are increasingly engaging with the historiographical fabric woven by the New Historians, integrating empirical expertise with indigenous archival and field craft. Such cross-border scholarly exchange, framed by both professional societies and exploratory field seminars, generates a dynamic corpus that refuses to rest within disciplinary or geographic enclaves. The dialogue between locally grounded research and overarching comparative frameworks generates refinements that challenge and reconfigure dominant historical schemata, effecting a fundamental reorientation within the broader historiography of the Levant.

The reach of this scholarly synthesis, however, is not contained within the seminar room or the archive. Research findings have begun to filter into diplomatic training curricula, public history projects, and policy advisory discussions, confronting previously unexamined historiographical presuppositions that underpin conflict and negotiation alike. The effect is a gradual yet discernible reframing of symbolic reference points, both within contested communities and among external stakeholders. Such dispersion of scholarly enquiry demonstrates the continuing efficacy of rigorous historical research as a catalytic ingredient in sustained dialogue and conflict resolution, thereby nurturing the prospect of a more critically self-aware and participative collective memory.

Intellectual Rifts within Israeli Society

Intellectual rifts have emerged throughout Israeli society as confrontations with divergent historical narratives sharpen communal fault-lines. The animating contest pits long-cherished chronicles of national emergence against the unsettling interrogations launched by the so-called New Historians. An introverted examination of archives, oral testimonies, and previously dormant documents has unsettled received explanations of the 1948 war, the aftermath of the 1967 occupation, and the occasional hush of the national memory. As the contest has migrated beyond seminar rooms and archives, it has come to script the grammar of popular debate, legislative proposal, and everyday conversation, exposing the frayed seams of the Israeli collective memory.

The building of respective camps marks this entangled public and scholarly field. One camp cherishes the heroic saga of sacrifice and improbable triumph, arraying itself around the founders' rhetorical legacy and the early disciplinary canon; the other, animated by disciplinary canons forged across the 1980s and 1990s, urges a candid reckoning with violence, dispossession, and silenced voices. Evidence-laden repartee inevitably hardens into rhetorical trench warfare, each side augmenting its citadel with social, scholarly, and popular fortifications. Universities, museums, veterans' groups, and even kibbutzim have become arenas for diagnostic confrontation. As a result, trust is eroded, alliances recalibrated, and public trust in a shared past fractures into multiply contested, emotionally entangled recollections.

Scholarly fractures have thus mirrored larger societal fissures, transferring heightened tensions from the public sphere into the intellectual domain, where they compact old cultural fault lines into fresh academic debate. The reverberations exceed university gates, shaping, in turn, party loyalties, cultural identifications, and everyday affiliations. Competing historiographies now function as ideological biomarkers, crystallising the wider fracture over national identity and attesting to the difficulty of constructing unity from the sediment of historical dissensus.

Engagement with these fractures forces subjects to re-visit

the terrain of their historical consciousness and the partisan allegiances that shape it. When multiple historiographies inhabit the same text, the necessity of interrogating once-unquestioned convictions arises, with the result that settled certainties dissolve into productive doubt. The result, for many, is a persistent and disquieting inner dialogue, in which the lassitude of received knowledge is replaced by the labour of memory reconstruction.

The fractures thus stage a larger pedagogical challenge: to engineer a shared narrative that does not erase, but rather manages the coexistence, of incommensurate truths. The scholarly response must now pivot from disaggregation to dialogue, and from polemic to deliberation, if a common discursive space is to be inhabited by communities that have long rehearsed the same past in mutually exclusive registers. Only through sustained and reciprocal exchange can the fractures be reframed as sites of collective healing rather than as cemented boundaries of permanent estrangement.

After the discoveries made by the New Historians, public debates in Israel have crystallised into decisive sites where competing memories reform the substance of national consciousness. Revised perspectives, once confined to scholarly margins, now confront previously uncontested memories, thereby revealing and intensifying the fissures running through the collective identity. Such debates extend well beyond university lecture halls, embedding themselves in everyday discussions, electoral preferences, and variations in national sentiment.

Amid shifting topographies of mass communication, the narration of critical moments—chief among them the events of 1948 and the exodus of Palestinians—has become almost scandalous. Each recitation unsettles inherited convictions and summons strong, often visceral, reactions. Twitter, Facebook, and televised cabarets now serve as the public square, where counter-narratives compete not merely for rhetorical victory but for the power to constitute a nationally accepted account. In this critical context, the debates do not merely mirror Israel's ideological fractures; they are formative, exerting a decisive influence on the trajectories of memory and policy that the nation will pursue.

Additionally, the ramifications of these public controversies radiate beyond the nation's borders, recalibrating international representations and diplomatic calculus. The contest over historical narratives is inseparable from Israel's global standing, swaying diplomatic loyalty and shaping multilateral discourse. When interpretations of the past shift, so does the country's leverage on the world stage. Debates in the public arena thus become the primary field on which claims to both domestic and international legitimacy are contested and measured.

More fundamentally, public controversies operate as crucibles in which the collective memory of the polity is remade. They determine which episodes ascend into the mnemonic canon and which recede. As competing accounts are affirmed, recalibrated, or repudiated, the contours of national identity are re-forged and the moral imperatives that govern social conduct are re-specified.

Such debates, therefore, surpass the realm of scholarly discourse and become decisive acts of memory and intention. They encapsulate the enduring effort to mediate incompatible testimonies, to mend long-standing fractures, and to chart a coherent forward direction. The ramifications of these exchanges have the capacity to alter the axiomatic self-conception of the polity, marking the debates as the decisive theatre for shaping Israel's ethical and political self-image.

Consequences for Public Policy and Educational Institutions

The influence of emerging historical narratives on both public policy and educational structures is profound and unavoidable. Once these reconstituted understandings of past events become widely adopted, they directly confront policies and curricula that have for decades rested on accepted versions of history. The resulting processes of revision and re-evaluation compel legislators and educators to confront difficult and often contested topics with renewed caution and intellectual rigour.

At the policy level, the rise of competing interpretations has triggered sustained public debate and institutional debate. Decision-makers must now confront the challenge of harmonising these varied accounts while crafting policies faithful to the fuller, often more ambiguous records that new scholarship presents. Such deliberation has encouraged legislators to reconsider the framing of issues once presumed settled and has complicated the negotiation of treaties, reparations, and commemorative measures. The augmented awareness of history's intricacies is producing measurable recalibrations in both diplomatic posture and legislative practice, with consequences that extend to the formation of regional alliances, the sequencing of aid, and the management of transnational grievances.

Contemporary historiographical upheaval has likewise transformed educational systems in significant, if often underestimated, ways. For decades, curricular documents, instructional guides, and student textbooks have transmitted historiography that frequently reproduces dominant state-endorsed interpretations. The emergence and circulation of competing historiographical strands, however, now require pedagogical authorities to interrogate and to reformulate these established resources. The deliberate integration of divergent narratives not only provokes pedagogues to re-evaluate pedagogical continuity; it actively invites learners to confront plural perspectives, thereby sharpening their capacity to evaluate the causative and contingent elements that underlie complex historical trajectories.

The pedagogical embedding of these counter-narratives further engenders reflective and empathetic dispositions among students. Confronted with contradictory interpretations, learners acquire the analytical faculties necessary for discerning the relative weighting of evidence and for adjudicating the plausibility of competing claims. Such educational practice broadens both intellectual boundaries and civic expectations, creating classrooms that privilege enquiry over consensus and that model the open-minded disposition requisite for pluralistic societies.

Thus, the influence of revised historiographical frameworks upon educational legislation and practice exceeds the simple transmission of factual information. It reconfigures the argumentative terrain of public deliberation and gradually reconstitutes the very institutional and discursive environments in which historical knowledge circulates. In so doing, it cultivates a population of discerning and empathetic citizens capable of recognising and engaging constructively with the irresolvable complexities that history irrevocably presents.

Stories from the Ground: Personal Narratives Amidst Contention

Personal accounts emerging amid acute historical contention merit careful study, for they reveal dimensions of human experience often eclipsed in public discourse. In the Israeli-Palestinian conflict—one of the most polarising chronicles of our time—individuals living the events translate rumour, trauma, and aspiration into testimony. These voices transcend partisan acrimony, exposing the gaps and grey areas that categorical analyses frequently obscure. Human agency, frailty, and desire thus are foregrounded, allowing historians and observers to reckon with the conflict not merely as a series of policies and casualties but as a mosaic of living, contested narratives.

From within the contested territories and beyond, storytellers recount what they lived, witnessed, or inherited. Survivors of bombardments, residents of besieged enclaves, and refugees in exile compose a polyphonic testimony. Their accounts, often supplemented by worn photographs or generations of oral practice, carry the weight of acute emotional memory and civic engagement. Syllables tremble as they describe children lost, homes demolished, or protections withheld, yet the same voices resiliently evince a stubborn yearning for dialogue. In this duality—of devastation and perseverance—the human scale of the conflict quite literally comes into focus, reminding analysts and policy-makers that statements of law or strategy are heard, and felt, within the contours of everyday intimacy.

These individual accounts thus contribute decisively to the communal memory that shapes how societies collectively remember their pasts and how they pass those memories down through time. Infused with the cadence of oral tradition, they keep memories of historical injustice alive, reminding both individuals and communities that the consequences of those injustices remain palpable. At the same time, the narratives become vehicles of empathy, permitting encounters between divergent historical perspectives that might otherwise remain irreconcilable.

In occasions of repair and challenge alike, such testimonies directly counter stereotypes and reductive narratives. They forcefully disrupt the habit of interpreting the past through monocausal lenses by humanising the figure commonly deemed 'other' and by laying bare mutual dreams of dignity, safety, and belonging that cut across ethnic, religious, and national divides. The invitation to witness each other's fundamental human hopes thus prompts sustained critical enquiry into previously unexamined biases and nurtures a climate more conducive to dialogue and, eventually, to the fragile but necessary project of reconciliation.

We must duly recognise and respect these ground-level testimonies, aware of the courage and exposure required to disclose such intimate experiences. Their importance transcends the solitary voice; they disclose the common struggle for truth, justice, and healing that follows any grave historical rupture. In the course of grappling with the intricate landscape of historical comprehension, these lived accounts become essential beacons, constantly redirecting our attention to the abiding human spirit that survives amid competing discourses.

The Role of Arts and Literature in Reflecting Conflicts

Art and literature have historically served as vital vessels for articulating and reflecting the fractures within societies, including those that are inextricably woven into the tapestry of historical memory. In the Israeli-Palestinian conflict, the creative domains have proved especially resonant, furnishing a site where individuals confront the tumult of conflicting loyalties and traumas, and where collectives are urged to reckon with uncomfortable certainties. The artistic and literary sectors have thus performed a crucial function in re-subjectifying those whose lives are otherwise instrumentally consumed by the conflict, eclipsing political segmentation in the quest for empathy and mutual comprehension.

Poetry, the visual arts, music, and prose have each operated as an artistic errand through which the conflict's severing effects are registered in the corporeal and emotional matter of lived lives. Creators have charted personal affliction and collective wound in the same breath, producing textured testimonies that unsettle dominant discursive formations and summon reflective pause. In attending to intimate corporeal and psychic dimensions, such works furnish a counter-apparatus for apprehending the conflict's intricacies, compelling observers to reckon with the contingencies that political discourse routinely obscures.

Prose fiction, in particular, has cultivated a literary domain where authors assemble intricately woven lives that are conserved in the crux of the conflict. In doing so, they elucidate the multivalent texture of existence under siege, where quotidian aspirations and larger political logics fuse and collide, inviting readers to contemplate the precarious assemblage of hope and loss that any durable resolution must eventually confront.

Whether in novels, autobiographical accounts, or verse, literature possesses the power to inscribe the human cost of war in indelible phrases that outlive the lifeless figures of casualty lists or the arid language of treaties. Skilled narrators weave sentences that pull forward once-marginalised witnesses, granting readers the rare gift of attending to the private tremors that political calamity inflates to history's scale. In so doing, they refuse the consolation of abstraction, demanding that empathy contends with the singular beating heart.

In parallel, the visual arts insist, often with a silence louder than argument, that the body politic be represented in the body of the person. Brushes, chisels, and lenses translate barricades, exile, and exposed skin into pigments, clay, and light, surveying the territory where courage and fragility splash against one another. The resulting canvases, installations, and photographs refuse schematic interpretations, framing instead the paradox of survival—its cost and its stubborn glow—by asking viewers to locate their own unrecognised faces within hunger, flight, or mourning.

Beyond the gallery and the printed page, sound rises, puncturing borders that diplomats draft. Traditional laments, newly minted symphonies, and spare roadside anthems circulate memories of missing children and unconsummated tomorrows, stitching disparate souls into a single trembling archive. The refrain of a travelling musician in a dusty square or the choral ascent of a children's exile choir does not translate into propositions; it vibrates beneath language, naming an intractable allegiance to both the land from which one flees and the porous futures one still dreams.

Melodies have borne witness to the exile of the uprooted and the trembling hopes of the reconciled, traversing borders and attuning listeners to the fragile realities that pulse beneath the long political silence.

The arts and literature therefore remain vital sites of confrontation with conflict, inviting reflection, cultivating empathy, and, in the best instances, urging the impatient soil of justice to yield change. By circulating views outside the fortress of orthodoxy, by lifting marginalised utterances, by cultivating a shared, somatic stillness in the audience, these practices can dissolve the emotional barriers that doggedly separate rival identities. By the same token, when we trace interdisciplinary engagements with the Israeli-Palestinian conflict, it becomes clear that cultural producers do not merely adorn the struggle; they actively shape the sediment of memory and desire, reframing the unending confrontation through images, sounds, and narratives that refuse to let either pain or hope remain mute.

Moving Forward: Reconciliation through Understanding

Emerging from the recent wave of confrontational scholarship and sweeping public argumentation is the fragile, yet promising possibility of reconciliation founded upon understanding. At this decisive moment, the cultivation of empathy and compassion stands out as an indispensable practice, capable of penetrating the hardened accounts that nourish enmity and estrangement. Authentic reconciliation, therefore, obliges all concerned parties to undertake a reciprocal quest for understanding, in which the layered and ongoing influence of past experiences upon the collective memory is openly acknowledged.

Key to this effort is a disciplined recognition of plural perspectives, which permits an expansive interrogation of the conflicting narratives that have produced reciprocal grievance. When participants enter into dialogue that intentionally honours the subtleties and contradictions of rival interpretations, they create a shared space in which mutual comprehension may take root. Such engagement requires disciplined habits: attentive listening, an eagerness to entertain propositions previously repudiated, and an unyielding resolve to abandon inherited biases for the sake of a reconstructed future.

Reconciliation grounded in understanding requires a deliberate and systematic re-examination of educational systems and public conversations, insisting on the integration of varied historical accounts and the cultivation of critical analytical capacities. When curricula are re-designed to prioritise historical enquiry and disciplinary rigour, contemporary learners are equipped to grasp the layered causality of contentious events; this achievement, in turn, lessens the allure of unilateral narratives and nurtures a sympathetic regard for differing vantage points.

Arts and literature complement this educational imperative by functioning as persuasive mediators in the reconciliation process. Works of drama, visual culture, poetry, and fiction represent the intimate, often contradictory emotions wrought by conflict, inviting audiences to inhabit positions across the spectrum of suffering. In this imaginative re-location, communities can comprehend the shared, if conflictingly expressed, dimension of humanity, even amid violence.

Finally, the reconciliation that rests on understanding requires a sustained commitment both to remembering injustices and to collaboratively imagining a future marked by reciprocal respect. By acknowledging the facts of past violations and by mapping the legacies they leave behind, societies initiate a restorative process; such a process, when pursued with transparency and compassion, encourages durable peace and unbreakable solidarity.

Moving ahead requires an unwavering dedication to cultivating empathetic ties that rise above the burden of past injustices while harnessing the generative force of mutual comprehension. By engaging historical records with reflective modesty and compassionate discernment, societies can carve out the ground for true reconciliation, thereby lighting a horizon that rests upon the values of connectedness, insight, and common human dignity.

***

References For Further Reading

1. Intellectual Battles and Public Debate (New Historians and Scholarly Reception)
   - Morris, Benny. (1987). *The Birth of the Palestinian Refugee Problem, 1947-1949*. Cambridge University Press. A seminal work challenging myths about the 1948 Palestinian exodus.
   - Pappé, Ilan. (2006). *The Ethnic Cleansing of Palestine*. Oneworld Publications. Argues that the 1948 events involved systematic displacement of Palestinians.
   - Shlaim, Avi. (2000). *The Iron Wall: Israel and the Arab World*. W.W. Norton & Company. Examines Israel's foreign policy and relations with Arab states.
   - Segev, Tom. (2000). *One Palestine, Complete: Jews and Arabs Under the British Mandate*. Metropolitan Books. Explores the Mandate period and early tensions.
   - Flapan, Simha. (1987). *The Birth of Israel: Myths and Realities*. Pantheon Books. Debunks myths about Israel's founding.

2. Critiques of New Historians

- Karsh, Efraim. (1997). *Fabricating Israeli History: The 'New Historians'*. Frank Cass. Accuses New Historians of distorting history.

- Teveth, Shabtai. (1990). "The Palestine Arab Refugee Problem and Its Origins." *Middle Eastern Studies*, 26(2), 214-249. Critiques Morris and Shlaim on refugee issues.

- Finkelstein, Norman G., and Masalha, Nur. (1991). "Debate on the 1948 Exodus." *Journal of Palestine Studies*, 21(1), 66-114. Challenges Morris's interpretations.

3. Public Perceptions and Media Representations

- Miladi, Noureddine (Ed.). (2023). *Global Media Coverage of the Palestinian-Israeli Conflict: Reporting the Sheikh Jarrah Evictions*. I.B. Tauris. Compares media narratives across regions.

- Tiripelli, Giuliana. (2016). *Media and Peace in the Middle East: The Role of Journalism in Israel-Palestine*. Palgrave Macmillan. Explores media's role in shaping perceptions and peace efforts.

- Dunsky, Marda. (2008). *Pens and Swords: How the American Mainstream Media Report the Israeli-Palestinian Conflict*. Columbia University Press. Analyzes U.S. media bias.

- Peterson, Luke. (2014). *Palestine-Israel in the Print News Media: Contending Discourses*. Routledge. Linguistic analysis of print media coverage.

4. Governmental Critiques and Political Tensions

- Sachar, Howard M. (2007). *A History of Israel: From the Rise of Zionism to Our Time*. Knopf. Covers political history and tensions.

- Oren, Michael B. (2002). *Six Days of War: June 1967 and

the Making of the Modern Middle East*. Oxford University Press. Examines the 1967 war's political impacts.

- Black, Ian. (2017). *Enemies and Neighbors: Arabs and Jews in Palestine and Israel, 1917-2017*. Atlantic Monthly Press. Analyzes a century of tensions.

5. Intellectual Rifts within Israeli Society

- Kimmerling, Baruch. (2001). *The Invention and Decline of Israeliness: State, Society, and the Military*. University of California Press. Explores societal fractures.

- Shapira, Anita. (1999). *Israel: A History*. Brandeis University Press. Discusses internal debates, including New Historians.

6. Consequences for Public Policy and Educational Institutions

- Ben-Josef Hirsch, Michal. (2007). "From Taboo to the Negotiable: The Israeli New Historians and the Changing Representation of the Palestinian Refugee Problem." *Perspectives on Politics*, 5(2), 241-258. Examines policy shifts due to New Historians.

- Podeh, Elie. (2000). "History and Memory in the Israeli Educational System: The Portrayal of the Arab-Israeli Conflict in History Textbooks (1948-2000)." *History & Memory*, 12(1), 65-100. Analyzes education impacts.

7. Stories from the Ground: Personal Narratives Amidst Contention

- Tolan, Sandy. (2006). *The Lemon Tree: An Arab, a Jew, and the Heart of the Middle East*. Bloomsbury. Intertwined personal stories.

- Barghouti, Mourid. (2000). *I Saw Ramallah*. Bloomsbury. Exile and return narrative.

- Karmi, Ghada. (2002). *In Search of Fatima: A Palestinian Story*. Verso. Memoir of displacement.
- Said, Edward W. (1999). *Out of Place: A Memoir*. Knopf. Identity and exile.
- Shavit, Ari. (2013). *My Promised Land: The Triumph and Tragedy of Israel*. Spiegel & Grau. Personal and historical reflections.
- Abulhawa, Susan. (2010). *Mornings in Jenin*. Bloomsbury. Family saga amid conflict.

8. The Role of Arts and Literature in Reflecting Conflicts
- Curthoys, Ned, & Hesse, Isabelle (Eds.). (2022). *Literary Representations of the Palestine/Israel Conflict After the Second Intifada*. Edinburgh University Press. Explores post-Intifada literature.
- Harlow, Barbara. (1987). *Resistance Literature*. Methuen. Literary resistance in conflicts.
- Kelly, Jennifer. (2023). *Invited to Witness: Solidarity Tourism Across Occupied Palestine*. Duke University Press. Art in activism.

9
Historical Truth as a Pathway to Peace

Historical Truth as a Pathway to Peace: Challenges and Possibilities

Historical Truth As A Foundation for Reconciliation

Lasting reconciliation can be achieved only when societies confront the historical truths that gave rise to their present conflicts. Historical truth thus becomes the bedrock upon which a sober examination of origin injuries can be built. When societies confront past injuries through a comprehensive reading that respects the diversity of victim and perpetrator memories, they expose the fragile strands of meaning that continue to bind the present to the past. Such confrontations, far from being exercises in moral accounting, allow communities to disentangle the traumatic layers that complicate contemporary disputes.

Exposing the historical truths of a conflict also contests the persistent myths nurtured by selective memory. When governing elites or militant groups re-edit the past to absolve their own abuses while demonising the adversary, they plant the seeds of lasting estrangement. Critical questioning, publication of archival evidence, and oral history projects expose these distortions, eroding the cynicism in which grievances are cultivated. By rescuing the past from the custody of propaganda, societies disarm the intergenerational reproduction of hatred and clear the path for truth-telling that evaluates injuries rather than indulging in retributive nostalgia.

Beyond its evidentiary function, historical truth creates the possibility of a mutual epistemic space in which formerly opposed groups can negotiate the meaning of their jointly contested past. When reconciliation becomes a shared enquiry into the past, its protagonists lose the temptation to speak past one another and instead expose the governing principles that inspired their actions. Such mutual testimony, carried out in public fora or in the privacy of truth commissions, transforms collective memory from a weapon of the strong into a shared inheritance that obligates all to remember differently. The resulting shared recognition serves as a fragile, yet indispensable, platform for further negotiations, joint memory initiatives, and, ultimately, coexistence.

Engaging with historical truths permits a rigorous interrogation of prevailing hierarchies and structural inequalities. Addressing past injustices enables communities both to redress historical grievances and to cultivate a future characterised by greater fairness. Such confrontation is not evidence of fragility, but rather an affirmation of ethical resolve and a steadfast dedication to justice and the protection of human dignity.

In the final analysis, a clear apprehension of the past serves as a navigational instrument for reconciliation advanced not only for the present moment but for durable peace. By confronting the disquieting dimensions of history, societies can establish the foundation for shared recovery and for change that is genuinely transformative. While the incorporation of historical truths is fraught with difficulty, the returns on that investment—in the form of lasting coexistence and genuine mutual comprehension—are beyond appraisal.

Examining the Role of Narratives in Shaping Perceptions

Narratives fundamentally mediate the transmission and reception of historical events, thereby moulding the contours of group identity and intergroup perception. When the pursuit of historical truth is framed as a condition for sustainable peace, a precise and critical exploration of narrative dynamics becomes indispensable. Investigation of narrative formation, circulation, and reception permits a productive engagement with persistent rivalries and with the divergent claims that animate them.

Narratives function as potent, though ideologically inflected, carriers of historical knowledge. Through the disciplined art of storytelling, a given polity conveys its version of the past, thereby securing collective memory, affirming cultural continuity, and imbuing earlier experiences with reconstructed significance. Such versions, however, are rarely ideologically neutral; they may harden into weapons of division, reproducing and magnifying collective injuries. The simultaneity of preservation and polarization compels rigorous scrutiny of how competing representations may either obstruct or facilitate peace.

Beyond the level of competing opinions, the sway of narratives is institutionalised in curricula, in cultural artefacts, and in the axioms of nationalist discourse. These framings, collectively termed historical consciousness, guide the manner in which societies remember, forget, or selectively rewrite the past. The consequences are consequential and enduring, for they condition both the public mood and the policy choices later adopted in the name of memory or reconciliation.

Engaging with the dynamics of narrative creation and dissemination reveals the mechanisms that subtend collective belief and concerted action.

Analysis of narrative processes illuminates the dynamic interdependence of history, memory, and power. Prevailing accounts typically issue from authoritative nodes and endeavour to authenticate selective readings of the past while reinforcing prevailing hierarchies. Counter-narratives emerging from subjugated or marginalised groups often languish at the periphery, permitting the selective oblivion of their testimonies and achievements. Such asymmetries compel a commitment to historiographical pluralism, whereby the record strives to embrace disparate standpoints and to present the recursive heterogeneity of past occurrences.

Media institutions, furthermore, exercise a decisive role in the calibration and circulation of narrative frames. Their technological reach and editorial choices can elevate specific interpretations while eclipsing rivals, refracting past events in a manner that decisively moulds public sentiment and informs the formation of collective memory. Accordingly, capacity for media literacy and the cultivation of a critical stance toward historical narrative are prerequisite to apprehending the delicate gradations that compose complex historical realities.

Through sustained investigation of narrative vectors, scholars and practitioners alike may acquire the analytical clarity necessary for grasping the intricate relations between historical comprehension and processes of reconciliation.

Acknowledging the intricate character of narratives and their broad impacts enables us to pursue a more sophisticated and inclusive conception of historical truth, thereby fostering the conditions necessary for enduring peace and reciprocal comprehension.

Bridging Historical Divides: Case Studies from Global Conflicts

An examination of global conflicts reveals converging pathways by which the acknowledgment of historical truth can reconcile even the most polarized societies. The South African Truth and Reconciliation Commission (TRC) epitomises this process, intertwining the confession of past abuses, conditional amnesty, and public testimony to transform private grief into collective memory. This architectonic approach produced a narrative of apartheid that, while contested, provided a common frame for historical accountability and a measure of political and emotional reintegration. In parallel, the aftermath of the Rwandan genocide illustrates how hybrid justice—composed of court trials, Gacaca community courts, and ritual mourning—contributed to a layered remembrance. The mourning itself, infused with confession and forgiveness, functioned both to rehumanise perpetrators and to redress the categorical denial of victimhood. Together, these instances underscore that public, structured confrontation with historical wrongdoing can stabilise and eventually unify divided polities. Such reconstruction depends not on the erasure of past fractures, but on transparent acknowledgment of their origins and consequences. Comparison of these processes with the Israeli-Palestinian conflict reveals common structural challenges: competing historical narratives, segmented memory cultures, and sovereignty struggles. The durability of both past and present divisions rests on how societies, and their governing institutions, elect to narrate their histories.

The New Historians' Contributions to Israeli-Palestinian Understanding

The Israeli-Palestinian conflict has entered a new phase of scholarly investigation, thanks primarily to the cohort of historians collectively known as the New Historians. Pioneered by scholars such as Benny Morris, Ilan Pappé, and Avi Shlaim, this movement has fundamentally unsettled long-cherished national narratives and brought to light a range of previously suppressed historical data. Their work has questioned the selective memory that has often guided both popular and academic discourse regarding the origins and development of the conflict.

The foremost contribution of this school of thought rests upon a disciplined re-examination of the documentary record and a refusal to accept the parameters of earlier historiography. By sifting through newly released archives, previously inaccessible military archives, and the oral testimonies of combatants and civilians, the New Historians have pieced together a historiographical puzzle that is neither unmarred by ideological baggage nor entirely neutral. Yet, their analytic rigour has yielded a textured portrait of the past that obliges scholars and policymakers alike to confront uncomfortable realities. Such incursion into the officially sanctioned memory has, in turn, prompted a wider scholarly re-assessment of ideological dichotomies and has opened the floor for a dialogic recounting of both Israeli and Palestinian experiences.

At the core of their contributions lies a steadfast resolve to face disquieting realities without softening their bitter edge, thereby offering a historiography that refuses to abbreviate the knots of the past. Their scholarship has rendered visible the trajectories of uprooted populations, the collateral toll exacted by military campaigns, and the dense constellation of socio-political drivers that have fostered intermittent conflagrations for decades. By directing analytical attention to these residual, often occluded facets, the New Historians have enlarged the interpretive perimeter and encouraged a recognition that multiple, coexisting realities must animate any rigorous apprehension of the past.

Having rendered the neglected visible, the New Historians move with equal deliberation to contest the myths that have calcified in popular memory into impermeable shields of opinion. Employing a deliberately calibrated hermeneutic of dispassion, they sift evidence and thereby puncture the sedimented tropes that have animated hostilities and fortified exclusionary lenses. The effect is to deepen the scholarly arena while simultaneously insisting upon the ethical weight of historiographical choices. By foregrounding the coercive hierarchies embedded in narratives, they underscore how the circulation of historical memory bears decisive, if frequently unrecognised, consequences for the fragile enterprises of reconciliation and conflict transformation.

Additionally, the New Historians' fidelity to documentary evidence and their insistence on reconstructing the past in light of the best available scholarship have created the preconditions for dialogues capable of transcending zero-sum imaginings. Their assembled enquiries, which frequently disclose the coexistence of mutually antipathetic interpretations, invite a recognition that any durable prospect for Israeli-Palestinian coexistence must cadge from the recognition of these irreconcilable tellings. By mapping the multidirectional trajectories of colonial, nationalist, and imperial projects, they prompt observers to perceive the region's past not through exclusive lenses, but as a braided texture in which empathy for the stranger learns to coexist, if only provisionally, with allegiance to a particular claim.

In the aggregate, the New Historians have redirected the conversation on Israeli-Palestinian relations from polemical shorthand toward a rigorous, evidence-based discursive practice. Their warranty of precision—whether in the re-examination of demographic data, the retrieval of displaced voices, or the scrutiny of governmental archival silence—encourages a historiography in which settler and displaced subject are no longer tacitly exchanged for a monolithic myth. The cumulative effect is an interpretive climate that privileges the recognition of overlapping grievances and the construction of shared temporal horizons, thus laying the frail, albeit discernible, axioms for a politics of recognition capable of displacing the above zero-sum.

Challenges Facing Historians in Politically Charged Environments

Historians operating within politically charged climates confront a series of formidable barriers that undermine both the integrity of their work and the public circulation of verified historical knowledge. Foremost among these is the systematic embedding of political imperatives within the very construction of historical narratives, especially when contested pasts are harnessed to legitimise competing national identities or ongoing political struggles. In such arenas, any deviation from the officially sanctioned version of the past invites escalated scrutiny, vitriolic critique, and institutional repercussions directed at the scholar, thus imposing a coercive definition of the permissible field of enquiry.

Equally, the historian's craft is fundamentally endangered by the twinned threats of source insecurity and source integrity. Tactical efforts to obscure, erase, or falsify records by politically aligned groups compromise the documentary trail upon which objective reconstruction depends. In the resulting landscape of, at best, incomplete files and, at worst, forgeries, the historian must navigate divergent, mutually exclusive narratives that each command their own curated bodies of evidence. The task of unearthing the vitreous core of fact thus becomes geomorphically obstructed. Compounding these archival impediments, confrontation with retaliation intensifies when historians probe highly polarising subjects. Censorship, degrees of social or institutional intimidation, and explicit threats to bodily security or professional livelihood converge, forcing scholars to weigh the personal cost of exposure against the scholarly imperative of incomplete silence.

The intricate character of historical scholarship conducted in politically charged climates obliges researchers to grasp critically how collective memory, trauma, and pervasive propaganda shape societal understandings of past events. Scholars must disentangle layers of communal pressures and inherited biases, remaining aware of the emotionally charged attachments that particular narratives evoke. This situation obliges historians to sustain a careful equilibrium between honouring conflicting positions and preserving disciplinary objectivity, as they pursue a narrative that aspires to be simultaneously comprehensive and balanced.

Simultaneously, external forces—partisan agendas, ideological predispositions, and market forces—can shape both the authentication and the circulation of historical documentation. When historical knowledge becomes a political weapon, it is often deployed to legitimise current policies or ideological goals, thus reinforcing errors and obstructing the open enquiry to which the discipline is committed.

Confronting these layers of complexity, historians must cultivate a combination of intellectual rigour, personal resilience, and principled ethics. Their devotion to scrupulous documentation, coherent analysis, and explicit methodological transparency becomes crucial in safeguarding the credibility of their enquiry and in furthering a richer comprehension of the past. In so doing, scholars can clarify the past's contradictions and contribute to the uncertain but vital prospects of reconciliation and peace in societies marked by the legacy of historical conflict.

Public Receptivity and Resistance to Revised Histories

The public reception of newly contested historical narratives unfolds as an intricate negotiation between social predispositions, personal convictions, and the sedimentation of cumulative memory. When professional historians interrogate the underpinnings of long-accepted interpretations, the responses of broader society typically stratify along a spectrum of varying degrees of welcome and repulsion. A crystalline grasp of these reactive modalities remains indispensable for gauging the ultimate efficacy of emergent scholarly insights, especially when those insights aspire to underpin mechanisms of reconciliation. Receptiveness to newly articulated chronologies derives, *inter alia*, from the salient intersections of cultural self-definition, partisan allegiance, and autobiographical memory. Constituencies may perceive long-familiar accounts as irreducible components of collective selfhood; any proposed reformulation thus activates a defensive reaction, couched in the rhetoric of existential jeopardy. The resultant affective allegiance to conventional constructs invariably solidifies in politically charged settings, where the historiographical corpus has been appropriated as a mediating vessel for confrontational national identities. Beyond the acquisitional substrate of the individual, the mediating forces of pedagogical and journalistic domains command analytic attention. Curricular sinews and editorial optics collaborate in sculpting public attitudes toward reconstituted narratives. When pre-established interests or factional imperatives surreptitiously guide the circulation of historiographical knowledge, discordant interpretations confront institutionalised valves of resistance, inhibiting the dialectical exchange that reconciliation necessitates.

At the same time, there exist segments of the public that demonstrate a willingness to reconsider established historical accounts, recognising that such amendments may facilitate more in-depth understanding and heightened empathy. This willingness typically arises from a readiness to confront unsettling realities and to honour the intricate, often contradictory, nature of past events. Moving towards reconciliation and broader societal inclusion through the practice of historical revisionism demands that scholars chart a careful course through the varied terrain of public openness and reticence. Historians can, by fostering open and respectful conversation, reach diverse constituencies, alleviating anxieties and suspicions while emphasising the significance of verifiable history as a communal heritage that underpins the construction of a more cohesive future. It is at the intersection of collective memory, individual and communal identity, and public moral consciousness that the capacity of amended narratives to instigate meaningful social transformation is most vividly affirmed.

Educational Curricula as a Tool for Fostering Reconciliation

Curricula are central to how societies educate their future citizens, and are therefore uniquely positioned to promote reconciliation after periods of conflict or systemic injustice. When educational frameworks responsibly integrate contested historical events, they move beyond rote memorisation and invite students to grapple with competing truths. This process requires training teachers to present materials that transcend dominant national myths to include previously marginalised voices and perspectives, inviting learners to evaluate evidence, recognise bias, and appreciate the contingencies that shape all historical narratives. Such pedagogical plurality serves to instil the habits of mind and heart that reconciliation requires.

At the same time, an explicit commitment to revising and expanding school history presentations can disrupt the transmission of inherited prejudices. When curricula invite learners to interrogate why certain versions of the past were previously sanctioned and others silenced, they create conditions for critical reflection that can loosen the hold of inherited identity-based animosities. Classrooms thus become laboratories for civic dialogue, where students simulate the difficult negotiation that unresolved pasts demand of future societies. This emphasis on dialogue, rather than mere consensus, nurtures an ethic of ongoing enquiry and mutual respect that, over time, can consolidate the practical foundations of a reconciled and pluralist polity.

Incorporating updated historical narratives into school curricula poses significant, yet surmountable, hurdles. Certain political or cultural constituencies often mobilise to defend traditional accounts, frustrating attempts to offer a comprehensive and equitable historical picture. When guardians of orthodoxy mobilise to protect established narratives, the space needed to introduce and interrogate non-dominant perspectives is constricted, thereby obstructing the slow but necessary movement towards collective reconciliation.

Selection and presentation of contested historical truths demand both accuracy and moral sensitivity. The framing, emphasis, and omissions within textbooks, curricula, and classroom discussions decisively shape students' cognitive, emotional and ethical responses. Consequently, teachers are obliged to create pedagogical contexts wherein scholarly rigour, critical questioning, and empathetic listening cohere, whilst honouring the varied lived experiences that the past continues to provoke.

Ultimately, well-constructed curricula serve as instruments of reconciliation by cultivating learners who interrogate inherited truths and appreciate plural perspectives. By committing to a comprehensive, inclusive instructional stance, educators can transmit the dispositions of empathy, analytical acuity and a pedagogical vocation to pursue truth. In so doing, they enable educational institutions to exert a meaningful, if iterative, influence upon the reconciliation processes and durable peace in societies still animated by the legacies of past conflicts.

Media Representation of Historical Truths: Impacts and Limitations

In contemporary informational ecosystems, media discourse exerts a decisive influence on collective perceptions of past injustices, on the interpretive frameworks with which societies engage their own histories, and on the foundational conditions for eventual reconciliation or rupture. Although some media interventions can advance critical historiography, the very same technologies can circulate reductive or instrumental accounts, underscoring the ambivalence of their political and ethical effects. This ambivalence emerges most acutely when the media confronts historiographical controversies over the responsibility, memory, or aftermath of violence.

The consequences of mediated historical representation extend far beyond immediate audience reaction. Linear platforms, documentary series, online forums, and viral images collectively construct a polyphonic yet often asymmetrical memory scape that favours certain narratives over others. Iconic footage or resonant headlines have the capacity to sediment collective memory, immunising certain interpretations against subsequent scholarly correction. Conversely, when media strategically assembles documents, oral histories, and counter-testimonies, it can destabilise hegemonic accounts, illuminate silenced agency, and inaugurate public spheres for dialogue. In such instances, the media may record historical contests and mediate their interpretive resolution, thereby influencing memorial policy, pedagogical curricula, and, by extension, conflictive group identities.

Yet, these gains remain contingent and reversible. Structural commercial imperatives, the pursuit of sensationalism, and algorithmic reinforcement of polarising content can distort or simplify complex pasts. Commemorative programming may afford disproportionate airtime to antagonistic recollections, further entrenching antagonistic identities. The impermanence of online discourse compounds these risks, as archival practices lag rapid glissades of attention. In such environments, truths that demand measured scholarly exposition can be subsumed under mnemonic capsules that obscure causality, agency, and temporal specificity. The consequent representations, although widely circulated, may lack the evidentiary and contextual rigour necessary for historical adjudication, leaving public memory vulnerable to fabrication, aggrandisement, or denialism.

In summary, while media have the capacity to illuminate and contest historical truths, their interventions occur under conditions that can either fortify or undermine scholarly and ethical imperatives. Only through critical media literacy, sustained scholarly engagement, and institutional safeguards can the potentially constructive function of the media in mediating history be realised.

Media coverage of historical events is frequently shaped by biases, prevailing political agendas, and profit motives. Emphasis on dramatic presentation and the reduction of intricate historical processes into catchphrases can obscure factual accuracy and entrench reductive stereotypes. The constraints of print and broadcast formats—where limited airtime and column inches prevail—tend to compress historical realities, favouring generalisations that confirm rather than challenge prevailing misinterpretations.

The rising reach of 'fake news' and the constant circulation of unchecked data present a further and acute threat to the credible dissemination of historical fact. Misinformation of this sort impedes efforts of reconciliation and the reconstruction of communal trust, since propaganda, rather than enlightenment, can intensify polarisation and make acts of mutual understanding and forgiveness more elusive. The present context thus demands that media practitioners uphold rigorous ethical standards and that audiences develop a discerning media literacy capable of apprehending historical accounts both critically and contextually.

Attention to the constructive and limiting capacities of media representations is therefore indispensable in the pursuit of durable peace and reconciliation. Affirming the media's capacity to foster collective healing demands equal and continued vigilance to ensure that its communication does not repeat and amplify division or falsehood.

By harnessing media to amplify authentic historical narratives, feature marginalised voices, and nurture critical enquiry, society can move toward the urgent goal of fostering empathy, understanding, and ultimately, reconciliation.

Policy Recommendations: Integrating Historical Insights into Peace Processes

For sustainable peace and reconciliation, intentional embedding of historical awareness within peace accords and post-conflict recovery narratives is non-negotiable. Recognising that collective memory and identity can lock societies into cycles of violence, contemporary mediators must acknowledge the persistence of historical grievances and distorted recollections. Peace formulators should thus orient policy recommendations around the realisation that misunderstandings of the past, if left unexamined, become the scaffolding of future hostility. Accordingly, measures intended to cultivate empathetic coexistence must begin with an evidence-based appraisal of past events.

Central to this endeavour is the creation of bi-communal

historical commissions that bring together professional historians, curriculum designers, and delegates of the previously antagonistic groups. Operating under the principle that understanding does not eliminate disagreement, these bodies are charged with systematically documenting, comparing, and, where possible, reconciling competing national, ethnic, or ideological histories. Commission work must foreground contested episodes, spotlight under-represented viewpoints, and, through iterative dialogue, produce a composite historical account that can inclusively memorialise the past. Such a reconciliatory narrative strengthens the credibility of peace accords by embedding a culture of mutual respect and prepares societies for sustained partnership across difference.

Educational reform remains a linchpin in embedding historical consciousness within peace-building initiatives. Curriculum design ought to emphasise balanced, context-rich narratives that move beyond polarising nationalist or ethnocentric frames. Teachers, as trusted mediators, must guide learners through sensitive historical controversies, fostering critical reflection and cultivating empathy. By reconstructing events and locating their enduring consequences within a broader socio-political landscape, schools can help to disrupt cycles of intergenerational trauma and nurture a durable culture of peace.

Concomitantly, public policy must foreground the unfettered circulation of historically verifiable information across diverse media. Given the media's capacity to mould collective memory, strategic investment is required to promote responsible and ethically coherent representations. This can involve strengthening independent journalism, amplifying marginal perspectives, and systematically rebutting disinformation that entrenches sectarian divisions. By curating an information environment saturated with credible historical data, media actors can equip societies to confront the past with resilience and to engage in authentic reconciliation.

Additionally, international and regional organisations that mediate conflict must systematically embed historical scholarship within their peace building frameworks. By actively recruiting historians and conflict specialists who are versed in the longue durée, these organisations can unearth the underlying structures that have perpetuated violence, thus refining the specificity and effectiveness of their intervention logics. Joint archival and oral history projects, underwritten by regional actors, can produce a common corpus of evidence that mitigates selective memory and supports transnational dialogue. Such initiatives can subsequently serve as the empirical foundation for policy-driven programmes that disaggregate and reconceptualise historical grievances.

To summarise, the operationalisation of historical knowledge in peace processes demands a coordinated effort that traverses education, diplomacy, media, and multinational cooperation. By foregrounding the veracity of past injustices while fostering pluralistic accounts, policymakers can stabilise the social imaginary and diminish the salience of historical animosities. The recommendations thus advanced affirm that a deliberate encounter with history is not merely archival, but a transformative social practice capable of animating a future animated by empathy, reciprocal recognition, and enduring coexistence.

Concluding Thoughts: Towards a Future of Coexistence

The quest for historical truth as a stepping-stone to lasting peace is laden with complications, resistances, and subtleties. Traversing the interwoven thickets of contradictory narratives and opposed outlooks, it becomes ever clearer that the cultivation of coexistence surpasses a scholarly undertaking; it emerges as a moral necessity for anyone who cares for the world that is to come. Weaving historical awareness into peace negotiations invites the possibility of born empathy, genuine understanding, and decisive reconciliation, thus supplying the moral soil wherein lasting respect and solidarity may take root. We must accept that historical truth is never monolithic; it frequently contains painful and unsettling facts that demand both reckoning and, sometimes, restitution. Integrating such truths within peace building is required to adjust collective memory and to rupture the recurrent spirals of animosity. The viability of a shared future depends upon our communal readiness to confront the past without reduction, willing to sit with the disquiet it brings while appropriating the energy it offers for constructive change. Furthermore, the cultivation of commemorative customs that reverently attend both to the suffering endured by victims and to the moral weight borne by perpetrators is, in itself, a necessary dimension of the healing journey.

Such commemorations remind us with painful clarity of the human cost of war, forging a shared determination to prevent the recurrence of past atrocities. In mapping the journey to coexistence, we must nurture spaces for authentic dialogue and plural storytelling, elevating those voices long obscured by dominant accounts. This openness demands a radical rethinking of pedagogy, equipping learners with the analytical discernment to separate fact from fabrication while nurturing a culture imbued with intellectual modesty and receptiveness. The influence of the media on public conscience remains decisive; reported attention to past events must be measured, fair, and principled, for it can recalibrate societal attitudes and disrupt the cycle of grievance seeded by misrepresentation. Ultimately, the striving for coexistence summons a profound moral and ethical reckoning: an unswerving resolve to acknowledge and interrogate history's darkest passages and to compose a shared, reconciled future. Contending with the layered truth of the past and its bearing on peace, we must continue our unwavering pursuit of a tomorrow characterised not by the residues of bitterness, but by coexistence, compassion, and an enduring, collective peace.

***

References for Further Reading

1. Historical Truth as Foundation for Reconciliation
- Rotberg, Robert I. (Ed.). (2006). *Israeli and Palestinian Narratives of Conflict: History's Double Helix*. Indiana University Press. Explores how conflicting historical truths can be confronted for reconciliation.
- Longman, Timothy. (2017). *Memory and Justice in Post-Genocide Rwanda*. Cambridge University Press. Discusses truth-telling and memory in reconciliation processes.
- Graybill, Lyn S. (2002). *Truth and Reconciliation in South Africa: Miracle or Model?*. Lynne Rienner Publishers. Analyses truth commissions as foundations for societal healing.

2. Examining the Role of Narratives in Shaping Perceptions
- Dajani Daoudi, Mohammed S. (2009). "Israelis and Palestinians: Contested Narratives." *Israel Studies*, 18(2), 53-69. Examines how narratives mediate identity and perceptions in the conflict.
- Rotberg, Robert I. (Ed.). (2006). *Israeli and Palestinian Narratives of Conflict: History's Double Helix*. Indiana University Press. Focuses on narrative dynamics in the Israeli-Palestinian context.
- Dornbach, Márton. (2016). *Receptive Spirit: German Idealism and the Dynamics of Cultural Transmission*. Fordham University Press. Discusses narrative transmission and historical consciousness.
- Collini, Stefan, Mandler, Peter, & Stapleton, Julia. (Various years). Works on national histories and narratives, as referenced in nostalgic reflections on historiography.

3. Bridging Historical Divides: Case Studies from Global Conflicts

- Fox, Nicole. (2021). *After Genocide: Memory and Reconciliation in Rwanda*. University of Wisconsin Press. Investigates memorials and survivor experiences in post-genocide reconciliation.
- Clark, Phil. (2010). *The Gacaca Courts, Post-Genocide Justice and Reconciliation in Rwanda: Justice without Lawyers*. Cambridge University Press. Analyses community courts and hybrid justice in Rwanda.
- Mack, Edward C. (Ed.). (2018). *Reinventing Theology in Post-Genocide Rwanda*. Georgetown University Press. Examines the Catholic Church's role in genocide and reconciliation.
- Wilson, Richard Ashby. (2001). *The Politics of Truth and Reconciliation in South Africa: Legitimizing the Post-Apartheid State*. Cambridge University Press. Explores the TRC's impact on political reintegration.
- Mack, Edward C. (Ed.). (2018). *From Apartheid to Democracy: Deliberating Truth and Reconciliation in South Africa*. Penn State University Press. Studies the TRC through rhetorical and deliberative lenses.
- Boraine, Alex. (2000). *A Country Unmasked: Inside South Africa's Truth and Reconciliation Commission*. Oxford University Press. Insider account of the TRC process.

4. The New Historians' Contributions to Israeli-Palestinian Understanding
- Morris, Benny. (1987). *The Birth of the Palestinian Refugee Problem, 1947-1949*. Cambridge University Press. Key revisionist work on the 1948 events.
- Pappé, Ilan. (1992). *The Making of the Arab-Israeli Conflict, 1947-1951*. I.B. Tauris. Challenges traditional narratives on early conflict origins.

- Shlaim, Avi. (1988). *Collusion Across the Jordan: King Abdullah, the Zionist Movement, and the Partition of Palestine*. Columbia University Press. Examines diplomatic collaborations.

- Segev, Tom. (1986). *1949: The First Israelis*. Free Press. Critiques early Israeli society and myths.

- Morris, Benny. (1990). *1948 and After: Israel and the Palestinians*. Clarendon Press. Further explorations of post-1948 dynamics.

- Pappé, Ilan. (2010). *Out of the Frame: The Struggle for Academic Freedom in Israel*. Pluto Press. Discusses New Historians' challenges and contributions.

5. Challenges Facing Historians in Politically Charged Environments

- Johnson, Walter. (2003). "On Agency." *Journal of Social History*, 37(1), 113-124. Warns against concepts that avoid addressing political environments.

- Collini, Stefan. (2012). *What Are Universities For?*. Penguin. Reflects on historians' roles in politically charged settings.

- Charette, James. (2020). "State of the Field: The History of Political Thought." *History*, 105(367), 644-668. Surveys challenges in politically influenced historiography.

- Gibson, James L. (2004). *Overcoming Apartheid: Can Truth Reconcile a Divided Nation?*. Russell Sage Foundation. Addresses biases and source integrity in post-conflict history.

- Karsh, Efraim. (1997). *Fabricating Israeli History: The 'New Historians'*. Frank Cass. Critiques New Historians in a charged context.

6. Public Receptivity and Resistance to Revised Histories

- Gibson, James L. (2004). *Overcoming Apartheid: Can Truth Reconcile a Divided Nation?*. Russell Sage Foundation. Assesses public responses to truth processes.

- Cole, Catherine M. (2010). *Performing South Africa's Truth Commission: Stages of Transition*. Indiana University Press. Explores public theater and receptivity to historical revisions.

- Leonard, Devin. (2016). *Neither Snow Nor Rain: A History of the United States Postal Service*. Grove Press. Discusses how narratives shape public memory (tangential but relevant to media and history).

- Gallagher, Winifred. (2016). *How the Post Office Created America: A History*. Penguin Press. Examines institutional shaping of public historical perceptions.

7. Educational Curricula as a Tool for Fostering Reconciliation

- Paulson, Julia (Ed.). (2011). *Education and Reconciliation: Exploring Conflict and Post-Conflict Situations*. Continuum. Analyses education's role in reconciliation.

- Korostelina, Karina V., & Lässig, Simone (Eds.). (2013). *History Education and Post-Conflict Reconciliation: Reconsidering Joint Textbook Projects*. Routledge. Focuses on curricula in Europe and the Balkans.

- Russell, S. Garnett. (2019). *Becoming Rwandan: Education, Reconciliation, and the Making of a Post-Genocide Citizen*. Rutgers University Press. Examines post-genocide education in Rwanda.

- Korostelina, Karina V. (Ed.). (2017). *History Education and Conflict Transformation: Social Psychological Theories, History Teaching and Reconciliation*. Palgrave Macmillan.

BREAKING THE WALL OF SILENCE

Discusses models for curricula in reconciliation.

8. Media Representation of Historical Truths: Impacts and Limitations
   - Starr, Paul. (2004). *The Creation of the Media: Political Origins of Modern Communications*. Basic Books. Explores media's historical role in shaping truths.
   - Berger, Stefan, et al. (Eds.). (2008). *Narrating the Nation: Representations in History, Media and the Arts*. Berghahn Books. Analyses media's impact on national narratives.
   - Knapp, James A. (2003). *Illustrating the Past in Early Modern England: The Representation of History in Printed Books*. Ashgate. Discusses visual media and historical representation.
   - Grey House Publishing. (2020). *Opinions Throughout History: Truth & Lies in the Media*. Grey House Publishing. Surveys media's role in historical truth from colonial times.

9. Policy Recommendations: Integrating Historical Insights into Peace Processes
   - Haass, Felix, Hartzell, Caroline A., & Hoddie, Matthew. (2022). "Citizens in Peace Processes." *Journal of Conflict Resolution*, 66(4-5), 597-607. Advocates for citizen inclusion in peace policies.
   - Dayal, Anjali. (2021). *Incredible Commitments: How UN Peacekeeping Failures Shape Peace Processes*. Cambridge University Press. Provides insights into UN peacemaking and historical integration.
   - Lederach, John Paul. (1997). *Building Peace: Sustainable Reconciliation in Divided Societies*. United States Institute of Peace Press. Recommends historical awareness in peace building.

- Bratt, Duane. (2023). "Knowledge Production on Peace: Actors, Hierarchies and Policy Relevance." *International Affairs*, 99(5), 1839-1859. Examines how historical research informs policy.

- Nilsson, Desiree. (2023). "How Research Travels to Policy: The Case of Nordic Peace Research." *International Affairs*, 99(5), 1953-1972. Discusses bridging academia and peace policy.

10
Israeli Society
Struggling With an Uncomfortable Past

A State at Crossroads

Israeli society now stands at a decisive point in its historiographic journey, confronted by the dense stratigraphy of its past. The rediscovery and reinterpretation of pivotal episodes have provoked a sustained and sometimes disquieting self-scrutiny, fracturing formerly settled chronologies and ideological frames. While the nation confronts the shadow of its past, it concurrently navigates urgent contemporary dilemmas, generating an atmosphere marked by solemn enquiry and self-questioning. This moment of dislocation provides a particularly generative site for examining the porous crossing of cultural memory, collective identity, and the generative, persistent work of historical consciousness. The dense weave of Israel's chronicle, threaded through polychrome strands of victory and catastrophe, of martial valour and moral ambivalence, has produced a collective memory resource that steadies shapes, but also contests, the nation's self-image. From the inaugural declaration of sovereignty in 1948 to the contemporary, unresolved stratification of the Israeli-Palestinian encounter, every archive of memory has been integrated into an ongoing prefiguration of the collective story. At this point of articulation, citizens and policymakers alike are obliged to revisit earlier episodes through a tempered and multilayered optic that recognises the embedded complexities and the braided contradictions of the record. Such a recomposed discourse dislodges inherited heuristics, inciting a sustained reappraisal of figures, moments, and strategies that for decades have been canonised as the core of national identity.

The acknowledgment of former injustices, together with the reexamination of previously unquestioned convictions, signals a readiness to pursue honest, if sometimes painful, conversation. This reflective process is not limited to universities and think tanks; it reverberates in civic culture, artistic production, and private deliberation. Such widespread scrutiny compels a sustained enquiry into how yesterday's choices structure today's dilemmas and raises the imperative to interrogate the values, ethical obligations, and visions bequeathed to coming generations. At the confluence of history, memory, and identity, Israeli society encounters a moment of reckoning, foregrounding diverse and often contradictory narratives that converge to constitute a shared sense of self. The cumulative effect is a society poised at a decisive moment, where navigation of historical contradictions is inextricably linked to the remaking of communal identity and to a continuing, negotiated definition of Israeli membership within a chronically shifting historical horizon.

Cultural Memory and Collective Identity

Cultural memory serves as an intricate fabric interlacing a nation's historical milestones, inherited customs, and shared emotions. In Israel, this weave extends from biblical antiquity to contemporary life, narrating a continuum that informs collective identity. Memory does more than preserve; it shapes ethical orientations, habitual practices, and the nation's sense of itself relative to the globe. Acting as a bridge across time, it confers on each generation the reassurance of continuity and the promise of belonging. In everyday Israeli life, memory is ritualised in commemorative ceremonies, emblematic symbols, and public displays that translate the shared story of hardship and triumph into tangible experience. The jubilant observances of Independence Day and the hushed reverence of Holocaust Memorial Day are emblematic markers that strive to consolidate the nation's heterogeneous groups around a single historical consciousness. Yet, the story is neither homogeneous nor finished. Constantly re-scripted in response to changing circumstances, collective memory remains an arena of lively contestation. Multiple, sometimes contradictory, narratives coexist, each representing the distinct vantage points of various communities, political factions, and regional origins. These competing accounts frequently engage one another in public discourse, reformulating the meanings attributed to decisive moments such as the establishment of the state and the series of Arab-Israeli conflicts.

When cultural memory becomes intertwined with collective identity, it not only shapes the self-perception of Israelis, but it also colours the ways they assess their global standing and their engagements with other nations and cultures. A scrutiny of how cultural memory is constructed in Israel yields important insights into the internal pluralisms of its society and the difficulties it encounters in negotiating competing historical trajectories. Such an analysis also illuminates the methods by which Israel's discrete social groups continuously alter their self-understanding in relation to the persistent legacies of the past.

Education and Historical Narrative: A Complex Relationship

Education remains a central arena in which people internalise conceptions of history and collective identity. In Israel, where national consciousness is inseparable from historical memory, the nexus between schooling and historical narrative presents distinctive complications.

The framing of past events within the national curriculum noticeably shapes pupils' interpretations of their country's biography. Long-standing debates in Israel have focused on how textbooks represent the foundational period and later military confrontations with neighbouring states. Instructors and policymakers confront the dual obligation of delivering a scholarly, rigorous record while simultaneously cultivating a cohesive sense of national pride and social solidarity among adolescent learners.

Critics maintain that the curriculum reproduces a selectively heroic interpretation of history, celebrating national triumphs yet marginalising the underlying conflicts and contentious realities. According to them, the consequent unilateral emphasis on national glory entrenches a reductive patriotic outlook, impairing learners' capacity for critical examination and layered analysis of the past.

In contrast, defenders of the existing framework argue that fostering a robust patriotic identity, and an accompanying capacity for endurance, remains a moral imperative shaped by the nation's volatile birth and maturation. They contend that narratives celebrating the courage and sacrifices of national figures and ordinary citizens must be central, presented as the moral imperative of an uninterrupted struggle for sovereignty and flourishing.

Nonetheless, amid these polarized perspectives, an expanding chorus acknowledges the imperative for a broadened, pluralistic historiography in the classroom. Initiatives have begun to weave in the testimonies and interpretations of subordinated groups and internal critics, alongside the conventional narratives. By exposing students to the intersecting strands of past experience, the revised programmes endeavour to cultivate not only compassion and analytical acumen, but also a principled respect for competing interpretations of communal memory.

The rapid evolution of digital media and communication technologies has increased the availability of alternative historical narratives, allowing students to encounter a broader array of perspectives that extend beyond conventional pedagogical frameworks. This circumstance has prompted renewed scholarly enquiry into the significance of digital and media literacy as foundational competencies that enable learners to navigate, contextualise, and critically appraise the multiplicity of historical sources now at their disposal.

While the educational sector continues to reform in response to shifting societal expectations and emerging pedagogical imperatives, the interplay between the teaching profession and the formation of historical consciousness remains a principal site of analysis and practice. Educators are thus challenged to mediate between the cultivation of national allegiance and the promotion of a dispassionate, evidence-based apprehension of the past, so that graduates may emerge as reflective and democratically engaged citizens, able to confront the ambiguities and traumas inscribed in their collective heritage.

Generational Perspectives on Past Conflicts

In the longer trajectory of Israeli society, generational perspectives on past military confrontations exert decisive influence on modes of national-minded self-understanding. One reflexive manifestation of this influence is the selective transmission of directed mnemonic acts, anchored especially on the Israeli-Palestinian divide. Different age cohorts, shaped by the sequential interweaving of global and local pressures, cushion and reframe the legacy of earlier hostilities, yielding internally differentiated modes of adjudicating conflictual memory.

Among those now identified as the historical older generation—individuals forged in the years immediately preceding and following the establishment of the Jewish state and in successive confrontations—memory is usually ratified by a triadic triangulation of individual biography, institutional pedagogy, and public ritual. The salient ideational clusters are forged in tangible experiences of siege, emergency, and consolidation which, in the absence of formal coping discourses, become assimilated as normative data for identity. The concomitant narrative blends emotive arcs of trauma and resilience with a polysemous sense of homeland imperilment, reaffirming the trajectory of survival as coterminous with state success. As a result, surviving cohort members seldom distinguish between personal trauma and collective memory, for survival itself is read as the normative justification of past military choices.

In contrast, the younger cohort, having matured amid rapid technological progress and expansive global networks, adopts a more discerning and layered stance toward the presentation of historical events. Their access to a breadth of information and a pronounced sense of social accountability encourages them to interrogate canonical historiographies and to participate in transnational dialogues. Typically, they articulate a commitment to reconciliation and seek to dismantle seemingly immutable accounts, hoping to articulate a prospective civic order founded on coexistence and reciprocal comprehension.

The resulting divergence between older and younger memory-keepers cultivates intergenerational friction and animated public debates within Israel. This interaction between variegated recollections animates a vibrant contestation of the past and its bearing on present-day political and social configurations. It further highlights the mutable character of collective memory and the extent to which generational transitions shape the ongoing re-articulation of national identity.

The ongoing influence of earlier wars on Israel's socio-political environment renders it necessary to engage systematically with how each generation remembers those conflicts. Only through deliberate intergenerational conversation can societies overcome memory-based fractures and nurture empathic recognition of differing lived realities. Such dialogue may yield a collaborative memory whose contours exceed those of any single generation. Paying close analytical attention to these shifting generational lenses amounts to a practical first step in moving toward a pluralistic reconciliation of Israel's contested pasts.

The Role of Media in Shaping Public Perception

The impact of media in this process can neither be overstated nor simplistically stated. Over time, journalistic, audiovisual, and documentary channels adopt, reinforce, and occasionally contest dominant accounts of conflict, thereby negotiating the borders of acceptable remembrance. Their selections of imagery, voices, and framing techniques not only mirror existing ideological divides but also operate as instruments that crystallise and disseminate collective memory. In a polity where present-day policies remain thoroughly saturated with earlier wars, these media practices acquire strategic weight; the framing of the past, once embedded in the public sphere, becomes a necessary context for interpreting the present and informing the prescriptions of the imagined future.

Understanding how the Israeli-Palestinian conflict is mediated is critical, not only for academic analysis, but for grasping why historical memory has become a battleground of its own. Israeli media—ranging from televised news cycles to documentaries, commentary, and print journalism—holds the capacity to shape collective memory and, indirectly, policy. The rise of social media has only intensified this influence, allowing historical claims to circulate rapidly and often without editorial gatekeeping, thus complicating how demographic segments of the Israeli populace come to terms with their nation's past.

Framing pivotal episodes like the Nakba of 1948 and the Six-Day War is therefore more than a pedagogic matter; it is a political act with long-lasting consequences. Choices about terminology, the prominence of particular images, and the sequencing of events determine which narratives become dominant in the public imagination. This editorial alchemy can either confirm existing convictions or create the conditions for a critical reassessment of what those convictions are based upon. Furthermore, persistent media reproduction of selective historical myths, alongside reductive stereotypes, reinforces binary understandings of the conflict and thus reinforces intra-Israeli divisions, making shared civic discourse and policy consensus more elusive.

The interaction between political interests and media portrayals of past events merits rigorous analysis. When media organisations are openly or covertly aligned with partisan agendas, the likelihood increases that their accounts of the past will be selectively framed or rhetorically embellished, thereby producing a spurious consensus about historical reality. This convergence of political will and communicative practice compels scholars and citizens alike to approach mediated historical material with a vigilant scepticism, mindful of the interests that may be at play.

Given the entanglement of these factors, the promotion of media literacy and independent analytic thinking is a civic necessity. When citizens are systematically trained to interrogate the evidential bases and narrative strategies that inform the representation of historical events, they cultivate capacities for deliberative judgment that strengthen public debate. Simultaneously, the insertion of plural and marginalised perspectives into the media sphere serves to pluralise historical accounts, diminishing the monopolistic grasp of any single political narrative and fostering, in turn, deeper intercommunal empathy.

In the ongoing negotiation of its contested past, Israeli society confronts the media not merely as a peripheral actor but as a decisive agent in the collective process of memory, recognition, and prospective reconciliation.

Political Discourse and Historical Controversy

Political discourse regarding historical controversies in Israel is deeply entwined with the broader competition over the control of the collective memory that underwrites the state's identity. Interpretations of pivotal events are calibrated to serve present political ends, transforming memory itself into an instrument of contestation. This section examines the recursive relationship among rhetorical deployment, historiographical contestation, and the enduring replication of discord.

Contemporary Israeli partisanship consistently situates memory as the first battleground on which political credibility is established. Parliamentary factions and extra-parliamentary movements disaggregate the past, retrieving discrete episodes that bolster their strategic goals, excluding rival readings. Such forensic selectivity is then elevated to official discourse, where it informs school curricula, media broadcasts, and official documentaries, thereby conditioning the parameters within which policy is debated. The disparity between interpretive licences granted to one's own memory and the delegitimising indictment of the opponent's past serves, in turn, to polarise public cognition and to frame diplomatic interlocutors.

Heightened, collective contestation over historiographical detail reinforces social cleavages and stagnates reconciliation initiatives. Contending versions of the past occupy the same argumentative space as present policy proposals, leaving little intellectual margin for a convergent, shared narrative. The result is an ongoing fracturing of the public sphere, in which every historical adjudication begets diagrammatic walls between constituents, while the political elite refrains from publishing a future vision that could supersede the grievance-archetype furnished by the unequal remembrance of the same events.

Furthermore, the convergence of contested historical episodes with current political agendas presents a persistent threat to the autonomy of the academy and the ethical obligations of the historian. Scholars attempting to revisit and recalibrate foundational narratives frequently encounter a regime of intimidation that includes institutional censorship, public vilification, and the mobilisation of political machinery against them. When the interrogation of the past is folded into partisan imperatives, a corrosive atmosphere arises that both distorts evidence and throttles the collegial exchange that is the lifeblood of historiographical advancement.

Beyond national boundaries, the entanglement of historical quarrels with political rhetoric exerts potent effects on international diplomacy. States and institutions interpret Israeli historical controversies chiefly through the prisms of realpolitik, modulating their approaches to aid, embargoes, and the frameworks of mediation. The resonance of specific historiographical claims on global opinion and policy formulation underscores the necessity of disentangling scholarly enquiry from instrumental political objectives; the echo of domestic historiographical strife is thus magnified into the international arena, where its consequences for mutual recognition and conflict mitigation accrue in inextricable relation to the framing of the past.

Navigating the intersection of political discourse and contested history requires a sophisticated grasp of the diverse and often contradictory forces at work. Achieving such a grasp involves a careful reconciliation of two imperatives: first, a recognition of how history shapes contemporary circumstances, and second, a commitment to dialogue that is genuinely open and inclusive, refusing to be confined by partisan boundaries. By confronting the intricate and layered nature of historical controversies as they coalesce with political stories, Israel may work toward the creation of a space where constructive engagement, empathetic listening, and the gradual articulation of a co-owned historical memory can flourish.

Public Monuments and Their Symbolism

Public monuments manifest the values, collective beliefs, and historiographical choices of the societies that create them. Within the Israeli context, such monuments act as agents of collective memory, continuously negotiating the meanings assigned to the past. The symbolism encoded in each structure often indexes dominant social attitudes toward the events and personages it commemorates. Whether depicting the grandeur of a military achievement or honouring a contentious political figure, a monument quietly announces axioms about national identity and collective orientation.

A salient instance of this dynamic is the itinerary of memorials devoted to both the fallen and the living agents of Israel's recurrent conflicts. These sites of commemoration, while recognising sacrifice, simultaneously propagate paradigmatic tales of survival and moral fortitude. Conversely, the very act of their creation and the ritual of their upkeep can generate dispute, especially when past actions, now scrutinised under more selective or critical lenses, appear ritualised and sacrosanct. The resultant friction between honouring memory and interrogating legacy provokes public discourse about the validity of canonical commemorative projects and invites calls for historiographical pluralism—an insistence that the commemorative landscape encompass a broader spectrum of experiences, traumas, and interpretations.

In addition, public monuments are increasingly envisaged as instruments for reconciliation. Contemporary proposals frequently advocate for memorials that recognise the pain endured by every group embroiled in previous hostilities. Such memorials aim to disrupt the dominance of unilateral historical accounts, inviting instead the compassion and insight of heterogeneous populations. When public environments are reconstituted as arenas of communal mourning rather than of singular veneration, the result is a deliberate choreography of collective mending and social cohesion.

Beyond their physical existence, monuments in Israel exert a symbolic capital that penetrates the political and diplomatic spheres. They can reorient national narratives by foregrounding specific events or figures, thereby swaying public sentiment and inviting legislative re-evaluation. Conversely, the deliberate dismantling or reconfiguration of a given monument is itself a rhetorical gesture, signalling a polity's readiness to re-read its own chronicle and to entertain a more differentiated, reflexive apprehension of the past. Such gestures may publicly index the recalibration of communal values and the acceptance of historical complexity.

Public monuments derive their significance not merely from their material presence, but from the narratives they embody and the dialogues they provoke. Within the contemporary Israeli context—where the permutations of memory and identity remain hotly contested—these monuments assume an ongoing responsibility for the configuration of collective memory and the facilitation of processes aimed at reconciliation. Thus, the critical examination of their placement, design, and reception becomes an indispensable dimension of the broader enquiry into how a society negotiates its multifaceted past.

Grassroots Movements Seeking Reconciliation

Grassroots movements within Israel and the Palestinian territories continue to illuminate the pathway to reconciliation, creating space for healing despite the weight of prolonged confrontation. Emerging from an unwavering commitment to mutual recognition, these collectives reaffirm the enduring strength of civil society even when state-level diplomacy falters. The Bereaved Families Forum stands as a striking illustration of this commitment: Israeli and Palestinian parents, siblings, and spouses alike, forever marked by the death of a loved one, choose to configure their sorrow as a foundation for solidarity. The presence of both Hebrew and Arabic mourning rituals at their gatherings symbolises not only shared loss but also the rejection of loss as a weapon. Together, these families petition for a political landscape that can protect rather than forfeit life.

Central to the efficacy of such movements is the premise that dialogue—intimate, courageous exchange—can alter the currency of enmity. Organisations like Combatants for Peace and the Parents Circle-Families Forum convene space for men and women who have at one time borne arms, or who have become professional mourners, to narrate the moments that reshaped their identities. In these circles, memories of ambush, of burial, of regret become the lexicon of a new, common grammar. The affirmation of one another's suffering, despite earlier convictions that the other was the embodiment of the threat, disrupts both caricature and conflict. For many, these sessions yield not consensus but an unmistakable reconciling currency: recognition. Through successive meetings, participants initiate the slow, tentative reweaving of a social fabric long sustained by the rhetoric of division.

In addition, grassroots organisations have sought to mitigate the socioeconomic inequalities reinforced by the protracted violence. Initiatives centred on educational partnership, economic collaboration, and community-led development have taken root, determined to dismantle walls of mistrust and to weave reciprocal relationships among fragmented populations. The Hand in Hand Centre for Jewish-Arab Education in Israel, for example, pursues a model of bilingual instruction in which students become proficient in both Hebrew and Arabic while grounding their learning in common civic values and shared cultural narratives.

Yet, the journey toward lasting reconciliation is punctuated by formidable impediments, including popular apathy, institutional marginalisation, and violence from both extremist fringe and militant groups. Grassroots organisers frequently confront animosity from hardline constituencies that perceive any dialogue toward coexistence as betrayal. Unfazed, the activists redouble their efforts, underpinned by an ethical resolve for justice. Their relentless resolve illuminates the way forward and encourages wider constituencies to confront the entangled legacies of their respective histories.

In summary, community-based efforts championing reconciliation illuminate possible pathways beyond the entrenched Israeli-Palestinian conflict. Through relentless dialogue initiatives, redress of social inequities, and cultivation of reciprocal comprehension, these movements illuminate the contours of a horizon in which coexistence may eventually replace inherited enmity. The complications confronting the future remain formidable; nevertheless, the dogged dedication and fortitude of local activists attest to the unwavering capacity of the human spirit to persist amid formidable obstacles.

Academic Freedom vs. National Loyalties

Academic freedom and national allegiance frequently intersect—often contentiously—within the domain of historical scholarship. Researchers who illuminate marginalised perspectives or interrogate dominant historiographic assumptions frequently confront a complex triage of obligations. They are driven, firstly, by fidelity to the principles of empirical verification and interpretive rigour, yet simultaneously subject to the sociopolitical forces that demand fidelity to the prevailing national script. Such an impasse invites interrogation of the procedural sovereignty of research, alongside the extra-scientific constraints engendered by loyalties that politicians and citizens alike deem indispensable.

Academic freedom faces added pressure from deeply held national loyalties, particularly in societies still negotiating the legacies of contentious pasts. Efforts to illuminate buried evidence and to reassess systemic wrongs inevitably collide with the official scripts of history endorsed by the state. In this setting, the pursuit of evidence and the critique of silence become, themselves, politically fraught. Scholars consequently walk an epistemic tightrope, striving to uphold the axiom of scholarly detachment while they are simultaneously urged to embrace—and therefore legitimize—the national narrative that the state defaults to in moments of crisis.

The mutually reinforcing relationship between academic liberty and national allegiance generates ramifications beyond the cloisters of the university and the archive. It contaminates curricular design, public debate, and the internal governance of universities. Textbooks in secondary schools are often constructed to legitimize the national story; teachers who venture to interrogate such versions of the past discover that the penalties for divergence are both administrative and social, coming from both state directives and organized segments of civil society that contest even the faintest insinuation of disloyal historiography.

The obstacles that arise from national allegiances are undeniably significant; however, historical experience confirms that they can be effectively addressed. Across time, scholars and social movements have defended academic freedom, frequently at considerable personal cost, and their unwavering commitment underscores the critical value of preserving the integrity of historical interpretation outside the reach of political coercion.

In confronting the interplay of academic liberty and patriotic loyalty, it is essential to cultivate conditions in which countervailing historical viewpoints are not merely tolerated, but actively honoured. A polity that guarantees scholars the latitude to contest established judgements and to investigate disquieting facts effectively enlarges its own self-understanding. Such a discerning and inclusive historiographical stance, in the final analysis, possesses the capacity to outstrip the limitations of national identification and to mediate competing memories.

Toward an Inclusive Historical Dialogue

The advancing of an inclusive historical dialogue confronts persistent obstacles posed by entrenched national attachments and competing memories. Achieving such dialogue demands a collective commitment across every segment of society to recognise and credit divergent accounts, including those that unsettle the dominant collective memory. Central to this undertaking is the establishment of a civic atmosphere in which varied voices may enter the public record and receive equitable attention, free of intimidation or suppression.

Reform of educational policy occupies a decisive place in this process. National curricula serve, in a decisive way, to form young citizens' understandings of the past, and a rigorously balanced presentation of significant themes and episodes cultivates the critical acuity required to engage multilayered memories. Simultaneously, the deliberate inclusion of marginalised and subaltern perspectives in school syllabi assists in dismantling entrenched stereotypes, replaces distortion with documented fact, and nurtures a culture of empathy between pupils who bear different genealogies of memory.

Media institutions play a decisive role in shaping public conversations about historical memory. Journalists and broadcasters have the capacity to direct debates in ways that foster inclusivity and intellectual openness. When they amplify a spectrum of historical perspectives and model civil exchanges, they assist in cultivating a deeper and more textured comprehension of the past, thereby reducing social rifts.

Public monuments and memorials, meanwhile, possess a potent symbolic charge in the collective memory of societies. A considered re-examination of such sites can constitute a decisive act of acknowledgement toward the plurality of lived histories. Whether by erecting supplementary memorials or by re-contextualising the originals, these practices announce a readiness to integrate once-marginalised accounts, thereby widening the ambit of historical discourse.

At the same time, community-led movements committed to reconciliation and dialogue can generate durable transformation. By hosting environments within which citizens may confront past legacies in open, constructive dialogue, these enterprises cultivate sites of healing and mutual comprehension. They empower neighbourhoods to face disquieting truths and collaboratively to forge a historical narrative that honours the complexity and plurality of lived human experience.

The endeavour to establish a genuinely inclusive historical discourse necessitates a fundamental rethinking of national identity itself. A commitment to a narrative that candidly confronts the past's intricacies while validating the distinct experiences of every community represents not a fracture of loyalty, but a bold advance towards a future anchored in veracity and mutual comprehension. Through sustained participation in this reconstitutive undertaking, polities may move beyond entrenched cleavages and create a shared memory that accommodates the entire constellation of human encounters.

***

References

A. Overviews: Israeli Historiography & the "New History" Turn

1. **Segev, Tom** – _1949: The First Israelis_ (Free Press, 1998).
Journalistic narrative that first popularised internal Israeli critique of 1948 myths; still a gateway text for undergraduates.

2. **Silberstein, Laurence J.** – _The Postzionism Debates: Knowledge and Power in Israeli Culture_ (Routledge, 1999).
Maps the academic culture wars of the 1990s that cracked open the official story.

3. **Shapira, Anita** – _Israeli Historical Revisionism: From Left to Right_ (Frank Cass, 2002).
Insider's anatomy of why the "New Historians" provoked establishment backlash.

4. **Zerubavel, Yael** – _Recovered Roots: Collective Memory and the Making of Israeli National Tradition_ (Chicago, 1995).
Classic ethnography of how Independence Day, Lag Ba-Omer, and Holocaust Memorial Day rituals were constructed and contested.

B. Generational & Biographical Perspectives

5. **Feldman, Yael** – _Glory and Agony: Isaac's Sacrifice and National Narrative_ (Stanford, 2010).
Literary study of how the Akedah trope has been mobilised across Israeli fiction, theater, and film to negotiate guilt and heroism.

6. **Almog, Oz** – _The Sabra: The Creation of the New Jew_ (California, 2000).
Tracks the cultural archetype of the native-born Israeli and its gradual erosion under post-1967 critique.

7. **Shenhav, Yehouda & Hever, Hannan (eds.)** – _The Oxford Handbook of Israeli Literature and Society_ (Oxford, 2022).
Multigenerational essays on how Hebrew, Arabic, Russian, and Amharic writers re-narrate 1948 and its aftermath.

C. Education, Curriculum, and Textbooks

8. **Podeh, Elie** – _The Arab-Israeli Conflict in Israeli History Textbooks, 1948-2000_ (Bergin & Garvey, 2002).
Systematic content analysis of how 1948, the Nakba, and refugees were (not) represented.

9. **Naveh, Esther & Yogev, Esther (eds.)** – _Histories and Identities: Israeli Educators Grapple with Contested Narratives_ (Syracuse UP, 2022).
Ethnographic cases of teachers who smuggle alternative sources into classrooms despite Ministry of Education guidelines.

10. **Goldberg, Tsafrir & Ron, Yiftach** – "Teaching the Nakba in Jewish-Israeli Schools," _Journal of Curriculum

Studies_ 54:6 (2022), 1-20.

Empirical study of pilot programmes and parental backlash.

D. Media, Commemoration, and Digital Memory

11. **Liebes, Tamar & Kampf, Zohar** – _Transforming Media Coverage of Violent Conflicts: The New Face of War_ (Palgrave, 2010).

Chapters on how 1948 footage and terminology re-circulate in 21st-century news cycles.

12. **Neiger, Motti & Zandberg, Eyal** – _Media Memory and the Israeli-Palestinian Conflict_ (Palgrave, 2022).

Covers Yom HaZikaron ceremonies, Facebook commemorations, and viral TikTok reenactments of Deir Yassin.

13. **Handel, Ariel** – "Digital Nakba: Virtual Returns and the Politics of Memory," _Jerusalem Quarterly_ 87 (2021), 6-27.

Explores 3-D reconstructions of destroyed villages and their reception inside Israel.

E. Public Monuments, Museums, and Spatial Politics

14. **Azaryahu, Maoz** – _Tel Aviv, the First Century: Visions, Designs, Actualities_ (Indiana, 2012).

Urban biography that unpacks how Independence Hall, Rabin Square, and Nakba graffiti coexist in the cityscape.

15. **Young, James E.** – _The Texture of Memory: Holocaust Memorials and Meaning_ (Yale, 1993) – esp. chapter on Yad Vashem and its ripple effects on 1948 memory.

Comparative framework for analysing how state memorials police or pluralise narratives.

16. **Dumper, Michael & Larkin, Craig** – _Martyrdom and Memory in the Israeli-Palestinian Conflict_ (Routledge, 2022).
Studies roadside shrines, military cemeteries, and "alternative tours" that challenge official geographies of loss.

F. Grassroots Reconciliation & Civil Society Initiatives
17. **Bekerman, Zvi & Zembylas, Michalinos** – _Teaching Contested Narratives: Identity, Memory and Reconciliation in Peace Education and Beyond_ (Cambridge, 2012).
Comparative cases including Hand-in-Hand schools, Wahat al-Salam/Neve Shalom, and Combatants for Peace dialogue groups.

18. **Savir, Uri** – _The Process: 1,100 Days that Changed the Middle East_ (Vintage, 1999).
Insider memoir of Oslo backchannels; still relevant for understanding why grassroots work fills the vacuum left by failed diplomacy.

19. **Hall-Cathala, David** – _The Peace Movement in Israel, 1967-1987_ (Macmillan, 1990).
Genealogy of the first Israeli NGOs that dared to memorialise Palestinian loss.

G. Academic Freedom, Censorship, and the Law
20. **Beinin, Joel & Stein, Rebecca L.** – _The Struggle for Sovereignty: Palestine and Israel, 1993-2005_ (Stanford, 2006).
Chapters on university purges, "Nakba Bill" (2011), and the

chilling effect on scholars.

21. **Rabinowitz, Dan & Abu Baker, Khawla** – _Coffins on Our Shoulders: The Experience of the Palestinian Citizens of Israel_ (California, 2005).
Discusses how Palestinian-Israeli historians navigate loyalty tests inside Israeli academia.

22. **Gross, Aeyal** – "Academic Freedom in a Militant Society: Israel and the Occupation," _Law & Ethics of Human Rights_ 14:2 (2020), 235-273.
Legal analysis of anti-BDS legislation and its impact on research about 1948.

11
The Fall of The Extremist Narratives at the Hands of the New Historians

Extremist Narratives: A Historical Context

Extremist narratives have persistently conditioned public perception and statecraft across the region. Emerging within epochs of crisis, these discourses fused militant ideology with highly selective historiography, constructing superscriptions of the past that decisively oriented both sentiment and policy. Encoded with axiomatic certitudes yet purged of contesting evidence, the narratives fabricated not merely disagreement over historical fact but a quasi-sacred memory that rationalised political and military enterprises. Over successive conflicts and interruptions, the narratives have playbook-like endowed adversarial policies with ostensible historical licence, instilling durable animosities and ritualised animosities. Their reiterative circulation within education, media, and parliamentary debate has furnished successive generations with ready-made moral accounts of the present. Grounded less in empirical debate than in mythologised conviction, the narratives have consolidated collective memory that mandates fidelity at the expense of self-critical revision. Their influence, accordingly, has overflowed scholarly historiography, saturating civic discourse and operationalising in martial slogans. What appears as historiographical debate often bifurcates, sotto voce, into contest over legitimacy itself: the narratives are indistinguishable from the modalities by which the region remembers itself. Disentangling political present from militant past thus requires acknowledging the narrative's constitutional role in constituting both memory and policy.

The analysis requires scrutiny of the disruptive energies once exercised by extremist voices and the persistent markers they have imprinted on collective memory. Illuminating the reach of such narratives simultaneously opens the enquiry toward the counternarratives that refused their hegemony and that proposed alternative interpretations capable of reframing the evidential landscape. This interplay provides the groundwork for a measured revaluation and energetic reinterpretation of the evolving past. Situating extremist claims within the larger historical milieu that nourished their ascent is essential for understanding why successive efforts to modify the inherited paradigm have confronted formidable barriers, a dynamic that now invites a scholarly upheaval informed by critical reflexivity. To appreciate the rise of the New Historians and their decisive reconfiguration of historiographical practice, the investigator must first chart the dense weave of hegemonic narratives that long dictated the rate and shape of the debate, for only from that thorough immersion can the contours of their eventual collapse, catalysed by the new historiographical wave, be fully discerned.

The Birth of the New Historians' Movement

The emergence of the New Historians' Movement constituted a decisive moment in the historiography of Israel and Palestine. Led by a generation of researchers trained in the disciplines of history, sociology, and critical theory, the movement sought to interrogate, dismantle, and re-evaluate the dominant retelling of the State of Israel's founding and its immediate aftermath. Motivated by a principled dedication to the corroboration of historical accuracy, its proponents sifted through government and military archives, press records, and refugee testimonies, thereby exposing previously relegated evidence and contesting long-held consensus. Their enterprise was animated by the conviction that the period had been rendered misleadingly monochromatic, and that a more textured portrait of competing actors and incommensurable human experiences was attainable. The decisive impetus for this historiographical shift derived from the multifaceted sociopolitical milieu in which Israeli universities were embedded during the 1970s and 1980s. The 1967 war, the subsequent territorial settlement, and the gradual militarisation of the national discourse encouraged a critical reevaluation of the nation's past. Encounters with the testimonies of Palestinian displacement, the Arab and Jewish nationalist historiographies, and international scholarly debates encouraged a new cohort of historians to subject the founding myths to disciplined interrogation. The intellectual environment thus engendered an emergent cadre of scholars who possessed the analytic training and institutional commitment to overturn the conventional scholarly consensus.

Moreover, the domestic turbulence and external crises stemming from the Arab-Israeli conflict compelled historians and commentators alike to reassess prevailing narratives, culminating in a heightened insistence on disinterested and self-critical scrutiny of the past. Within that environment, the collective known as the New Historians grasped the moment to loosen the dogmatic fetters that had long constrained scholarly enquiry. Their inquiries, while simultaneously galvanising fierce contests among specialists, also attracted broad public notice, receiving both lauding and censure. The impact of their labours, however, exceeded disputation; they irrevocably reframed the scholarly terrain, facilitating a historiography both wider and more egalitarian in its purview. In venturing into previously sensitive domains and interrogating accepted prohibitions, the New Historians' enterprise positioned itself as a prelude to a more intricate and variegated comprehension of the region's intertwined pasts. This historiographical upheaval inaugurated self-reflection within Israeli civic discourse and radiated into global academic arenas, stimulating a sustained and expansive discourse on the entanglement of historiography, public memory, and the formations of national identity.

Challenging Orthodox Perspectives: Key Debates

The New Historians' Movement decisively reshaped the scholarly investigation of the history of Israel, especially the moment of state creation. Historians including Benny Morris, Ilan Pappé, and Avi Shlaim confronted the longstanding consensus that had pervaded both the academy and the public sphere. At the heart of this intellectual rupture was a critical reassessment of the foundational myths that had long gone unquestioned, provoking fierce and expansive debate both within scholarly journals and in the wider polity.

Central to this contest was the characterisation of the Zionist enterprise and the trajectory that culminated in the establishment of the State of Israel. Established narratives typically celebrated the determined ingathering of Jewish settlement as a noble reclamation of an ancestral homeland, framed in terms of an exalted David-and-Goliath heroism. The New Historians, however, applied a systematic and often archival-driven critique to this schema, exploring the negotiated purchase of land, the incremental but consequential dislocation of Arab populations, and the multi-layered military calculus that guided the embryonic state. In so doing, they illuminated aspects of the state's inception that had long been obscured, thereby destabilising the glorified horizon within which the founding had previously been situated.

The New Historians reinvigorated contentious debate over the Palestinian exodus of 1948, introducing interpretations that directly contradicted the long-dominant view of voluntary Arab flight. By scrutinising newly released archives, interviewing key actors, and re-evaluating Israeli State documentation, they underscored patterns of intentional removal and systematic intimidation that accompanied the uprooting of Palestinian societies. These findings unsettled established readings of the exodus, forcing a reconfiguration of historical responsibility and legal-moral liability across the fields of diplomatic history and human rights scholarship.

A second focal point of the controversies was the way nationalist historiography has shaped Israeli collective memory and national identity. The older paradigms, animated by accounts of redemptive conquest and defensive valour, sustained a heroic national mythology that served to bolster political unity and public morale. The New Historians, by contrast, problematised this heroic narrative, prompting an overdue confrontation with historical disquiet. Through a critical unmasking of cherished fables and a confrontation with the less-commemorated dimensions of state formation, they instigated a public re-examination of memory, encouraging an ideological recalibration that unsettled even the most entrenched registers of political culture.

The New Historians' rigorous analyses have moved well past scholarly circles, triggering a major reevaluation of long-accepted narratives about the founding of Israel. By persistently exposing concealed facts and challenging silence around sensitive issues, they have compelled a deep reconsideration of the interwoven dynamics of authority, land dispossession, and collective memory. The resulting critically dialogue with traditional accounts has pushed Israeli historiography itself into fresh epistemological space, marking the beginning of a sustained effort to reconcile accurate reporting of the past with ethical responsibility.

Benny Morris: Archival Scholarship and Its Public Consequences

In contemporary historiography, Benny Morris commands attention both for the precision of his archival labour and for the controversies that have attached themselves to his findings. Morris's early studies of the 1948 War, particles of which were mined from the newly accessible Israeli state archives, have rerouted scholarly and popular understandings of the conflict, exposing the friction between documentary evidence and collective memory. The publisher's trade and the lecture hall testify to the bilingualism of his influence: for politicians and journalists, his name has become shorthand for the treacherous truth that can emerge from meticulous analysis; for historians, it underscores the merit and the peril of exposing inconvenient evidence. Morris's work is animated, above all, by the conviction that the discipline demands fidelity to what the record can both confirm and contest, however explosive the conclusions. By insisting that the records of Jewish paramilitary behaviours and Palestinian dilemmas be read alongside one another, he has complicated binary explanations of national trauma and has forced audiences to account for the contingent, often brutal, decisions that structured the season of flight. The weight of his archival corpus, however, is not solely in the catalogue of events; it challenges the terms by which memory, narrative, and accountability are ordinarily negotiated, prompting historians to reconsider the historiographical devices that mediate between past and public. Morris's combination of erudition and courage in pursuing the archival record has, in this sense, not enlarged the library of the Israeli-Palestinian conflict so much as it has redrawn the limits of acceptable evidence in any attempt to narrate the tumult.

Furthermore, Morris's impact reaches well beyond the academy, affecting wider civic and political discourse, where his scholarship has elicited both public reflection and personal reckonings. The persistence of his arguments compels a stern re-examination of earlier decisions and their long-lasting consequences. His scrupulous attention to archival evidence, coupled with an unflinching confrontation of divisive episodes, secures Morris's position as a pivotal scholar in the continuing re-evaluation of the Israeli past.

Ilan Pappé and the Provocation of Academic Orthodoxy

Ilan Pappé, an Israeli historian broadly identified with the New Historians, has positioned himself as an incisive critic of the historiographical orthodoxy governing interpretations of the Israeli state's genesis. His scholarship has elicited vigorous debate, and even censure, particularly his framing of the 1948 Palestinian exodus as an act of ethnic cleansing. By scrutinising the founding of Israel alongside the systematic uprooting of Palestinians, Pappé has disturbed the intellectual equilibrium of prevailing Zionist historiography. His resolute insistence on anchoring interpretation in an expansive corpus of newly accessible archival records and oral testimonies from both Jewish and Palestinian witnesses has expanded the methodological aperture of the field and syndetic narrative, while, concurrently, contesting the foundational Zionist chronotope. In The Ethnic Cleansing of Palestine, Pappé combines archival excavation with a narrative of intentionality, thereby displacing the apologetic tropes typical of earlier Israeli histories. Through a detailed examination of Israeli military directives, government correspondence, and local administrative files, he has exposed the congruence of military, political, and settler-colonial imperatives, situating the 1948 dynamics within a calculated calculus of demographic engineering. Pappé's commitment to a porous multidisciplinary framework—including political theory, memory studies, and moral philosophy—underscores his contention that the discipline must confront vexed and morally charged dimensions of the past, even at the periphery of scholarly convention and personal conviction.

The resonance of his scholarship extends well beyond the university setting, energising ongoing discourse about the ethical duties of historians and warning against the consequences that historiographical choices hold for live arguments over justice and reconciliation in the Middle East. Ignoring disciplinary boundaries, Pappé insists that the production of knowledge cannot remain indifferent to its social consequences, thereby breathing new life into academic research while simultaneously inviting sustained meditation on how competing narratives are forged under the pressure of military and political domination. By pressing scholars to confront the fraught temporality of their subjects, he unsettles the traditional portrait of the historian as a neutral observer and reveals how the assumed foundations of factual accuracy are always already layered with contesting ideologies. Pappé's continued insistence on a self-reflexive and politically engaged scholarship compels a fresh interrogation of the archives and a relentless critique of the ideologies that colour their reading, ensuring that the past remains a site of political significance for the present and the possible.

Avi Shlaim's Diplomatic Insights and Military Strategy Analyses

Avi Shlaim, a leading figure in the New Historians movement, occupies a critical, yet nuanced, scholarly vantage point from which to interrogate the orthodox renditions of Israeli diplomacy and military praxis. His work, whose scrupulous documentation and analytical breadth have earned him a wide and deserved readership, exposes the contingencies and contradictions at the heart of sixties and seventies Israeli decisions. Through sustained examination of newly released archival correspondence and a series of interviews with principal actors, Shlaim has recovered evidence that alters, and in some cases upends, earlier simplifications. His enquiry, however, refuses the label revisionist, since it does not seek merely to correct the record but to reconstitute the explanatory framework itself. The texture of his argument thus shifts the focus from actors alone to the interwoven fields of power, diplomacy, and war. In so doing, Shlaim elucidates how international patronage, domestic factionalism and military logic converged in the shaping of pivotal confrontations. His detailed dissections of specific diplomatic overtures, battlefield decisions, and their international reverberations reveal a realm in which contingency and calculation are inseparable, and the resulting portrait is at once illuminating and unsettling to settled perceptions of Israeli agency and rationality.

In addition, Avi Shlaim's work exemplifies how rigorous historical research continues to inform and sharpen contemporary discussions. By examining both diplomatic tactics and military operations, he offers a perspicuous analytic framework that illuminates how past events continue to inform present power relations. Shlaim's careful reconstruction of successive crises underscores the layered interplay of intentions, decisions, and unforeseen repercussions that constitutes the region's historical formation. His achievement consists, therefore, not merely in recounting the past but in demonstrating that sustained, critical enquiry is essential for any responsible evaluation of the present and for forecasting the future trajectories that those contemporary actions may engender.

Host scholars of the New Historians have similarly unsettled national memory by confronting and reinterpreting the supposed consensus version of recent events. Their work exposes the selective processes through which societies remember some episodes while quietly omitting or re-framing others. By foregrounding archival material previously ignored or occluded, these historians invite wider publics to question the reliability of long-settled understandings. In so doing, they have expanded the domain of acceptable debate and have encouraged a re-evaluation of symbols, vocabularies, and rites that previously sustained a uniform national identity. The circulation of their arguments in both academic and mass media therefore exemplifies how historiography may intervene in and eventually alter the character of common memory.

Iconoclastic Views: The Impact on Popular Memory

One notable consequence of iconoclastic scholarship is the consequent alteration of communal memory concerning previous wars and their legacies. Revisionist readings put forward by the New Historians have compelled students, educators, and the public to interrogate deeply ingrained convictions and to recalibrate their grasp of specific episodes. Accordingly, collective memory, once guided largely by authoritative but partial narratives, has been obliged to accommodate the newly foregrounded evidence, thereby engendering a thicker and more stratified comprehension of the record.

In addition, the iconoclastic arguments of the New Historians have generated a wide-ranging and, at times, acrimonious public deliberation. By interrogating the hegemonic historiography and marshalling fresh documentation to lend credence to alternative reconstructions, these researchers have precipitated deliberation in academic, media, and civic forums. Such vigorous exchange has not only deepened the quality of public argument but has also been instrumental in recalibrating present-day orientations toward the corpus of matrices that historiography attempts to interpret.

Iconoclastic historiography has similarly left a decisive imprint upon both the formal curriculum and the structures of scholarly debate. Alternative explanatory models articulated by the New Historians have obliged curriculum designers, textbook authors, and researchers to rethink the pedagogical and analytical plotting of the past. The cumulative effect has been the formation of a more textured, heterogeneous, and, crucially, self-questioning rendition of past conflicts, thereby cultivating a more aware and discerning engagement with their inhering complexities.

Associated perspectives on historicity have strikingly remapped the depiction of past events in cultural media—literature, visual art, and audiovisual production alike—in the contemporary age. The deconstruction of canonical frames has afforded creators novel angles of enquiry and imaginative latitude, permitting them to interrogate, reword, and represent these events in ways that productively pluralise cultural memory and expand its representational vocabularies.

Ultimately, the insurgent scholarship of the New Historians has indelibly recalibrated the collective memory of the nation, provoking sustained critique and fresh appraisal of received chronicles. Its resonance does not linger only in academic debate, but has diffused throughout public discourse, shaping enduring public dispositions and collective attitudes toward the past.

Reassessing Historical Accuracy: Evidence vs. Ideology

As the New Historians methodically question the dominant historiography, the issue of historical accuracy gains unprecedented urgency. Their thorough re-examination of key episodes confronts the traditional consensus, insisting that the verification of the past must hinge solely on documentary confirmation rather than on pre-existing ideological commitments. Long before these earlier interpretations had come to be regarded as canonical, they had already been infused with nationalist imperatives that crystallised collective memory. The New Historians, by contrast, invoke a methodical, forensic sensibility, scouring unconsulted archival holdings and calling forth taciturn witnesses to re-frame the object of study. The result is a visible rupture that juxtaposes durable ideological formulae against the obstinate evidence that such narratives had tended to ignore.

The task thus re-imposed, however, is anything but facile. The commitment to recovering historical accuracy obliges the researcher to move across a swamp of entrenched interests and institutional resistances. Such navigation is only possible by subjecting the documentary record to a magnanimous, but unrelenting, critique. Archival fragments, memory, and artefacts are isolated, catalogued, and interrogated; the lenses of state, ideology, and collective memory are simultaneously dismantled. Through this iterative process, the historian endeavours to render the saturated surface of collective recollection transparent, so that the coarse and unadorned material of the past becomes diplomatically discernible.

Moreover, by systematically reconstructing historical phenomena because of documented evidence, the New Historians expose the covert distortions of data that have been employed to bolster dominant ideological constructs. Such exposure dislodges the scaffolding of credulity upon which long-cherished convictions have rested, obliging a polity to face the disquieting verities it has habitually disavowed and to reconsider the axioms upon which its collective identity has been erected. The encounter between verifiable data and partisan doctrine generates a field in which the alloy of historical verity is repeatedly tempered, invalidating received dogmas and yielding a more complicated and, ultimately, a more truthful comprehension of the temporal continuum.

In this context, the elevation of documented fact above sedimented belief alters the terms of historical debate, confronting authoritative constructs with the unyielding mandate of evidential rigour. The New Historians excavate, re-contextualise, and publicly confront the traces of the past, thereby demanding that historiography be re-anchored upon data that no ideological preconception can dislodge. This reorientation defers the designation of historical accuracy to a variable field that is irrepressibly reconstituted by the rigorous and non-negotiable force of evidence, thereby deepening our cognisance of the past and announcing the opening of a decisive phase in historiographical enquiry.

Public Reception and Intellectual Resistance

The introduction of the New Historians, along with their revisionist reconfigurations of Israel's past, has ignited a polemical crossroads that intersects scholarly debate and everyday discourse in palpably divergent ways. This chapter examines the contrapuntal phenomena of public reception and scholarly pushback that have framed the New Historians' ingress into collective memory.

Central to the controversy is the New Historians' disruption of sedimented national master narratives. Their re-examination of the 1948 conflagration and the attendant processes of displacement has undermined the staple tropes that historians, educators, and commemorative practices long sustained, thereby provoking visceral and disciplined resistance alike. Within the academy, the reception has fissured along partisan fault lines: some scholars commend the reconstituted archive as a necessary corrective to commemorative amnesia, while others denounce it as tendentious, selective, and corrosive to the historical continuity the polity requires. Beyond the seminar room, the public has mirrored this polarisation, subjecting the historians to condemnation, avid readership, or both, in crude registers of memory and forgetting.

The empirical claims announced in seminal monographs and subsequent compilations have, in consequence, attracted sustained counter-investigation. Conservative historians and commentators—many of whom sympathetic to foundational historiography—have raised epistemological questions about the provenance, synthesis, and interpretive filters the New Historians employ. They contend that the archival assemblages, though legally acquired, transmit a jurisprudential mode of argument that prioritises guilt over nuance and that the authors' political backgrounds compromise the necessary detachment of the scholarly vocation. Illustrative debates about the Palestinian refugee experience, the systematicity of the Haganah's operations, and the compositional structure of the Israeli archives have thus acquired both pedagogical and disciplinary stakes, repeatedly re-injecting the controversy into the scholarly mainstream.

Facing critiques from eminent historians and prominent political representatives, the New Historians have been compelled to defend their archival methodologies and scholarly integrity within an atmosphere of pointed suspicion and vigorous debate. The need for incessant and detailed rebuttal has reinforced the recognition that the historiographies emerging from the region cannot be disentangled from the partisan dynamics that currently animate Israeli public life. Interpretive choices, whether regarding the 1948 War or subsequent state policies, are, accordingly, subjected to the same partisan reading that would shape policy or electoral behaviour today.

Media channels and public spectacles have, accordingly, become both forum and arena for the replication and refutation of New Historical writing. Impassioned symposia, baroque literary controversies, and the immediacy of televised discussion have permitted the continual re-examination of contested archival evidence. More consequentially, they have also illuminated the fractures within contemporary Israeli society, revealing how disagreements over the past are immediately linked to divergent imaginaries of the nation's present and future. The effect has been that the New Historians' narratives have crystallised into a symbol for broader negotiations over identity, memory, and authority.

In tracing the arc of public reception and scholarly rebuttal, one registers how the New Historians' impact is now felt outside the seminar room. Their writing has entered the discourse of political activism, educational policy, and cultural production, compelling citizens and officials alike to confront the past with an explanatory pressure seldom matched by earlier generations of historians.

Their lasting impact and persistent sway over how history is conceptualised and how national identity is experienced will be the essential vantage point from which subsequent phases of historiographical investigation and collective reflection must be discerned.

Conclusion: The Enduring Impact and the Path's Ahead

The culminating phase of this enquiry discloses a field in motion, shaped equally by scholarly innovation, civic debate, and the practices of the state. The New Historians have irrevocably redrafted the chronicles of Israel's inception, and in the process have prompted a fundamental reconceptualization of collective memory and of the identitarian projects that derive from it. Extremist genealogies are now subjected to a withering interrogation that in turn steers the evolving historiography toward a calibrated, polyphonic confrontation with the past. The New Historians' readiness to unsettle institutionalised interpretations has itself become a historiographical signal, obligating successors to interrogate, rather than inherit, evidentiary canon and to expose, rather than suppress, disquieting verities. Yet, their critical outputs have also incited a broader social confrontation, obliging individuals, educational bodies, and civic institutions to renegotiate the terms of their attachment to the past and the historiographical edifice that sustains national, and transnational, narrative frameworks.

The continuing influence of the New Historians is observable in the recalibration of public discourse and the drafting of policy. Their revisionist orientation has catalysed contests within the discipline and the wider public, producing an acute sensitivity to the opacities embedded in master narratives. This sensitivity imposes an emergent scholarly and civic duty to scrutinise settled doctrines and unexamined premises, thereby nurturing an ethos of enquiry that is both progressively expansive and acoustically plural. Within this shifting terrain, the New Historians are bequeathing an expansive orientation that advances a historiography more attuned to marginalised voices and to the ethical necessity of grappling with dissonant and rival truths.

Anticipating forthcoming scholarly pathways, the New Historians have established an enduring intellectual ethos that prizes academic bravery and the relentless questioning of inherited certainties. This ethos, in turn, invites early-career historians, educators, and policymakers alike to pursue narratives that, rather than fortifying dogmatic boundaries, foreground an unwavering fidelity to empirical evidence and to the lived experiences of the governed. The aftershocks of their audacious research continue to resonate within the present-day world, urging renewed scrutiny of the origin myths that shape both national identities and the collective imaginaries by which societies orient their futures. At the same time, the lasting influence of the New Historians requires their successors to regard the recuperation of silenced or marginalised accounts as a professional and ethical imperative, since such accounts possess the capacity to reveal the polyvalent character of historical phenomena and to nurture the gradual cultivation of mutual recognition and negotiated reconciliation.

Ultimately, the eclipse of extremist historiographies by the New Historians denotes more than a correction of the formal record; it denotes a seismic reordering of the modalities by which polities negotiate their temporal horizons—past, present, and future alike.

References For Further Reading

A. Foundational & Critical Studies on "Extremist" or Hegemonic Memory

1. **Kimmerling, Baruch** - _Politicide: Ariel Sharon's War against the Palestinians_ (Verso, 2006).
Dissects how militarised nationalist discourse became state common-sense, marginalising dissenting historiography.

2. **Ram, Uri** - _The Globalization of Israel: McWorld in Tel Aviv, Jihad in Jerusalem_ (Routledge, 2008).
Explores the interplay of neoliberal consumerism and ethno-religious extremism in shaping Israeli memory politics.

3. **Peri, Yoram** - _Generals in the Cabinet Room: How the Military Shapes Israeli Policy_ (USIP, 2006).
Traces how ex-generals translate battlefield narratives into civilian policy scripts, constraining historical debate.

4. **Shenhav, Yehouda** - _Beyond the Two-State Solution: A Jewish Political Essay_ (Polity, 2012).

Deconstructs the "demographic anxiety" trope and its extremist deployment since 1948.

B. The New Historians – Core Monographs & Collective Portraits

5. **Shlaim, Avi** – _The Iron Wall: Israel and the Arab World_ (Norton, 2001).
Classic diplomatic history that foregrounds Israeli expansionism and refugee creation, framed in archival detail.

6. **Morris, Benny** – _Righteous Victims: A History of the Zionist-Arab Conflict, 1881-2001_ (Vintage, 2001).
Sweeping synthesis that still anchors the New Historians' corpus; pair with his later autobiographical reflections.

7. **Pappé, Ilan** – _Ten Myths About Israel_ (Verso, 2017).
Short, polemical primer that translates New Historians' findings for a popular audience.

8. **Shafir, Gershon & Peled, Yoav** – _Being Israeli: The Dynamics of Multiple Citizenship_ (Cambridge, 2002).
Sociological lens on how competing nationalist narratives are institutionalised in law, land policy, and memory.

C. Archival Method & Evidentiary Debates
9. **Gelber, Yoav** – _Palestine 1948: War, Escape and the Emergence of the Palestinian Refugee Problem_ (Sussex, 2006).
Conservative rebuttal to Morris/Pappé; indispensable for understanding evidentiary fault lines.

10. **Sela, Avraham & Kadish, Alon** – "The New Historians: A Critical Appraisal," _Israel Studies_ 15:2 (2010), 1-52.
Special issue featuring archival audits, declassified minutes, and methodological critiques from both camps.

11. **Khalidi, Rashid** – "The Palestinians and 1948: The Underlying Causes of Failure," in _The War for Palestine_, 2nd ed. (Cambridge, 2007).
Palestinian historian's assessment of how New Historians corroborate or diverge from Arab archives.

D. Memory Wars in Education, Media & Law
12. **Firer, Ruth** – "The Presentation of the 1948 War in Israeli School Textbooks," _Holy Land Studies_ 3:1 (2004), 55-74.
Content analysis showing how extremist tropes ("empty land," "voluntary flight") were institutionalised.

13. **Gross, Zehavit & Maoz, Ifat** – _The Israeli-Palestinian Conflict in the Israeli Psychology Curriculum_ (Springer, 2021).
Examines how psychological discourses of fear and trauma reinforce extremist historical scripts.

14. **Lentin, Ronit** – "Israel's Holocaust/Nakba Law: Memory, Lawfare, and the Criminalisation of Counter-Memory," _Ethnic & Racial Studies_ 41:11 (2018), 2016-2034.
Legal-ethnographic study of the 2011 "Nakba Bill" and its chilling effects on public commemoration.

E. Digital & Visual Cultures of Extremist Memory
15. **Kuntsman, Adi & Stein, Rebecca** – _Digital Mili-

tarism: Israel's Occupation in the Social Media Age_ (Stanford, 2015).

Tracks how memes, viral videos, and emoji militarise historical grievance in real time.

16. **Handel, Ariel** – "Military Memes and the Digital Reenactment of 1948," _Journal of Visual Culture_ 20:2 (2021), 165-184.

Case-study of TikTok and Instagram reels that remix archival footage into extremist narratives.

F. Grassroots & Artistic Counter-Memory

17. **Bishara, Amahl** – _Back Stories: U.S. News Production and Palestinian Politics_ (Stanford, 2013).

Anthropology of Palestinian citizen-journalists who contest Israeli extremist memory from within the state.

18. **Yosef, Raz** – _The Politics of Loss and Trauma in Contemporary Israeli Cinema_ (Rutgers, 2011).

Film analysis showing how Israeli filmmakers (Waltz with Bashir, Lebanon) subvert martial heroism.

19. **Slyomovics, Susan** – _The Object of Memory: Arab and Jew Narrate the Palestinian Village_ (Penn, 1998).

Ethnography of coexistence initiatives that curate 1948 memory against extremist erasure.

G. Academic Freedom & Reprisals

20. **Beinin, Joel & Hajjar, Lisa** – "Palestine, Israel and the Arab-Israeli Conflict: A Primer," Middle East Research & Information Project (2023).

Continuously updated dossier on academic boycotts, visa

denials, and tenure cases.

21. **Rabinowitz, Dan & Abu-Zahra, Nadia** – "Weaponising Antisemitism: The IHRA Definition and the Silencing of Nakba Scholarship," _Race & Class_ 64:1 (2022), 3-24.

Critical account of how allegations of extremism are mobilised to police academic speech.

12
Israel: A Lie Debunked
A Society About To Implode

The Historical Divisions of Israeli Society

The historical imprint of Israeli society emerges from a sustained record of movements, migrations, and stratifications that stretch back millennia. From antiquity, varying degrees of ethnic, sectarian, and political contention provided the brittle groundwork on which later communal fault lines would crystallise. Jewish, Arab, Druze, and Bedouin groups persisted alongside—rather than assimilating into—one another, the resulting mosaic exhibiting a remarkable variety that alternately enriched and embittered civic life.

Twentieth-century milestones, notably the British Mandate, the 1948 Declaration of Independence, and the successive confrontations of the 1967 and 1973 wars, realigned territorial borders and accentuated pre-existing cleavages. Each rupture imposed new waves of trauma on particular sectors of society, while the attendant population transfers, state-building programmes, and military stratifications entrenched spatial and economic discontinuities. A formalised class hierarchy then crystallised, whereby centres of capital accumulation and infrastructural investment coincided with particular demographic groups, leaving peripheral communities to navigate a less forgiving economic environment.

The Aliyah movement, with successive migrations from Europe, North Africa, the Middle East and later, the former Soviet Union and Ethiopia, composites yet another stratum of differentiation. Each wave carried exclusive customs, languages, and senses of belonging, which the colonial apparatus of settlement and state consolidation wove into a polity simultaneously aspiring to unity and to hierarchisation.

Waves of immigration from Europe, North Africa, the Middle East, and Ethiopia have infused Israel with distinctive cultures, each settlement adding its dialect, cuisine, religious calendar, and mnemonic of loss and renewal to the communal table. This aggregation of difference, while enhancing the nation's pluralistic character, has concurrently produced friction, as groups insist upon the visibility and continuity of their inherited customs even when these contrast with the main Israeli vernacular surrounding them. The attempt to harmonise multiple calendars, dress codes and jurisprudential sources within a single legal and civic framework has, at times, rendered difference into a focal point of grievance rather than a quiet enrichment.

Compounding these cultural frictions is the protracted contest over land and sovereignty. The fate of Jerusalem, at once the religious capital of Jewry, Christendom and Islam, crystallises deeper claims, while the interactions with the Palestinian territories and their inhabitants have institutionalised rival narratives into both legislation and everyday rhetoric. Views on security, settlement, negotiations and conciliatory initiatives are seldom isolated opinions; rather, they crystallise into mutual disbelief, fault lines within families, professional rivalries, and educational silos. These ideological gulfs, codified in national documents and in the street, render the discussion of the shared future a cacophony of competing futures, each anchored in a selectively rehearsed history.

Historically, then, the fragmentation of Israeli society must be apprehended as an interwoven matrix rather than a succession of discrete clefts. Cultural traditions, religious loyalties, stratified political loyalties, and uneven patterns of capital distribution have fused into a single ongoing pluralistic experiment, one in which fragmentation is not an interruption of harmony but its continuing, dynamic stage. Only through careful excavation of these interlocking origins can the analyst render the present fragmentation legible and, perhaps, chart productive paths toward reconciliation that respect the resilience of difference without denying the claim of collective sovereignty.

Economic Inequality and Class Stratification

Economic inequality and class stratification continue to interlace within the overall fabric of Israeli society. The nation's economic cartography resembles a heterogeneous quilt whose uneven patches of advantage and disadvantage were quilted across successive decades. At the summit of this cartography, a limited echelon of capital accumulates wealth and prestige, while a large portion of the populace contends with fragile livelihoods and circumscribed mobility. The persistence of this economic rift—between the affluent few and the exposed many—has marked successive decades and reverberated across the nation's political, educational, and health domains.

The genealogical trajectory of the present inequality can be located in the formative decades of statehood, when successive waves of immigration and nation-building shaped both rural and urban economic nodes. The arrival of migrants bearing heterogeneous cultural and vocational legacies facilitated the segmentation of the economy: certain groups quickly secured high-demand licences, urban employment, and state contracts, while others were channelled into low-wage sectors with few advancement pathways. Grasping how these early allocations of capital and obligation were calibrated remains essential to understanding the contemporary persistence of group-based advantage and disadvantage.

Class stratification today reveals the solidification of this early distribution. The economic spectrum is marked by a shrinking circle of families concentrated within the highest income deciles, whose educational, cultural, and financial capital beget a recursive advantage. In juxtaposition, the lowest quintile—often composed of sizeable families and migrants from peripheral towns—experiences cumulative indebtedness and limited relation to either political leverage or mobility-enhancing institutions.

This division involves far more than differences in income. It infects educational opportunity, access to medical services, and, more broadly, the very measure of life quality. In all of Israel's largest cities, one need only observe the urban cartography to grasp the situation: gated neighbourhoods rise immediately beside unmaintained blocks, framing a visible, unarguable chart of two diverging realities on a single city map.

At the same time, the compound forces of globalisation, rapid technological change, and unregulated market competition have only intensified the divide, pushing Israel's cleavages deeper and wider. When these forces merge, they exacerbate the drift toward economic polarisation, driving the gulf ever wider between the affluent strata and the groups locked in persistent, downward mobility. Such enlargement of the divide not only affirms how deeply inequality is woven into the national fabric but also highlights the extraordinary difficulty of reversing or even reducing the breach.

The currents of class stratification are now inseparable from wider social phenomena, shaping not only allegiance to political parties but also the texture of local community ties and the feasibility of genuine upward economic movement. Economic disparity inscribes itself in every public sphere, triggering critical enquiry into the morality of wealth distribution, the moral imperative to correct unequal starts, and the feasibility of policies that genuinely embrace the entire populace. Such debates do not merely circulate as political rhetoric; they illustrate the systemic routes by which material difference translates into institutional distinction, stimulating both fierce argument and strategic advocacy.

Given this portrait, a rigorous examination of economic inequality and its stratified consequences is not optional; it is a condition of intellectual and practical engagement with Israeli society as a whole. A critical, stepwise excavation of the valuation, mobility, and cultural practices that animate stratification reveals not only which groups are scoring visible and measurable gains but also which social mechanisms are reproducing relative deprivation. Only through this analytical labour can observers hope to clarify the limits and potentials embedded in the pursuit of a society that is demonstrably both just and cohesive.

Religious Fragmentation: Secularism vs. Orthodoxy

The religious landscape of Israeli society exemplifies the larger tensions that shape the state. The secular-orthodox divide continues to inform social relations, since Israel's designation as a Jewish state situates religious identity within the very frame of nationalism. This proximity, while conferring a sense of collective Jewish meaning, simultaneously produces fracture, as secular and orthodox sectors negotiate divergent claims to the public square.

Modern secularism, associated with broad contemporary and liberal values, calls for the disentanglement of religious law from state function. Proponents envision a multicultural polity in which the conscience of the individual—whether theistic, atheistic, or agnostic—retains sovereign standing. Orthodoxy, in contrast, calls for fidelity to Halakhah and traditional rituals, insisting that religious imperatives must govern public policy as well as private moral conduct.

The contention between the two is evident across multiple domains. In politics, legislation concerning divorce, the conscription of religious students, and the status of the Sabbath as a day of rest precipitates acute public conflict, exposing the incommensurable priorities that each camp endorses. Parallel fractures emerge in the education sector, where parallel curricula and institutional regimes respond to the distinct epistemological and identity-based imperatives articulated by secular and orthodox leaders.

Consequently, the fracture lines of religious plurality remain visible during day-to-day exchanges, colouring household customs, neighbourhood connections, and ritual life. The endeavour to establish a unified national identity must contend with these centrifugal forces, accentuating the protracted negotiation of how to fit divergent religious convictions into a common sense of citizenship and belonging.

At the same time, between these tensions, emerging partnerships and organised dialogue suggest a possible redress. Local-level projects and broader interreligious networks invite collaboration between secular and traditional groups, encouraging empathetic engagement and cooperative enterprise. Such initiatives testify to a durable anthropological impulse that outlives sectarian division, suggesting that Israel's variegated religious fabric may, with concerted effort, evolve toward a future that is both more unified and more respectful of its manifold sources of meaning.

Ethnic and Cultural Diversity: A Melting Pot or a Boiling Cauldron?

The intricate weave of ethnic and cultural diversity within Israeli society constitutes an enduring contest between coexistence and contestation. Communities defined by divergent heritages—Ashkenazi and Mizrahi Jews, Palestinian Arabs, Druze and Bedouin groups—overlay the territory, each contributing distinct languages, rituals, and collective memories. The envisaged Israeli 'melting pot' posits an eventual harmonisation, whereby varied traditions fuse into a singular civic identity. Yet, this aspirational formulation is often contested; critics assert that its rhetoric encourages a tacit pressure toward cultural homogeneity that risks erasing minority customs and historical narratives.

Juxtaposed to the 'melting pot' is the 'boiling cauldron,' a formulation that captures the ferocity of enduring antagonisms. Here, the emphasis falls on asymmetrical power relations, colonial legacies, and a legacy of wars, each of which exacerbates rather than reconciles difference. Episodes of interpersonal violence, institutional discrimination, and differential access to the state's resources galvanise this imagery, which serves to expose rather than elide the fractures. Within this frame, ethnic and cultural boundaries remain porous but oppositional; coexistence is present, yet undergirded by a persistent, unresolved contest over voice, recognition, and the terms of collective existence.

Engaging with the complex constellation of ethnic and cultural diversity obliges us to respect the layered histories that shape each community, while simultaneously confronting entrenched inequalities that sustain conflict. True progress surpasses the passive acceptance of difference; it hinges on actively nurturing the distinctive customs and languages of every group. This goal demands carefully crafted policies that ensure equitable access to political voice, social institutions, and cultural preservation, thereby validating the worth of all persons and communities embraced by the polity.

Equally, the work of bridging long-standing divides rests on disciplined practices of transparent dialogue and reciprocal recognition. When societies acknowledge the composite but often uneven historical experiences of their constituent groups, avenues open for empathy, restitution, and converging narratives that strengthen collective identity. Formal education remains the cornerstone of this effort, offering curricula that illuminate the shared humanity in varied cultural practices and thereby cultivating the dispositions of respect and inclusiveness that future citizens will require to sustain a vibrant, pluralistic democracy.

The ever-evolving character of Israeli society requires a discernible yet flexible strategy to reconcile the quest for a cohesive national identity with the safeguarding of cultural pluralism. The ideal of a 'melting pot' that respects constituent identities without dissolving them, yet is carefully insulated from the fractious potential of a 'boiling cauldron,' obliges policymakers to cultivate a sophisticated equilibrium. This equilibrium must recognise multiple, sometimes conflicting, layers of belonging while remaining oriented toward a shared future that is both integrative and pluralistically enriching.

The Political Chasm: Left, Right, and Everything In-Between

Israel's political environment is characterised by a large and persistent ideological chasm that runs from the far left through the centre to the far right, albeit with a multiplicity of intermediate positions that constantly reconfigure the overall spectrum. This chasm is animated by the shifting force of four interrelated domains: rival historical narratives, competing religious claims, existential security imperatives, and territorial controversies, any of which can tilt an individual or collective actor toward one political pole or to another. The left-of-centre parties generally call for a diplomatic resolution to the Palestinian question, favouring diplomatic gestures, the fortification of civil rights for minorities, and secular civic norms. Conversely, the right-wing coalition insists upon the imperative of deterrence, presses for an expansionist reading of national borders, and seeks to anchor Israeli identity within religious nationalism and traditional hierarchies. Centrist formations, often under stress, occupy the narrower space between these alternatives, striving to satisfy the divergent expectations of mixed constituencies. The resulting ideological contests have indelibly engraved themselves upon the formal governance structure, yet their reach is far deeper: public opinions, civic practices, cultural production, and private lives have all been reconfigured by persistent, often bitter, political rivalry. The chasm is thus both a political and an existential formation, whose ripples can be felt in the coffee-house debates as easily as in the plenary sessions of the Knesset.

Public discourse, media coverage, and educational frameworks are all subtly directed by the prevailing political environment, which in turn moulds both personal worldviews and collective community orientations. The Israeli parliament's proportional electoral system, which frequently produces multi-faction coalitions, serves as a structural mirror of the society's layered divisions. Such divisions spill over into ethnic and ideological fault lines that colour daily life, transforming political loyalty into a matter of intimate identification. Within this discord, however, the articulated pluralism fuels a persistent contestation of normative assumptions, contributing to the gradually evolving discourse over the nation's direction. The same political plurality, nonetheless, inhibits the forging of durable agreements, obstructing decisive collective action on pressing matters of governance and security. Historical, religious, and identity-based legacies entwine to institutionalise these divisions, revealing the intensity of both consensus and contest. Hence, the immediate ethical and pragmatic task is to identify frameworks that encourage respectful cross-partisan dialogue and nurturing reciprocal recognition, thereby enhancing the possibility of a more integrated and equitable civic order.

The Role of Education in Shaping Social Perspectives

Education functions as the foundational bedrock upon which societies are built, fundamentally influencing the formation of individuals' beliefs, values, and interpretive frameworks. Within Israel's complex social reality, the educational sphere's capacity to either sustain or contest entrenched social divisions remains a decisive factor. Schools surpass the role of knowledge transmission, evolving instead into influential settings in which youthful cognitive and affective dispositions are cultivated, and specific ideological predications are advanced.

In Israel, the educational landscape mirrors the society's inherent pluralism, encompassing heterogeneous systems—secular, religious Zionist, ultra-Orthodox, and Arabic-language models—each presenting distinct curricula and ideological underpinnings. While each stream is internally coherent, the divergence among them often reproduces and solidifies societal divisions; curricula are couched in particular historical, cultural, and political vocabularies. Consequently, students across the partitions encounter inconsistent narratives, absent a shared interpretive horizon; they confront varying renditions of the national past, engage with antithetical self-definitions, and assimilate dissimilar images of the 'other.' This segmented formation of knowledge and identity, whether through textbooks, pedagogic practices, or extracurricular activities, unwittingly deepens the stratification of the national polity.

Moreover, the pedagogical orientations employed within these institutions merit close examination. The ways in which contentious subjects such as the Israeli-Palestinian conflict, Jewish-Arab relations, and the construction of national identity are broached will profoundly shape the attitudes and worldviews of the pupils. Educators possess formidable influence in determining the stories that pupils internalise, and the strategies adopted in confronting these multifaceted matters can, on the one hand, cultivate empathy, analytical discernment, and receptivity to pluralism or, on the other, entrench stereotypes, bias, and ethnocentric dispositions.

In light of these considerations, the imperative for a curriculum that is inclusive, even-handed, and grounded in empathy is evident. Such a framework, one that promotes deliberation, respect for divergent viewpoints, and a rigorous examination of both past and present realities, can operate as an engine for reconciliation and social cohesion. When students are trained to participate in constructive dialogue, to empathise with the experiences of others, and to interrogate sources with a critical eye, education can fulfil its potential as a transformative instrument for mending societal rifts.

Furthermore, the scope of education must be viewed as extending well beyond the walls of formal schools and universities. Informal learning environments—such as community-led programmes, youth movements, and extracurricular pursuits—play a significant role in forming the attitudes of the young. When they design spaces for dialogue, foster intergroup contact, and cultivate cross-cultural literacy, these initiatives can powerfully supplement the formal curriculum, creating contexts in which mutual respect and peaceful coexistence can take firm root.

Ultimately, education's influence on collective worldviews in Israeli society is at once deep and intricate. Discerning how differing educational models configure social realities is an essential step in confronting entrenched polarities and in constructing a more serene and inclusive future.

Media Influence: Perceptions and Misperceptions

The media retain powerful assets in shaping public perceptions in Israel. Across traditional newspapers, televised forums, and digital platforms, the flow of narratives and information heavily weighs upon collective opinion. Yet, accompanying the capacity for comprehension also resides the hazard of misperception and distortion. News platforms mirror the political and social schisms endemic to Israeli society, fracturing audiences and entrenching pre-established convictions. Interpretations of historical moments, political personages, and social questions may diverge markedly among different outlets, exhibiting the profound divisions that prevail. Moreover, the disproportionate prominence granted to select voices leaves others muted, producing an unbalanced reflection of the empirical world. Such selective listening can either validate or contest pre-formed convictions, augmenting the perception of societal disunity. The sensational character of certain reportage may inflame these divisions further, cultivating an atmosphere conducive to misunderstanding and heightened tension. The ascent of social media introduces an additional dimension: algorithmic amplification and echo chambers perpetuate and narrow these biases, restricting encounters with contrary viewpoints. Given these realities, rigorous analytic and critical examination of media influence upon perceptions of unity and division becomes not only prudent, but imperative.

Grasping how media systems function enables us to disentangle the dense networks of partial narratives and erroneous information that surround public discourse. Such comprehension highlights media's role in amplifying social fracturing, thereby reaffirming the necessity of rigorous ethical standards and responsible reporting across the profession. When outlets actively cultivate spaces for a plurality of voices and rigorously interrogate competing viewpoints, they contribute meaningfully to the repair of social fissures and to the cultivation of mutual comprehension. An analytical unpacking of media's sway over both accurate and distorted perceptions reveals a cumulative process through which a more integrated and compassionate society becomes both imaginable and attainable.

Youth Voices: The Next Generation's Struggles and Aspirations

The voices of young Israelis ripple through the country's layered society, intertwining ambition, anxiety, and hope. Positioned between competing historical narratives, ongoing socio-political contestation, and a kaleidoscopic cultural milieu, this generation stands at an emblematic juncture. Its collective aspiration is kaleidoscopic, attesting to the varied registers of contemporary life in Israel.

Amid a fluid media ecosystem, young people are bombarded by streams of information curated by partisan interests. The result is a fractured knowledge landscape that shapes their apprehension of the country's deepening divisions. Some are seduced by the certainties of entrenched ideologies; others consciously cultivate a critical stance that values dissent, striving to span the widening chasm that separates the contending camps.

Education functions simultaneously as a refuge and a contested space. Classrooms invite students to interrogate historical accounts and to imagine alternate national self-understandings, yet the same rooms become arenas for ideological circling and contest. Debates over whose narratives are embodied in textbooks and whose voices are acknowledged reflect the broader negotiation between a loyalty to inherited symbols and a demand for expansive, plural recognition.

The economic circumstances confronting contemporary young Israelis present a sterner set of pressures than those encountered by earlier cohorts. Escalating housing prices, a shrinking set of secure career openings, and a market that rewards narrow and specialised competencies rather than generalist adaptability combine to narrow the space in which ambitions unfurl. The quest for durable livelihoods, upward mobility, and the possibility of a stable adult life repeatedly meets the limits imposed by an unforgiving present.

Concurrently, the fluid exchange between enduring religious legacies and emergent secular norms frames the space in which young people interrogate the ties of community, the claims of creed, and the imperatives of personal agency. This inward-facing enquiry frequently dovetails with broader national conversations, producing a vertical cross-section of convictions that refuses to settle into singular, static identities.

Social Movements: Bridging or Widening the Divide?

Social movements in Israel have been decisive agents in the country's evolving social landscape, simultaneously functioning as instruments of cohesion and catalysts of discord. Certain collectives have deliberately endeavoured to close the fissures that traverse Israeli society, while others, including peripheral groups, have inadvertently intensified the estrangement among its constituencies. The proliferation of social, political, and cultural grievances that animates these campaigns underscores the multi-layered character of Israeli social life.

Yet, the risk of widening the divide remains palpable. Activism centred upon the Israeli-Palestinian conflict, however coherently executed, has recurrently crystallised communal allegiance into oppositional grids, hardening boundaries of acceptance. Moreover, the rise of peripheral impulses—scaffolded by doctrines of revanche and Premiership of enmity—has fragmented the discursive space, eclipsing the more moderate calls to common ground and thereby subverting the teleology of reconciliation overtly proclaimed by mainstream initiatives.

Media framing of social movements is never neutral; its narratives can either consolidate heterogeneous groups into an enlarged collective or deepen pre-existing animosities. Yet, amid such mediatised polarisation, certain civic campaigns devote themselves to narrowing the rifts. Through interfaith dialogue, shared civic projects, and sustained cross-community cooperation, these initiatives refuse to succumb to despair and instead affirm the latent cohesion available to the Israeli polity. By centring the structural, historical, and economic drivers of conflict, they cultivate a social texture that, however tenuous, gestures toward a comprehensive citizenship. Thus, the legacy of movements in contemporary Israel is not reducible to the binary of rupture or repair; it is a mingled weave of fracturing and mending. As the state confronts a succession of compound adversities, the sustained presence of such initiatives will determine the future calibrations of social solidarity, fashioning both obstruction and conduit on the long, uneven path to shared, dignified coexistence.

***

References

BREAKING THE WALL OF SILENCE

A. Macro-Histories of Israeli Social Cleavage

1. **Peled, Yoav & Shafir, Gershon** – _Being Israeli: The Dynamics of Multiple Citizenship_ (Cambridge UP, 2002).

Foundational political-sociology of how 1948 war gains, citizenship laws, and labour markets fused ethnicity, class, and nationality.

2. **Kimmerling, Baruch** – _The Invention and Decline of Israeliness: State, Society, and the Military_ (California, 2001).

Tracks the unraveling of a hegemonic "Israeli" identity into competing ethno-religious sub-cultures after 1967.

3. **Rouhana, Nadim N.** – _Palestinian Citizens in an Ethnic Jewish State: Identities in Conflict_ (Yale, 1997).

Still the benchmark study of how Palestinian Israelis negotiate citizenship inside a state that memorialises their 1948 dispossession.

B. Immigration & Ethno-Class Hierarchies

4. **Shohat, Ella** – _On the Arab-Jew, Palestine, and Other Displacements_ (Pluto, 2017).

Essays on how Mizrahi immigration was racialised and instrumentalised against Palestinian memory.

5. **Lissak, Moshe** – _The Mass Immigration of the 1950s: The Failure of the Melting Pot_ (Yad Ben-Zvi, 1999).

Archival study of ma'abarot transit camps as crucibles of class and ethnic stratification.

6. **Ben-Rafael, Eliezer & Sharot, Stephen** – _Ethnicity, Religion and Class in Israeli Society_ (Cambridge, 1991).

Quantitative mappings of income, schooling, and political affiliation across Ashkenazi, Mizrahi, FSU, and Ethiopian cohorts.

C. Socio-Economic Inequality & Spatial Segregation
7. **Filc, Dani** – _The Political Economy of Health Care in Israel_ (Lexington, 2009).
Demonstrates how health budgets, kupat-holim membership, and residential zoning reproduce 1948-era inequalities.

8. **Yiftachel, Oren** – _Ethnocracy: Land and Identity Politics in Israel/Palestine_ (Penn, 2006).
Seminal on how land regimes and planning law convert military conquest into enduring ethno-class geographies.

9. **Dahan, Momi & Klor, Esteban F.** – "The Economic Returns to Higher Education in Israel," _Israel Economic Review_ 17:1 (2021), 1-40.
Econometric evidence of how parental origin (Mizrahi/Ethiopian vs. Ashkenazi) trumps academic merit in wage returns.

D. Religious-Secular Polarisation
10. **Lehmann, David & Siebzehner, Batia** – _Remaking Israeli Judaism: The Challenge of Shas_ (Oxford, 2006).
Ethnography of how Mizrahi ultra-Orthodox politics weaponise memory of 1950s discrimination to claim state resources.

11. **Goodman, Yehuda & Fischer, Shlomo** – "Religion, Class and the Politics of Redemption in Israel," _Theory &

Society_ 44 (2015), 447-480.

Traces how Haredi draft exemptions are justified by theological readings of 1948 and Holocaust trauma.

E. Youth, Class, and Generational Anxieties

12. **Nahon, Karin & Manoff, Marik** – _The Israeli Dream: High-Tech Start-Ups and the Mirage of Mobility_ (Stanford, 2022).

Sociological study of how "Start-Up Nation" discourse masks deepening inter-generational class immobility.

13. **Dahan Kalev, Henriette** – "Ethiopian Israelis in the Military: Integration or Ethnic Regimentation?" _Armed Forces & Society_ 45:4 (2019), 629-648.

Shows how compulsory service reproduces racialised hierarchies rather than erasing them.

14. **Grinberg, Lev Luis** – _Politics and Violence in Israel/Palestine: Democracy vs. Military Rule_ (Routledge, 2010).

Frames youth protest (social justice tents 2011, Ethiopian demonstrations 2015) as class-based revolt against 1948 legacy.

F. Education & Youth Identity Formation

15. **Gross, Zehavit** – "Civic Identity and Citizenship Education in Israel: Between Nationalism and Pluralism," _Journal of Education Policy_ 35:6 (2020), 799-823.

Surveys how Jewish, Arab, and religious streams inculcate divergent narratives of 1948 and economic justice.

16. **Yonah, Yossi & Shenhav, Yehouda** – _What Is Mul-

ticulturalism? On the Politics of Difference in Israel_ (Hakibbutz Hameuchad, 2008).

Proposes curricular reforms that braid Mizrahi, Palestinian, and FSU memories into civic education.

G. Media, Digital Youth Cultures & Echo Chambers

17. **Kuntsman, Adi & Stein, Rebecca** – _Digital Militarism: Israel's Occupation in the Social Media Age_ (Stanford, 2015).

Chapters on how Instagram and Telegram groups monetise ethno-national grievance among Israeli youth.

18. **Tsfati, Yariv & Peri, Yoram** – "Mainstream Media and Ideological Polarisation in Israel," _Political Communication_ 33:2 (2016), 187-205.

Experimental evidence that selective exposure to Channel 12 vs. Channel 14 deepens class-ethnic divides.

H. Grassroots & Artistic Youth Counter-Cultures

19. **Almog, Oz & Almog, Tamar** – _The Sabras: Profile of a Generation_ (Am Oved, 2018).

Oral histories with 1948 "founder generation" grandchildren who reject hegemonic militarism.

20. **Ravid, Barak** – "From Black Panthers to Black Lives Matter: Ethiopian-Israeli Activism in Historical Perspective," _Middle East Journal_ 75:3 (2021), 389-410.

Links 1970s Mizrahi protest to 2015 Ethiopian youth uprising, stressing continuity of racialised policing.

I. Policy & Think-Tank Reports (Open Access)
- **Adva Center** – _Annual Social-Economic Report on

Israel_ (Hebrew & English PDFs).

Indispensable data on poverty, housing, and education gaps by ethnicity and immigration wave.

- **Taub Center for Social Policy Studies** – _State of the Nation Report_ (annual).

Macro-economic analyses linking military expenditure to welfare retrenchment.

- **Israel Democracy Institute** – _Israeli Democracy Index_ (annual).

Survey data on youth attitudes toward democracy, religion, and 1948 narratives.

J. Digital & Multimedia Resources

- **Israel Social TV** – https://tv.social.org.il

Grassroots Hebrew videos on class, race, and housing struggles subtitled in English.

- **#YouthAgainstDictatorship** – TikTok archive curated by +972 Magazine.

Short-form clips of Ethiopian, Mizrahi, and Palestinian youth critiquing 1948 legacy and economic precarity.

- **"Acre Dreams" Interactive Map** – https://akko.huji.ac.il

GIS layers juxtaposing Ottoman, Mandate, and present-day property regimes to visualise spatial inequality.

Conclusion
Political Implications in Today's Israel in the Wake of Gaza Genocide

Unpacking Contemporary Political Landscapes

The present Israeli political landscape, shaped in the aftermath of renewed conflict, manifests as an intricate fusion of historical memory and immediate political exigencies. Past military and political episodes continue to resound in the Knesset and the public sphere, requiring scholars to disentangle the genealogies of memory from the exigencies of governance. This chapter contends that any strategic reading of Israel's future is predicated upon the reconstruction of memory's role in the present moment. By methodically tracing the sedimentation of memory, diplomacies, and civil aspirations, we can isolate the persistent logics that both constrain and enable political action. Central to the Israeli political discourse is the enduring sedimentation of salient historical events, each of which has ritualised particular collective self-descriptions and external antagonisms.

These sedimentation processes have produced a politically infused communal selfhood that continuously refracts domestic contestation and foreign policy. The analytical challenge, therefore, is to articulate how these enduring narratives both respond to and conflict with momentary political pressures, revealing the fault lines through which opportunity and crisis are produced.

This chapter examines the layered continuity of Israeli history and its enduring effects on current ideological frameworks, alliances, and policy formulation. It treats historical narratives not as inert background, but as active substrates interwoven with present phenomena. By methodically tracing the sedimentation of these narratives, the study documents how earlier events have crystallised into ideological commitments and pragmatic calculations that inform today's political choices. It organises the analysis around key chronological pivots, shifting geopolitical contexts, and internal demographic and cultural transformations, thereby constructing a diachronic map of political development. The chapter's aim is to render a synoptic, yet analytic, account that clarifies how reverberations of the past inform the logic of present governance and political debate, thereby advancing scholarly comprehension of the complexity and dynamism of Israel's current political field.

From Historical Narratives to Present-Day Realities

History equips us to grasp the intricate realities of contemporary Israel, especially following the Gaza programme of

BREAKING THE WALL OF SILENCE

extermination. A careful study of past events reveals the sequential development of political ideologies, societal dispositions, and the fixed, collective visions that now inform the state. Analysis of the canonical and revisionist texts, especially those advanced by the New Historians, helps to clarify how divergent narrations have reconfigured the social imaginary that undergirds Israel today. Such enquiry is far more than scholarly reflection; it illuminates the wellsprings of violence, the codification of state doctrine, and public reception to ongoing crises. Every treaty, uprising, and rupture, from the earliest confrontations to today's bloodlettings, inscribes itself upon the living present. Such an understanding makes transparent the fractures and polarities that pervade Israeli public life. Beyond politics, these accounts supply the vocabulary of collective memory, moulding the nation's self-image and conditioning reactions to adversity.

Consequently, the movement from historical chronicle to current circumstance is infused with intricacy, presenting a densely woven fabric of conflicting readings and disputed meanings. Grounded in verifiable past events, yet directed by the demands of the present, this advance embodies a negotiation of inherited legacies and emergent novelties. The forthcoming discussion will map the delicate interrelations binding past to present, enabling the audience to negotiate the stretch of Israel's evolving trajectory with augmented lucidity and analytical grasp.

The Role of New Historians in Shaping Political Discourse

Today's political conversations in Israel are increasingly informed by the work of a new cohort of historians whose scholarship has systematically opened space for rethinking the past. Their painstaking archival research and fresh documentary evidence have produced alternative interpretations of pivotal events that once seemed settled. By bringing to public attention previously submerged conflicts, contradictions, and silences, these historians force a re-examination of the collective memory that underpins contemporary national identity. Their analyses have ripened into a counter-narrative that, while anchored in critical rigour, unsettles popular and political consensus. Academic debate has certainly been enlivened, yet the resonance of these works travels well beyond the lecture hall: op-eds, popular documentary films, and civil society archives now circulate their findings, making revisionist evidence a staple of public argument. Politicians, aware that voting constituencies are newly receptive to complexity, have been obliged to prefix policy pronouncements with disclaimers that previously seemed superfluous. Peripheral voices long relegated to footnote—the testimonies of refugees, the minutes of district governors, the questions raised by British officers—have been rendered central, inviting the public to adopt a more critical and, crucially, more empathetic stance. Grassroots campaigns for memory, for the preservation of Palestinian cemeteries, and for the commemoration of non-combatants now borrow tactics and terminology from these historians, signage and lecture-video archives flooding social media. In this sense, the new historians have ratified the maxim that scholarly labour, when judicious and tenacious, can reconfigure political time—unsettling the past to make sense of the present.

The significance of their scholarship rests on its capacity to elicit critical reassessment and reflexive enquiry, thereby cultivating a more knowledgeable and ethically responsible stance toward current political exigencies.

Emerging Voices: The Rise of Pro-Peace Movements

Amid persistent tensions and hostilities, a decisive dimension of the present Israeli political milieu is the rise and consolidation of pro-peace movements. These coalitions, consisting of a heterogeneous assembly of citizens and organisations, have progressively confronted dominant discourses and state policies, advancing alternative interpretations and proposals anchored in mutual recognition and negotiated settlement. Manifesting a durable investment in dialogue and restorative justice, the movements embody an expanding constituency within Israeli society that insists on addressing the protracted Israeli-Palestinian impasse through non-military practices and collaborative governance.

Pro-peace movements have rallied around a commitment to understanding and empathy, asserting that only a peace anchored in the mutual recognition of legitimate rights and aspirations can withstand the test of time and justice for both Israelis and Palestinians. Through grassroots organising, targeted advocacy, and a wide array of civic initiatives, movement participants work to create and sustain channels of dialogue that go beyond entrenched animosities and mutual distrust. Their efforts are far from isolated; these activists connect across national and international frontiers, partnering with sympathetic organisations to expand reach, enhance legitimacy, and cultivate a deeper resonance for their shared objectives.

The renewed traction of these movements owes much to a sharper focus on human rights, social justice, and the moral indictment of cyclical violence and oppression. Their agenda encompasses equal access to resources, the defence of marginalised populations, and the repudiation of discriminatory policies, each considered a non-negotiable pillar of the vision for a just and inter-inclusive society. Strategic in communication, movement leaders mobilise public discourse by participating in civic forums, publishing analyses, and exploiting digital channels, thereby involving a diverse array of stakeholders, in circles that extend from the local to the planetary.

Within Israel, initiatives advocating for peace have confronted a range of interrelated difficulties: opposition from established political interests, the divisive currents of societal polarization, and the ever-present spectre of security threats. Nonetheless, these movements, undaunted, continue to articulate their aims and seek legislative and social transformation. Their perseverance not only demonstrates the persuasive power of their doctrine, but also embodies a sustained aspiration for a future characterised by coexistence, recognition of every individual's dignity, and a sustained culture of peace.

Thus, the emergence and persistence of pro-peace movements confirm the ability of grassroots solidarity and compassionate engagement to navigate and soften deep-seated cleavages, galvanising a shared, stepwise effort toward a more just, cohesive, and ecologically viable future for every resident of the region.

Gaza's Shadow: How Recent Events Influence Policy Making

Recent developments in Gaza have loomed over Israeli politics with the inertia of trauma. Their fallout has rippled outward, reordering both regional alignments and the terms of international engagement. Observers arrived at the scene and beheld indiscriminate destruction; from that moment, policymakers were obliged to contemplate the long-term effects of the carnage. Parliamentary halls and cabinet rooms became sites of urgent, sometimes agonising, debate over whether the preservation of deterrent capacity could coexist with any semblance of humane obligation. Governing elites have since learned that the memory of mass death does not wither, and that memory in the hands of the oppressed can achieve persistent, mobilising force. External and internal pressures now converge upon a leadership that once construed military efficacy as synonymous with national integrity. Reassessing that equation requires moving, however cautiously, beyond a reflexive equation of security with legitimacy. The ground left scorched by bombs has likewise scorched the lexicon of official rhetoric: advocates of reprisal find their strongest rebuttal now in the steady background hum of suppressed moral reckoning. The occasion has thus turned inward, inviting ministers, soldiers, and citizens to interrogate whether operating from the grammar of force can ever produce a polity at once secure and habitable.

The recent events in Gaza now overshadow every policy conference, reminding states and scholars alike of how quickly consent can dissolve and lives can be extinguished. The scale of civilian suffering and infrastructural ruin has forced a collective reassessment of the adequacy and morality of any strategy advancing, or merely perpetuating, a status quo. Beyond the immediate humanitarian peril, the conflict has realigned regional pulsations, fraying old partnerships and exposing the fragility of collective security statements, while making the politics of neutrality increasingly perilous. The aftershocks of the bombardments reverberate through parliamentary schedules and diplomatic wires, obliging capitals to refine, if not reorder, entire layers of policy architecture. In this charged atmosphere, the pursuit of solutions capable of surviving the next flashpoint has grown not only practical but morally mandatory, driving statesmen to seek diplomatic corridors that scale ambition beyond ceasefires toward genuine political reconstruction. Gaza, therefore, continues to impose itself not as a distant humanitarian dossier but as a living critique of any governance that underestimates the lethal power of omission.

Media, Perception, and Politics: A Complex Interplay

An inescapable and ever-deepening nexus is fostered by media, perception, and politics in the current Israeli-Palestinian conflict, through which violence, sympathy, and policy are refracted for multiple audiences. Media instruments, spanning television, blogs, and hashtag movements, are rarely neutral; they dramatise death, injuries, blockades, and retaliations in ways that carve frames of meaning, privileging certain truths over others. In the case of the continuing Gaza massacre, the stakes are even higher; the calculated eradication of civilian neighbourhoods and infrastructure passes through edit suites and algorithms that decide which graphic, which death toll, which child's face elicits circulation and moral momentum. News angles, accompanying footage, and the length of a sitrep cumulatively educate politics; they decide when outrage swells and when it subsides, and thus when governments are empowered to foreclose options or finally concede to humanitarian inquests. Media thus can cultivate a politics of radical empathy or entrench a politics of residual indifference, and each outcome redounds upon conscripts and diplomats alike. In an interconnected world, differential media ecosystems—each steeped in its own economic, ideological, and editorial loyalties—compete not merely for audiences but for the moral register that calibrates treaty drafts, arms sales and, ultimately, the geography of violence. A critical comparative reading of those ecosystems—of how Gaza's rubble is lit in London, how sirens are heard in Delhi, how grief is tweeted in New

York—therefore becomes indispensable, for it uncovers the tendentious processes by which certain interpretations of tragedy are licensed while others are foreclosed.

The advent of citizen journalism and other non-institutional news channels has enriched and complicated the informational environment, furnishing a mosaic of perspectives and framings that complicate the interpretive process. Consolidating this plurality is the sustained interaction between state actors and the information sphere, where governments and lobby groups customarily deploy media platforms as instruments for the strategic calibration of public opinion. Such explosive coupling of narrative, perception, and statecraft marks the territory as especially challenging for any analyst seeking to chart the Israeli-Palestinian dispute's multiple, and often contradictory, dimensions. Moreover, the transnational reach of contemporary platforms guarantees that any single act of representation ripples through diplomatic channels and civil societies far removed from the frontline, recalibrating external stances and international obligations. Coverage thus transgresses the role of neutral report; it actively circumscribes the spaces of permissible debate and fashions the agenda for elite and popular deliberation. The resultant weave—where media, constructed perception, and state calculation cohabitate—requires, at a minimum, a discerning and layered enquiry that acknowledges the coevalness of image, interest, and international consequence.

International Relations and the Impact of Global Opinion

The recent genocide in Gaza has sent dramatic aftershocks through the Israeli polity and tested the limits of domestic consensus. At this moment, the trajectory of Israeli governance depends on the extent to which public and elite opinion abroad has crystallised into credible opposition—both moral and transactional—to the present military and diplomatic course. From the UN, the EU, and a progressively larger number of national parliaments, a steady drumbeat of denunciation and humanitarian ultimata has been supplemented by talk of conditional arms supplies and legal proceedings. Such signals ordinarily create a narrowing bandwidth of acceptable Israeli policies, especially in a society sensitive to reputational damage and to the reputational politics of triadic security partnerships. Nevertheless, the empirical weight of each pronouncement has been measurably attenuated by the discord—between the Global South and the transatlantic camp, between energy-producing and energy-satisfied states, and, crucially, between leaders and publics whose memories of the pogrom traditions are less than a century old. A series of meridian distributions of sympathy, fault attribution, and conditionality thus confirms that the Israeli state is facing a polycentric arena of governance. The diplomatic and legal risks attendant on this polycentrism are considerable. New opposition blocs are likely to crystallise within the EU, ramifications for the quantum and conditions of US military aid remain open, and language deployed in the permanent tribunals—a domain that has, since the 1990s, cultivated a transnational logic—could yet trigger the isolation which Compulsory Membership in Treaties of Universal Application is designed to inhibit.

The heightened focus of the international community on Israel has further complicated its foreign policy calculations, compelling the state to balance its partnerships with principal allies while encountering deepening diplomatic seclusion on several fronts. These overlapping pressures reveal the extent to which transnational perceptions interact with the internal political arena, actively reframing public debate and guiding policy formulation within Israel. Consequently, a sophisticated grasp of the international system and the differential influence of international sentiment is essential for deciphering the changing contours of Israeli governance and the country's status in the global arena. Israel's modes of reciprocating to external reproach and backing will inevitably influence its future direction, thereby rendering the examination of global sentiment a decisive component in the study of the longer-term consequences of the Gaza genocide for the state and its relations with the broader international milieu.

Political Factions Within Israel: Bridging or Widening the Divide?

The reverberations of the Gaza campaign continue to shake Israeli society, placing the country's political factions before a decisive moment in their evolution. The ideological divergences that have long characterised Israeli politics now sharpen under the weight of recent violence. One camp insists on a hard-line posture, asserting that maximum deterrence and ruthless retaliation against perceived threats are the only guarantees of Israeli survival and sovereignty. This perspective privileges the immediate preservation of the state over any long-term settlement. In contrast, a rival assembly of opinion urges a moderated course, promoting diplomacy, multilateralism, and humanitarian routines as the foundations for a lasting regional order. Adherents of this position argue that security and legitimacy are mutually reinforcing, and that genuine engagement with neighbours and the broader community is the only antidote to isolation. The chasm between these paradigms complicates Israel's political terrain, as vehement, mutually exclusive convictions collide. Within this charged environment, parties wrestle with the dual mandates of protecting the state while also permitting, or at least not precluding, the fragile pathways to sustainable peace.

These factions confront both exterior pressures and the debilitating force of internal fragmentation, a dual burden that renders the already multilayered Israeli political arena still more opaque. In the course of calibrating their stances and strategies, they confront a constellation of pressures: the mutability of public opinion, the exigencies of coalition arithmetic, and the mediated spectacle that offers both dented mirrors and amplifiers to their rivalries. While some actors advocate a creeping reconciliation across the divides, others seize the gleam of discord as political currency, extending polarisation and erecting hurdles to constructive dialogue. Grasping this theatre thus demands an awareness that every choice publicly announced reverberates beyond the Knesset and beyond the Levant, conditioning the spectrum from regional equilibrium to the obligations of an increasingly interdependent globe. It is within the friction of these rival imperatives that the collective psyche is ceaselessly probed, as the polity of Israel strives to discern—and to enact—the course that the next decade of discordant history will demand.

Legal and Ethical Considerations: In Pursuit of Justice

The quest for justice within the Israeli-Palestinian conflict is under constant examination from both legal and ethical vantage points; the consequences of this examination reverberate well beyond the immediate region. At its most elemental, the problem pivots around the persistent challenge of securing both accountability and a plausible path toward reconciliation. Competing historical narratives and disputed territorial claims ensure that the pursuit of justice is never monolithic, but instead assumes ever-shifting and multidimensional forms. International legal standards, human rights treaties, and ethical doctrines together furnish indispensable prisms through which the conduct of Israeli and Palestinian actors can be assessed. Key norms governing the conduct of armed hostilities—principles of proportionality, distinction, and necessity—are exposed to relentless interrogation, particularly following what many observers have designated *the Gaza genocide*.

BREAKING THE WALL OF SILENCE

As the global community confronts its collective moral responsibilities, ethical considerations ascend to the forefront of discussions on the Israeli-Palestinian conflict. A thorough examination of the criteria established by just war doctrine alongside the evolving norms governing humanitarian intervention reveals the moral tension attendant upon safeguarding civilians while deploying means designed to achieve military objectives. The accumulation of historical injury, layered trauma, and the memory of prior oppressions complicate the quest for restorative justice, obliging actors to negotiate an equilibrium between the imperatives of accountability and the necessity of reconciliation. Response mechanisms rooted in international human rights law, war crimes accountability, and the prescriptions of humanitarian law respectively furnish the collective and individual avenues through which violations may be addressed, thereby safeguarding the norms that undergird a lasting and equitable peace.

Justice, although obstructed at every turn, constitutes the irreducible foundation upon which any future resolution must rest. An interrogation of both legal and ethical dimensions facilitates informed discourse and nurtures the prospect of a mutually envisioned future in which coexistence prevails. As the international community recalibrates its engagement with a conflict marked by immovable attachments, the obligation to retain universal legal frameworks while attending to the region's distinctive historical and cultural idioms intensifies. Within this tightly interwoven framework, the imperatives of law and ethics fuse to illuminate a pathway toward accountability related to occupation by force, war crimes, the reparation of wrongs, and, ultimately, a reconciliation that to transcend the accumulation of past injury, should be based on the UN resolutions recognising the right of the Palestinian people to independence and sovereignty on the territories occupied by Israel since 1948.

Looking Ahead: Any Prospects for a Peaceful Resolution?

At this decisive moment, efforts to achieve a peaceful settlement to the Israeli-Palestinian conflict remain immensely complicated. Reaching a workable agreement entails confronting entrenched Israeli discourses and long-standing resentments, which is not obvious. Yet, even within this difficult landscape, tentative signs of possibility remain, inviting renewed dialogue, deeper comprehension, and the eventual emergence of peace.

Advancing diplomacy continues to represent a promising strategic entry point. When Israeli and Palestinian leaders engage in sustained conversation—fortified by a supportive international community—they can incrementally nurture mutual acknowledgment, foster confidence, and explore shared strategic interests. The participation of key global powers so far excluded, like China and Russia, and concerned regional actors, like Egypt and Turkey, can also introduce fresh insights and calibrating pressures, enriching the dialogue and enlarging the margins for constructive compromise.

A credible peace framework must, at its core, invite the recognition of historical facts – as the new historians showed us - and the honouring of the victim's narrative, which has never been considered seriously in any previous negotiations. This process demands collective acknowledgment that, however difficult, honesty about the past is the condition for credible futures. The occupation of the Palestinian historic territories was a collective crime perpetrated by all those who orchestrated it, whatsoever the purpose. Today, it is still there. Blatant, it does not need evidence. It bears it within itself. You don't mend a horrific crime (the holocaust) by allowing another. Nevertheless, this is what happened. The Western governments are as implicated as the Israeli.

It is their responsibility to bring peace, while the responsibility of the Palestinian people is to continue the fight for freedom until its achievement.

Then, and only then, through disciplined, empathetic examination of memory and grievance, the parties may dismantle enduring misapprehensions and articulate a cooperative, reconciled vision that transcends conflict.

www.ingramcontent.com/pod-product-compliance
Lightning Source LLC
Chambersburg PA
CBHW020516080526
44583CB00013B/620